ADDICTED TO MURDER

The Authors

Colin Wilson

Colin Wilson burst upon the scene in 1956 at the age of 25, with his bestselling book *The Outsider*. In the course of a remarkable career as an explorer of the human psyche, he has written on a wide range of subjects, and his books continue to be translated into many different languages.

Dr Chris Missen

Dr Missen, the author of the preface, is a criminal profiler who has been widely interviewed on the subject of Dr Harold Shipman. Look out for *Taking Life*, Dr Missen's account of the cutting edge of criminal profiling, due out from Virgin Publishing soon.

Mikaela Sitford

The author won the BT North West Journalist of the Year and BT Regional Daily Journalist of the Year awards for her coverage of the Shipman story. She was the journalist responsible for breaking the story to the world.

ADDICTED TO MURDER

Mikaela Sitford

*With additional material
from Steve Panter*

Virgin

Manchester
EveningNews

First published in 2000 by
Virgin Publishing Ltd
Thames Wharf Studios
Rainville Road
London W6 9HA

ISBN 0 7535 0445 6

Typeset by TW Typesetting, Plymouth, Devon

Printed and bound by Mackays of Chatham PLC

Contents

Introduction

Although he has been found guilty of murder, an enormous question mark still hangs over the case of Dr Harold Shipman: specifically, why did he do it? In only one of Shipman's murders – that of Kathleen Grundy – did he hope to gain a legacy.

According to the experts at the FBI's crime lab at Quantico, Virginia, virtually all serial murder is sexual in origin. But, in Shipman's case, that view is difficult to sustain. It is true that his victims were all (as far as we know) women, but most were elderly, and there seems to have been no obvious sexual motive. The only hint of a possible sexual hang-up can be found in the case of a seventeen-year-old girl, Lorraine Leighton, who went to see him about a lump in her breast. After Shipman apparently made rude comments about the size of her breasts, she fled the surgery. Is it possible that Shipman's response was based on sexual frustration? If so, it is the only suggestion of sexuality in the whole case.

But what seems very clear from *Addicted to Murder* is that Shipman could be very touchy when it was a question of his self-esteem. The author of this book, a journalist who worked on the case, speaks of 'his arrogance, and intolerance of those who opposed him in any way'. And, although most of his patients thought him 'a lovely man', he was apparently less agreeable to his receptionists: one remembers how he turned white with rage because she had forgotten his coffee. This suggests a man with an extremely high opinion of himself, and more than a touch of paranoia. One receptionist described him as 'a divisive, despicable man'.

Such a person *would* be a good doctor, since his standing in life is all-important; ideally he would like to be at the top of his profession, universally admired. But for those who have nothing to contribute to his pre-eminence, he can scarcely bring himself to be polite. He is, in short, self-centred and ruthless.

But these qualities do not necessarily make a killer. In order to understand Shipman, we would need access to personal and psychiatric information which is not at present available.

I have always been fascinated by slightly paranoid personalities – people with an immensely high opinion of themselves, who secretly boil with resentment because they feel that the rest of the world fails to recognise their superiority. A friend of mine, the science-fiction writer A.E. Van Vogt, called them 'Right Men', because they have a deep compulsion to believe that they are always in the right. He also called them 'Violent Men' because if their self-esteem is violated, they fly into a rage.

One example will make the point. During the Second World War, a man called Paul Ogorzov murdered a number of women in Berlin, mostly by flinging them off moving trains. When he was finally caught, it was revealed that he had once approached a woman in a dark street and tried to grab her. She screamed, and a number of men, including her husband, came running out of nearby houses and beat Ogorzov so badly that he had to spend a week in bed. When he recovered, he determined that all women should 'pay', and began his murders. His self-esteem had been so outraged that nothing would satisfy it, short of the murder of those whom he felt were responsible – women.

Van Vogt noted the interesting fact that the 'Right Man's' colleagues at work might feel that he was a perfectly 'nice guy'. Only his family (and perhaps his subordinates) would be aware of the extent of his paranoia. His wildly exaggerated notion of his own superiority meant that he would brook no defiance or even disagreement. He was the dictator, the sultan, and his wife and children were his subjects. So his little castle of self-esteem was built on very narrow and shaky foundations. In fact, Van Vogt discovered, if the Right Man's wife refuses to put up with any more bullying and humiliation, and walks out on him, he often collapses into despair, and may even commit suicide.

What is the basis of this strange neurosis? It is the fact that precisely five per cent of any animal group is 'dominant' – that is, has potential leadership qualities. But five per cent is a lot – one in twenty. And there is simply not room for millions of 'celebrities' in our society. A large number of the dominant five per cent inevitably have to accept a position which they feel to be below their true worth. This chafes their ego and fills them with resentment. Playing the tyrant with their families may be their only chance of feeling 'superior'.

Was Shipman such a person? I strongly suspect so, although the author of this book mentions simply that he was a bully with his younger children. Only they – and his wife – could tell us the full truth about Harold Shipman.

But even if he was a Right Man, why should he commit murder? That question takes us into altogether deeper and murkier waters.

In 1991, a children's nurse named Beverley Allitt was arrested and charged with four child murders and numerous attacks – she was suffering from a psychological illness known as Munchausen's Syndrome. Munchausen was a fictitious German baron who told preposterous lies for self-aggrandisement and patients suffering from this syndrome have a compulsive need for attention which they try to satisfy by claiming to have a series of imaginary ailments. Beverley Allitt had been killing children in her ward, often by injecting insulin. In one case, she had apparently saved the life of a child who was in a fit after one of her injections, as a result of which she became a close family friend. This is what she wanted – to *be* somebody, to be admired.

In such a case we can see that the problem is low self-esteem. But in others it is far more difficult to pin down. In *The Serial Killers*, written with Donald Seaman, I cite many bizarre cases of 'medical murder'. In 1981, a Los Angeles night nurse named Robert Diaz was charged with killing twelve patients with injections of a heart drug, and sentenced to death. He lived an intense fantasy life, claiming that in previous existences he had been an Egyptian pharaoh and the Spanish hero El Cid.

In 1983, a Norwegian doctor, Arnfinn Nesset, was charged with murdering twenty-two elderly patients by injecting them with a deadly drug. Nesset had also embezzled small sums from his victims, but not enough to constitute a 'motive'. No major motive was ever established, although Nesset admitted to 'a morbid need to kill', and to 'schizophrenia coupled with self-assertion'. He was given a maximum life sentence.

In 1987, a male nurse named Donald Harvey, of Cincinatti, Ohio, admitted murdering twenty-four people in four years. The prosecutor remarked: 'It's all about power', bringing to mind the remark of a Quantico detective: 'Sex crime isn't about sex – it's about power'. Harvey, a handsome, popular young man, received three life sentences.

In 1989, nursing sister Michaela Roederer, of Wuppertal, Germany, was believed to have killed twenty-eight of her patients, selecting randomly who should live or die. And, in 1989, no fewer than four nurses in Vienna were charged with a total of forty-nine murders.

Criminologists are inevitably reminded of the German mass poisoner, Anna Zwanziger, executed in 1811. Anna had come down in the world, from being the well-off wife of a solicitor to being forced to take jobs as a housekeeper. As her employers kept dying of stomach complaints, Anna was forced to move on. Finally, new advances in the detection of poisons led to her downfall. But one authority records that she declared that 'arsenic is my truest friend', and that her eyes gleamed with joy when she looked at the white powder. It is obvious that she was, to some extent, a 'mental case', a woman full of resentment at her misfortunes. But it is also clear that she came to take real pleasure in exercising the power of life and death.

How is this possible? That is hard to explain. But we can find an interesting clue in the case of the poisoner Graham Young, who began administering small doses of antimony to his family when he was only fourteen. When released from nine years of juvenile detention he took a job with a photographic firm, and again began poisoning fellow workers 'for fun'. He was suspected because, at a factory meeting to discuss the mysterious 'bug' that was decimating the workers, he could not resist showing off his knowledge of poisons. After he was sentenced to life imprisonment, his sister commented on his 'craving for publicity and notice'.

Young was an intelligent man, whose intelligence made him scorn his working-class environment and his acquaintances. In a sense, you could say that his crimes were a *substitute* for fame. If he had become famous for some other reason – such as discovering unexpected talents in the arts, for example – there can be little doubt that he would have stopped poisoning immediately. His crimes were partly the outcome of his feeling that he had no outlet for his dominance.

I find one of the most interesting sections in this book is the author's account of how Shipman broke with his old medical practice, in which he had been a partner for fifteen years, and set up his own practice, poaching three receptionists, a district nurse and three thousand patients. She points out that Shipman left his old practice because he said he hated computers, yet promptly bought himself a computer. 'He was never a team player', the author comments, with considerable understatement, and this casual remark goes to the heart of the matter. He was never a team player because he felt superior to his colleagues, and when they had served their purpose (of helping him re-establish his position after losing it through drug addiction), he wanted to be rid of them: 'He had finally wrested control of his working life, happily ensconced in his own little empire'.

For this is what the Right Man craves – 'his own little empire' – where no one can contradict him, and he is responsible to no one. This is the position Shipman had always worked for – to be his own master. I would like to take a bet that it all dated back to some small incident many years before, when Shipman suddenly felt himself vulnerable to the criticism or disapproval of his partners, and made a private vow that one day he would have done with them, whatever the cost in bad feeling.

All this would have been impossible without Shipman's certainty that he would never be caught. Without that, he would never have killed a single patient. But then, it is an unfortunate fact that many killers have found it easy to get away with murder, and have simply continued out of habit. Only two counties away from Shipman, Fred and Rosemary West went on killing for almost two decades without being suspected, and were only finally caught because Fred West raped one of his own daughters. No one suspected them, because no one suspected a perfectly ordinary and stable family – such people do not kill. And even closer to Hyde was the territory of Ian Brady and Myra Hindley, the Moors Murderers. Who would suspect a couple in their twenties of being able to torture and murder children?

As for Shipman, he felt he had an even more effective disguise for his activities – why should a busy and popular doctor want to kill his patients? And even though Shipman had aroused the suspicion of one colleague – and been investigated by the police – before he killed Kathleen Grundy, and forged her will, he was simply confident that, whatever happened, he could never be *proved* a killer and a forger. His whole attitude to murder depended upon his absolute certainty that he would never be called to account.

How is this possible? The answer is that it *is* possible, particularly for doctors. I have no doubt, for example, that Dr John Bodkin Adams of Eastbourne killed all the patients he was accused of (and acquitted of) murdering, and that he did it out of sheer greed, like a small boy helping himself to sugar lumps from the larder. I doubt whether he ever, for a moment, thought of himself as a killer. Most doctors have to make decisions about life and death – when an elderly patient is dying in pain, for instance, they might consider withholding certain treatments to end the misery. And so Adams drifted into murder, and finally began to make sure that his patients also left him their cars or other valuable possessions.

I believe that Harold Shipman also drifted into murder, for the same kind of motives as Arnfinn Nesset and Donald Harvey – some odd psychological compulsion involving the sense of power. And if he had not been caught, he would still be killing, although his increasing carelessness would almost certainly have been his downfall.

And as he spends the rest of his life in prison, he can take comfort in the thought that, among British medical murderers at least, by virtue of his lack of apparent motive, he is virtually unique.

Preface
Shipman's predecessors

Harold Frederick Shipman is the latest in a long line of medical multiple murderers. While most of them have been nurses and care assistants, not a few surgeons and physicians have turned to serial killing as an alternative to prayer, or as an agreeable and inexpensive hobby. And they have a habit of getting away with it. Perhaps the ones we hear about are merely the tip of the iceberg. They are in the ideal position to kill when the devil drives, or as the fancy takes them, without a soul being any the wiser. Medics have knowledge of and access to deadly, obscure and undetectable drugs. They know how to disable apparatus. They sign the death certificates. Most important of all, to the older generation in particular, doctors are God's representatives on Earth. As such, they are omniscient, unimpeachable and infallible. Even when presented with a mountain of incontrovertible evidence, juries still cannot quite believe that a *doctor* could do such things.

Medical serial killers constitute a highly significant sub-group, illustrating many of the phenomenon's sharpest conflicts. The contrast between the street persona of the saintly, self-sacrificing healer of the sick and the secret self, a malevolent misanthropic predator, who relishes swatting human beings like flies, is so pronounced, the contradictions so stark, the partition of the psyche so extreme, the wonder is that any single personality can contain them both and still function. The inner stresses and strains and the centrifugal forces thereby generated must be enormous. One case in particular embodies many of the thorniest issues and ethical ambiguities surrounding the nature of serial murder.

Six months after the Iraqi Armed Forces had been evicted from Kuwait, the Emir belatedly returned from exile. One of his first public appearances was at a ceremony to honour outstanding members of the Resistance. Amongst the most distinguished Kuwaiti 'partisans', whose bravery was recognised by the award of the country's most coveted medal, was a 21-year-old nurse, whose exploits were already legendary.

As soon as the Iraqis had occupied Kuwait City, the High Command forcibly removed all patients from the capital's large, well-equipped hospital, which they commandeered for the exclusive use of sick and wounded Iraqi soldiers. The medical staff was also conscripted *en masse* to care for them. Informed that they were now subject to military law and that any infractions would result in summary execution, numerous Iraqi troops guarded the wards, supposedly monitoring all activities.

However, throughout the six months of Iraqi administration, the young nurse found ways and means of quietly snuffing out her patients. She introduced air bubbles into saline drips, substituted noxious agents for prescribed drugs, gave overdoses or stealthily disconnected vital apparatus, all without incurring the slightest suspicion from the nervous Iraqis. By the time the Iraqi war machine made a dash for the border, the nurse had accounted for at least twenty enemy soldiers.

News of her exploits spread like wildfire across the 'Desert Kingdom', inspiring and delighting the populace, who invested her with Joan of Arc-like qualities. Eventually word reached the Emir, who had lost face and favour by fleeing from the invading Iraqis, tail between legs, and made matters worse by not returning promptly. By personally and publicly signalling his approval and admiration for her 'valour', the Emir hankered after a little 'reflected glory'.

Was the Kuwaiti nurse a heroine or a villain? A staunch patriot and freedom-fighter or a sordid and cowardly *serial killer* who was able to combine 'business' (self-aggrandisement) with pleasure? Her victims, like the vast majority of Iraqi soldiers, were probably conscripts, who had no designs upon Kuwait and little desire to be there in the first place. Many, if not all, were seriously ill or wounded and even if conscious, were unable to resist. Enemy soldiers or not, they were her charges. They were helpless and in her care.

On the other hand, once recovered, these same teenage conscripts would doubtless have resumed their exhausting military routine of rape, pillage, torture and execution. The verdict is finely balanced. Perhaps she was both *heroic patriot* and *vicious serial killer*. The Kuwaiti nurse was rewarded with a decoration and legendary status. So is the choice of victim all that separates a national hero/heroine from a serial killer? If the exterminator's victims are also the mortal enemies of a (recognised and embattled) civil power, they are transmuted from the lowest type of criminal predator to the highest most revered national role model. If so, then the concept of serial murder (as opposed to the term) has no moral dimension whatever. It is merely a pragmatic distinction, contingent upon the social conditions and the governing elite's attitude – what it deems acceptable, or even desirable – at a particular moment in time.

Due to the nature of their work, medical serial killers seem to stir up these fundamental issues, often connected to their specific roles and duties. Murderous health care professionals may be divided into several distinct subgroups. In the main, the extent of their lethality is inversely proportional to their responsibilities. Nurses have been furtively doing away with patients for centuries, either upon request, or on their own initiative.

Most worked in hospitals, like Beverley Allitt in Lincoln, or the Viennese 'Graveyard Shift' under Waltroud Wagner and her seven-woman team, suspected of 160 killings but convicted of only a small fraction, who had devised a bizarre betting game of 'elderly patient roulette'. Others were employed in small clinics, such as Genene Jones Turk, linked to the sudden demise of 63 babies. Jones was addicted to the praise and acclaim she received when she brought a child back from the brink. So she began to engineer the crises, so she could step in at the last moment and be heroic. However on 63 occasions, her timing was slightly out and no one was more upset by these infant deaths than their dedicated emergency nurse.

In ages past, midwives, who like family doctors had no institutional ties and made regular house calls, could often be counted on to 'arrange' stillbirths for a woman in distress. In more rural, feudal regions, the village midwife was frequently a living pharmacopoeia, with an extensive knowledge of herbs and folk remedies. Not a few were burnt as witches because of their 'infernal potions'. Some midwives of this sort also had a collateral familiarity with poisons, which they might be prevailed upon to supply to discreet souls (normally women), for nefarious purposes. Reportedly, wives would continually pester them for 'a physic' to reduce their husbands' preoccupation with 'lustful connection' as they were exhausted from many childbirths. Love philtres that promised to enthral the heart's desire was perennially popular.

Nor were such activities confined to the distant past, as 'The Angel-Makers of Nagyrev' demonstrated, at the time of the First World War. Conscription had carried off most of the men of fighting age from this agricultural village, 70 miles south of Budapest. Without a resident doctor, the inhabitants relied upon Julia Fazekas, the matronly local midwife, to take care of their health needs.

The situation of the lonely ladies of Nagyrev, whose husbands and lovers were away at the front, was made slightly more bearable as the war progressed, by the siting of two prisoner of war camps on the outskirts of the village. These were not places where the inmates were kept under lock and key 24 hours a day. They were allowed to serve as farm workers and casual labourers for the locals.

They soon began to provide services of another kind to the village's unfulfilled womenfolk. In short order, even the plainest among them was able to call upon the services of two or three strapping Russian and Italian prisoners of war from the nearby camps which had an exceptional record of no escapes.

Thus the war years turned into one long debauch for captives and captivated alike. The ladies of Nagyrev were no longer lonely and most seldom thought of their menfolk any more. Nagyrev was a contented community. Life was one long erotic idyll. Then the war ended and the men came home. They received a frosty welcome. Most of the wives and girlfriends were of one mind. Their husbands and boyfriends were a poor second best. Furthermore, the camps had not been dismantled, though no guards remained. The inmates seemed in no hurry to return home. Snatched moments in fields, nervous trysts in barns and the like were an anti-climax for ladies who had spent entire days sampling the carnal delights of two or three exotic, sophisticated Italians in turn.

They simply could not readjust. Things could never return to their prewar state. The demobbed heroes of Nagyrev were deemed obsolete. They were not prepared to go anywhere, however, and when some wives suggested this helpful option, not a few of Nagyrev's men responded with alcohol and fists. The ladies decided that something must be done. The answer was the local midwife Julia Fazekas and 'Aunt Suzi' Olah, her dedicated assistant, who did the dispensing.

Having heard the same dilemma recited by a succession of village women and girls, Mrs Fazekas was spurred by a lucrative stroke of genius. She and Aunt Suzi travelled to the nearest town, visiting every pharmacist they could think of. When they returned to Nagyrev, their baskets were crammed full with flypapers, which they set to work boiling down. This process extracted the active ingredient – arsenic. This was to be the panacea for the restless wives and girlfriends whose menfolk enforced their conjugal rights and prevented their spouses and betrothed from resuming their ecstatically licentious lifestyles.

Little arm twisting was required and word spread. Soon the midwife and her helpmate were besieged by customers for their 'problem-solving potion'. Aunt Suzi dispensed it in generous doses, sending various nieces on errands to towns in the region to replenish their supplies. As soon as the wave of male mortality hit Nagyrev in earnest, Julia Fazekas, to avoid becoming a victim of her own success, realised that the paperwork must be in order, so that any unwelcome inquiries could be fobbed off with the correct documentation. To this end she contacted her cousin, a genuine licensed medical practitioner, who lived twenty miles away. For a consideration, which grew steeper by the month, the good doctor was prepared to furnish correctly completed death certificates and file them with the competent authorities.

Unfortunately, these unforeseen expenses necessitated a price hike, which had the unintended effect of increasing the murder rate, as the ladies decided to aid their ageing parents' long journey to the grave, so that they could claim their paltry legacies somewhat earlier than nature intended. From these ill-gotten gains they could then pay the midwife's higher price and have a supply of the elixir at hand in case the need arose, which it invariably seemed to. The villagers were, of course, unaware that boiled-down flypapers were the source of 'Dr Julia's' and Aunt Suzi's nostrum plus the wealth and power it brought them.

Thus, family members became 'legitimate' targets, if by their deaths the lust-crazed younger females could afford the 'medicine' to remove obstructive male partners from the scene and revert to their erstwhile daily routine of orgiastic decadence. The husbands of Nagyrev must have been a singularly dim-witted bunch, for they never seem to have questioned the origins of the epidemic, although it was exclusively confined to men.

On the other side, a number of Russian fighting men probably missed their homeland's revolutions and much of the ensuing civil war, while the Italians avoided the postwar chaos and street battles between the Red and Black, which ended with Mussolini's assumption of power. However, the repatriation of the POWs could not be postponed indefinitely. By January 1920, the camps had been evacuated and were due for demolition. All the internees were gone.

Yet the liberal dispensation of poison to unwanted persons did not stop. It had become a local tradition, a habit, the favoured method of solving problems, the weapon of first resort. Now the ladies, most of them widows, took lovers from nearby towns and hamlets, disposing of them (with Dr Julia's problem-solver) when their appeal faded, or if they were suspected of straying. Ageing relatives, unruly children and economically unwelcome infants went the same way. Periodic probes by the Hungarian gendarmerie into the drastically reduced life expectancy of men from the Nagyrev region always ended with the impeccably correct documentation and properly filed death certificates that Dr Julia's medically qualified cousin attended to . . .

And so the humdrum daily round of sensuality, profligacy and sudden mortality ground on, in Nagyrev and its environs, until 1927, when a furious dispute erupted between two of the village's more prominent widow-conspirators. This squabble was speedily settled when one of the contending parties was struck down without warning. Retribution was almost exacted, for later the same week, Mrs B., who had won the earlier argument by default or arsenic, was herself taken ill. She more or less survived, but only as a shadow of her former self, and only with great difficulty did Dr Julia prevent a full-scale vendetta from breaking out. A truce was declared but no one forgot.

Two years later, in the summer of 1929, the inevitable happened, when one of the 'toxic widows' who wished to do away with her latest flame, who had begun to bore her, miscalculated the dosage. As a result, her paramour became very sick indeed, but did not die. Neither was he as naïve or as asinine as most of his predecessors. As soon as the sickness hit him, he suspected he had been poisoned. Consequently, he brushed aside all his lady-friend's ministrations and once he was able to stand unaided, lurched off to the gendarmerie to press charges. Detectives confronted the Nagyrev widow in question, who, apparently too taken aback to speak, was lodged in a police cell. She broke quickly, naming a friend as accomplice, and the trail led inexorably to Dr Julia Fazekas and Aunt Suzi Olah. Clandestine surveillance and an undercover police operation were mounted.

As a consequence of these tactics, no less than 51 women from the Nagyrev area were arrested and charged. Skin-saving denunciations, hearsay and gossip were plentiful, but hard evidence was scarce, and proof more elusive still. Rural Hungary in 1929–30 was not a world leader in forensic science, and many of the victims had been interred for a decade or more. Their grieving families, as good, staunchly superstitious Roman Catholic stock, were obdurately opposed to exhumation.

In the event, 32 women were finally convicted of murder or related offences, some on multiple counts. Nine, including Aunt Suzi, her sister Lydia and the latter's unprepossessing, murderous daughter-in-law Julia Lipka, who had developed a passion for extermination,[1] were sentenced to death. An equal

---

[1] 'Credited' with at least ten poisonings, snuffing out aunts, siblings, a stepmother, her father, two children, her husband and a lover.

number were sentenced to life; eight received more than ten years hard labour and the remaining six, shorter jail terms.

'Doctor' Julia herself cheated the executioner by swallowing a lethal cocktail of laudanum and 'extract of flypapers' when the officers delegated to arrest her knocked on her door. She was dead by the time they broke it down. Heaps of used, half-boiled and new flypapers, plus jugs full of the valuable distillate littered her modest dwelling. Several other 'noxious substances' were also recovered.

The 'Angel-Makers of Nagyrev' are relevant to the Shipman case, not just because a midwife and her second cousin, a doctor (who somehow escaped) were both leading players in the affair, but because the midwife, Julia Fazekas, really did serve as the village's *de facto* GP (with Aunt Suzi as her dispensing chemist). Both the midwife and her loyal attendant made house calls if summoned with sufficient urgency and currency. Moreover, police searchers discovered large amounts of Julia Fazekas' 'problem-solver' (arsenic) all over her house, just as they uncovered quantities of diamorphine, which he was banned from keeping at hand,[2] at Shipman's residence.

The majority of medical serial killers have carried out their homicidal activities in an institution of some sort, whether a hospital, clinic or residential home. In such establishments, the patients are more accessible, more vulnerable, usually debilitated and frequently helpless.

---

[2] This rule had been imposed upon Shipman because in 1974 the fact that he had become addicted to pethidine (demerol), an opiate-like analgesic often supplied to women in labour, had come to light. Treated indulgently, Shipman was allowed to continue his medical career with that proviso. He could prescribe Grade A painkillers, like diamorphine, pethidine, palfium etc., but he could not keep them around.

Typically, the victims are the very old, the very young, or the very sick.

One of the more homogeneous institutional serial killer subgroups comprises homosexual nurses – mostly, though not exclusively, male. Some of these male nurses were incredibly prolific killers. Florida's Brian Rosenfeld (1995), terminated more than 25 patients, most of them old, and many of them helpless. Jeffrey Feltner (1989), another gay carer from Florida, was linked to fifteen suspicious patient deaths.[3] Roberto Diaz (1983), from Southern California, another of this ilk, tied to more than nineteen unexpected hospital fatalities, was charged with and convicted of a dozen. New York's Richard Angelo (1991) was probably responsible for up to fifteen patient slayings. The infamous Donald Harvey, strictly speaking an orderly or care assistant rather than a qualified nurse, roamed the wards of Ohio and Kentucky's Nursing Homes and hospitals, extinguishing patients as the fancy took him, for between seven and eight years before he was finally exposed in 1988. Like several others of his kind, his dubious activities and proximity to sudden death amongst the bedridden had been detected early on in his career. Anxious to avoid bad publicity, the hospital authorities decided to dispense with his services, rather than take legal action. They even provided a reference, failing to notify his next clinical employers of question marks surrounding his character. Harvey eventually admitted 58 murders.

Finally, this particular trend in the medical serial killer reached its peak in 1996, with Indiana intensive care male nurse Lynn Majors, who was seriously

---

[3] Though he was in fact only charged with seven. This is the usual practice, indicting the assailant for only those counts in which the evidence is watertight, or that he is willing to admit.

suspected of anything up to 165 lethal transactions with patients. In a hospital where he worked from 1994 to 1995, for the three years before he arrived, the mean intensive care mortality rate was 27 per annum. Then Majors joined the team and over the next eighteen months the level rose to 103 deaths per annum (*pro rata*). Majors is the only medical serial killer on either side of the Atlantic whose body count exceeds Shipman's overall total, but he had 'captive' victims in the intensive-care wards of large medical establishments. Shipman was a 'friar' rather than a 'monk', as he was out and about in the world and had a list of regular patients, many of whom venerated him like a saint, commending his conscientiousness, consideration and ostensible probity. But then, is it easier or harder for a pillar of the community to live a Jekyll and Hyde existence?

Catherine Wood and Gwendolyn Graham (1982), a lesbian duo who 'looked after' Alzheimer's patients in Walker, Michigan,[4] were exceptional in several respects. Wood later reported that she and Graham became sexually excited and insatiable whenever they took life (at least six times). Their reaction was a little reminiscent of turn-of-the-century virgin, serial killing New England residential nurse Jane Toppan, who dispatched more than 70 ageing wealthy patients with morphine, but was clever enough to combine it with atropine, preventing pinpoint pupils. This was another elementary precaution that Shipman never bothered, or was unable, to take. The evidence indicates he started

---

[4] One of the stranger common factors shared by these multicidal, often US, homosexual nurses was their geographical distribution. In contrast to habitual US female poisoners, the bulk of whom were 'Southern Belles', many if not most of the (gay) nurses lived and worked in the Great Lake states, such as Ohio, Michigan and Pennsylvania.

planning only after he had done the deed. Such behaviour is typical of a rage-dominated serial killer. Negligible reproaches, minor inconveniences and imagined slights appeared to ignite an implacable fury within him. If the protagonist was a middle-aged or elderly woman, she would probably be dead within a day or two.

Virtually all of Shipman's qualified doctor predecessors, like the majority of the nurse and care assistant 'terminators', carried out their depredations in the institutional settings where they were employed. In one or two instances, like that of Ulsterman Dr Robert Clements, who also used diamorphine as his weapon of choice, their profession was largely incidental. Clements, whose career in extermination spanned two and a half decades (1923–49), did his dirty work in the comfort of his own home(s). All four victims were his wives, for whose death certificates he furnished one of the signatures (and the cause), readily persuading a GP colleague to act as his co-signatory. This was precisely the technique that Shipman later adopted.

Clements, who chose to kill himself rather than submit to justice, was a late example in a tradition of dissolute philandering physicians, who really belonged to the Victorian era – characters like wife and mistress killer, Dr Alfred Walden. Or the mutton-chopped impregnator of maidservants, Dr Edward Pritchard, an upstanding citizen who fled from Hampshire to Glasgow to avoid awkward questions about a fire at his well-insured home, in which a bulging servant girl was informally cremated. Pritchard could not help but take his habits, his wife and his shrewish mother-in-law with him. But history promptly repeated itself. He felt obliged to abort a fifteen-year-old maidservant, for he was keen to continue their liaison. Another occasional maid fell down some stairs, dying a few weeks later, just as she seemed to be recovering. Then the dutiful Mrs Pritchard became seriously ill, causing her hovering harridan of a mother to move in, to keep an eye on her lecherous son-in-law and nurse Mary Jane Pritchard back to health. His mother-in-law's presence must have cramped Pritchard's style, but not his lust for his adolescent mistress. So the redoubtable Mrs Taylor, his mother-in-law, predictably fell ill after eating a tapioca pudding. The household cook also went down with a similar ailment, with symptoms a local doctor described as 'resembling the effects of a narcotic drug of the opiate variety . . .' Pritchard took fright when he realised that Mrs Taylor was beginning to improve. Abjuring morphine as to easy to spot and quantitatively unpredictable, he switched to antimony, which had the lethal results he was seeking. Both mother and daughter relapsed and died within a short time of each other. Pritchard was so inflamed with carnal lust for his young concubine that his wife died before he could arrange even a modest insurance policy on her life. Pritchard's problems should have been over, for the old lady had died first, leaving a tidy sum to Mary Jane. When she too died, just over a fortnight later, the legacy devolved to the grieving widower. The servant girl, now sixteen, moved into her master's bed and Pritchard seemed set fair. Then came the anonymous letter, arriving at the Procurator-Fiscal's (the Scottish Director of Public Prosecutions) office, just days after Mary Jane's funeral. It denounced Pritchard as a poisoner, mentioning in passing the fatal Hampshire fire, the cook's untimely illness and the accident proneness of Pritchard's invariably glamorous female household staff. The Glasgow police exhumed the bodies of mother and daughter at the dead of night, so not to alert the good doctor. Both were brimful with antimony. Scottish justice was expeditious, for less than six weeks later a hundred thousand people watched the sanctimonious surgeon swing.

Even Pritchard, who was not a cool, calculating murderer, eventually rejected morphine as the lethal weapon, as it was too easily detected. Other medics have tried to conceal their crimes in a number of different ways. Dr Marcel Petiot, a French physician resident in Paris throughout the war, gassed at least 64 desperate, fugitive Jews, in his own private gas chamber. Through a concealed porthole, Petiot liked to observe his victims' death throes. Claiming to be a member of the Resistance, Petiot would relieve them of their remaining worldly goods and assets, then show them to the guest room. Unknown to his scared and weary lodgers, it could be hermetically sealed from outside, through ingeniously designed gadgetry and a control panel. Once so arranged, no escape was possible from the poison gas that wafted in through a dummy ventilation shaft. Petiot had also constructed a small crematorium in his basement, to rapidly incinerate the incriminating corpses. It worked well, but Petiot, a lifelong thief and heroin user, was not inclined to dwell too long on details like servicing and maintenance. He did not have the chimney swept regularly, so it stopped drawing properly and began to clog up. Either unaware or past caring about such trivia, or perhaps having total confidence in his seemingly charmed life (echoes of Shipman?), he ignored the foul-smelling thick grey or black smoke which started to belch out of his chimney, nauseating the neighbours, who notified the gendarmerie. They visited Petiot, who, far from the Resistance man he professed to be, was in fact a valued police informant.

He mumbled about disposing of dead dogs and cats, the officers gave him a wink and a nod, and life returned to normal.

Petiot did nothing to ameliorate the choking fumes that still spewed forth from his house and hung like a shroud over the prosperous neighbourhood where it was situated. The police were not interested. Then one night residents noticed sparks and flames billowing out of the offending stack. Claiming to fear for their lives and property lest the entire street be consumed in some terrible Petiot-inspired conflagration, a deputation alerted the fire service, who hastened to the scene. Oblivious to the householder's threats and entreaties the firefighters crashed through doors and walls, axes in hand, hoses on full blast. Eventually someone brought some light to the darkened cellar, where the furnace was installed. At that point the emergency workers were able to identify what the odd bits of wood they had felt beneath their feet and nearly slipped on actually were. They were human bones, some with flesh, rather than leaves, still attached. More decaying bodies were found in the doctor's stables, as was a mountain of clothes and accessories. The vitriolic but witty Petiot proved to be a good turn at his subsequent trial and quite won over the visiting spectators, who were not averse to a little entrepreneurial anti-Semitism, especially when the perpetrator was so utterly shameless and unrepentant. Petiot had a razor-sharp intellect, making the prosecutor and judge appear decidedly leaden-footed, then whispering loud asides to the public gallery, commenting on their clumsiness. By the end of the trial, the presiding judge was so overcome with fury that he had to call a recess to compose himself. The jury did not dare let Petiot off under the circumstances, and he was duly guillotined in May 1946.

xxx

Dr Ronald Clark of Michigan had a small clinic and his practice was not unlike that of a UK GP. In the mid-sixties, while performing minor operations in his 'surgery', Clark developed a predilection for giving his female patients liberal amounts of analgesics and short-acting general (as opposed to local) anaesthetic. When they passed out, as they usually did, Clark would sexually abuse them in a highly imaginative and depraved manner. Sporadically Clark confused the dosages and drugs and as a result the patient concerned failed to revive. His nurses were just feet away, in the consulting room. His receptionists were in the waiting-room adjacent to the 'treatment room', on the other side (again one is reminded of Shipman's occasional incautious executions just a curtain or a door away from his support staff). This reckless conduct led to Clark's downfall. One day, a receptionist entered the treatment room at an injudicious moment and caught Dr Clark crouched naked over his patient's face. Exclamations and ejaculations ensued, and Clark realised he was finished if his shocked middle-aged receptionist was allowed to disclose what she had seen. He was therefore obliged to prevent this eventuality, which he did with a blow, prior to a lethal injection. A game of 'musical corpses' followed, as his semi-molested patient came round, in a somewhat dazed and uncomprehending state.

Clark pretended that his receptionist had died while undergoing minor surgery. The authorities had heard that one before, however, several times. The autopsy uncovered one or two inconsistencies, but insufficient to justify a prosecution. Consequently, the State Attorney General's Office initiated inquiries into Clark's background. The investigators did not have to delve very deep to unearth shovels full of dirt about Dr Clark. He was apparently an escapee from an Illinois lunatic asylum (as such places were then known), but, unsurprisingly, had not seen fit to mention the fact, either on his application to medical school, or on his application for a state licence to practice medicine. This was enough to put him behind bars, while a further probe was conducted. Slowly the whole sordid truth about Dr Clark's medical career unravelled, until he was once again detained in a locked ward until he was deemed sane enough to try.

Dr Mario E. Jascalovich, an Argentine citizen, known during his trial in 1976 as Dr X due to an injunction won by his attorneys, sought to conceal his involvement in 25 or more patient murders by different means, for unprecedented reasons. From 1964 to 1968, Jascalovich, a distinguished surgeon, was the sole Director of New Jersey clinic. In 1966 the board had tried to bring in another surgeon, an osteopath, Dr Stanley Briski, as co-director. In spite of his eminence, Briski's patients began to die off, even when the procedure he had performed on them was utterly routine. The board became alarmed and restricted Briski's privileges; this was tantamount to demotion. Briski became a nervous wreck and felt he had no option but to resign. For eighteen months Jascalovich again became undisputed top dog. Some of the clinic governors, however, still entertained doubts about Jascalovich, so they repeated the 'Briski experiment', recruiting Dr Anthony Harris, a highly respected vascular specialist, to act as joint Chief Of Medical Staff with Jascalovich. Then Harris's patients started to give up the ghost, for no obvious reason, even when they were more or less well again. Initially, Harris was baffled; the unheralded, mysterious deaths persisted. Autopsies were scrupulously performed on the dead, but no obvious cause of death could be established in most cases. Whenever it could, it turned out to be 'natural causes'. Harris wondered if he was jinxed, but unlike Briski he decided he was not. At that point, only one other logical explanation could account for all the strange fatalities. Harris arranged to be contacted immediately if another of his patients died in his absence. Sure enough, it happened. Harris dashed to the clinic and discovered Jascalovich quite literally lurking suspiciously at the scene, unable to account adequately for his presence. Harris's misgivings about his colleague grew apace when he noticed a notation on the recently expired patient's chart indicating that Jascalovich had treated him earlier that night. Asked about the circumstances, Jascalovich shrugged and became hostile.

Harris informed the Vice Chairman of the Governing Board, Dr Alan Lans, of his suspicions. Other members of the Board were notified and, as a body, they confronted Jascalovich, whose reply was an incoherent mumble about a 'conspiracy' to ruin him. In Jascalovich's presence, his locker was opened. Inside, the Board members found needles, syringes and eighteen virtually empty ampoules of curacit, a medically refined anaesthetic distillate of curare, the drug used by Amazonian Indians for hunting, which kills by paralysing muscles, including the heart. Everything was passed to the District Attorney, who investigated Jascalovich for three months, before unaccountably declaring that he had been cleared without a stain on his character.

That Jascalovich had achieved this outcome merely through an astute and timely combination of charm, outright denial and tall stories about researching new uses for the drug is hard to believe. Jascalovich was, of course, a relatively wealthy man. There the case remained for another seven years, until an investigative reporter on the *New York Times* reinvigorated it. Jascalovich's story was exposed as a fabrication. More incriminating records, charts, duty rosters and patient lists were located. Still the DA's office did not want to know, mainly because all three leading prosecutors had been parties to the original 'inquiry'. By threatening to publicise this point and to interpret their demeanour as obstructionism, the journalist succeeded in having the file passed to a fairly junior but 'clean' Assistant DA. Corpses were exhumed. Jascalovich was unworried, for he knew that curare breaks down quickly in the body, swiftly becoming untraceable. However, by some inventive science and careful research, the team of pathologists discovered that the poison was retained in the 'optical vitreous humour' (eyeball fluid), and it was identified as present in five cases (the others were too decomposed).

Jascalovich was charged and a 35-week trial ensued. At the end of that time, the jury, some of whom had inexplicably taken to the defendant, retired for just two hours and fifty minutes before returning with a 'not guilty' verdict, the perversity and circumstances of which remain a mystery to this day. Certainly, Jascalovich had a very able and expensive attorney, yet the case had seemed watertight. The State Medical Board took a less sanguine view, and Jascalovich lost his licence to practise in the state. Not long after these two events Jascalovich abruptly left for Argentina without paying his lawyer's bill. He died just four years later.

Jascalovich's motive (if he had one) was uniquely blatant, but according to sundry experts, including the FBI, it was in many fundamentals typical of the doctor serial killer, in that it was all about (the preservation of) power and status. Accustomed to Godlike adulation and authority, so the theory goes, the rogue medic can very easily slip into the role of playing God, with his desires becoming all-consuming, and the sick, the halt and the lame merely the means of satisfying those aspirations. If most were dead or chronically sick, then he would be doing them a mercy. Everyone would be a winner.

That was roughly how the prosecution depicted the rationale that they claimed had driven John Bodkin Adams, a Sussex GP, to do away with 21 of his female patients,[5] after most of them had changed their wills in his favour. The year was 1957.

Adams was a bloated, balding, bespectacled bachelor in his late fifties, with a taste for good living and the finer things of life. Well-heeled elderly ladies were disproportionately represented on his patient list. Adams' chief treatment for many of these ageing matrons consisted of doling out barbiturates and opiates, often over a considerable period of time and in generous doses, so that ultimately several developed dependencies of one sort or another and were totally reliant upon Adams for their supplies. Few, if any, actually appreciated the bleak realities of their predicament, or were able to envisage it in such stark terms. The drugs that killed them were usually barbiturates or diamorphine, which Adams sometimes acquired in less than honest ways. The ladies tended to finally expire (and most were bedridden) not too long after they named Adams as a major beneficiary in their wills. One matron had a Rolls Royce Adams much admired. Sure enough, she changed her will to bequeath it to her 'dear doctor'.

---

[5] Nine other cases had been put to one side and saved for a putative second trial.

Adams too finally came to grief due to the incredulity of relatives, who had expected to be left whole estates and then found them snatched away. He ended up facing 21 charges of murder at the Old Bailey. Another batch of cases would probably have followed. The trial was lengthy by English standards and the evidence looked grim for Adams. However an English jury in 1957 was not able to believe that a doctor, one of those semi-divine experts they all but worshipped, would even dream of committing one murder, let alone 21, and for reasons of self-enrichment at that. Moreover, the roly-poly jovial Adams did not look like a 1957 jury's image of a murderer. Adams had also been cunning. All those who died were demonstrably ill, some terminally, before they 'unexpectedly' died. Few were any longer mobile. This allowed Adams to argue that he had in a way contributed to their deaths, by giving them large quantities of heavy painkillers, so they could retain some dignity in death. His barrister thought up, or at least publicised, the fortuitous catchphrase 'easing the passing'.

The jury were not inclined to disagree, and in less than an hour returned with a verdict of not guilty, to jubilation all round except amongst the relatives, who pressed for the Prosecution Service to institute a second trial on the remaining nine charges. The Crown declined. Adams had more trouble with the BMA and was struck off for a short period because of the prescription irregularities, the significance of which the jury seemed not to appreciate.

The lesson was that a doctor could get away with multiple murder provided he was careful, clinical and discriminating in his choice of victim. He only needed a semblance of a defence for juries to feel sympathy.

This hard reality evidently eluded Harold Shipman, and perhaps never even occurred to him. For a doctor he did not seem overburdened with intelligence. The sloppiness of his depredations attests to that. He was not in the same league as his closest predecessor, John Bodkin Adams.

Although no standard blueprint of the seriously rogue doctor can be formulated, one or two common traits may be identified. They do not generally become homicidal until early middle age. They tend to have a lifelong reputation for light fingers. They tend to abuse drugs, in particular diamorphine or its cognates. Such medics are inclined to be brusque and acerbic in manner; have an arrogant demeanour, yet are able to command enormous loyalty. Often self-made men, they are apt to be acutely conscious of status, readily taking offence if not accorded the respect they deem their due. Given to brooding over minor or fancied slights, they harbour grudges indefinitely and may seem arbitrarily vindictive. Politically, they are frequently of the hard right, privately espousing a primitive form of social Darwinism. Above all, and hardest to actually appreciate in its most literal sense, is their utter lack of empathy. They are quite simply incapable of putting themselves in someone else's shoes. (Contrary to popular mythology, this is not a trait shared by all serial killers. Some lust-driven serial killers demonstrate an *enhanced* capacity for empathy.) This may be a failure of imagination. They may be severely practical, earthbound characters, with a very short-term frame of reference and somewhat stunted feelings. Many like to display their lack of squeamishness, their detachment in the face of horror and appalling suffering. This goes further than the essential dispassion or professional front that a doctor, especially a surgeon, must cultivate in order to do his job. It has a crass air about it, some element of showing off, almost relishing harrowing circumstances as an opportunity to exhibit what such medics believe to be leadership qualities.

One further feature worthy of comment is their inability to make it to the very top of their profession. Several have been very competent doctors, but none has been outstanding, though they are all inclined to give the impression that they should and would have gone further, were it not for some dastardly injustice not their fault. Then nothing is their fault. That and its concomitant, the persistent blame-shifting, may well be by-products of their singular want of empathy, which places them at the centre of the universe and makes their convenience the highest cosmic priority.

Shipman was like Petiot (who in many respects is the archetypal rogue doctor), in at least one other way. Both men were on short fuses, having hair-trigger tempers. Yet their fury did not manifest as a spontaneous lashing out. It was temporarily repressed. However, Shipman could not sit on his virulent anger for long before it burst out of its restraints. For a man of undoubted intelligence and ostensibly possessing considerable self-discipline, his impulse controls were severely impaired. This deficiency was undoubtedly worsening. The intermissions between killings were diminishing. His inhibitions were dissolving. His internal rage was intensifying and his ability to manage his homicidal urges had decreased markedly. Shipman was in the first stages of a typical serial killer's tailspin. One way or another he was on course for a crash. And crash he did.

1 Angela Woodruff

The scrap of paper fluttered in Angela Woodruff's shaking hand.

The last will and testament of her beloved mother, the former Mayoress of Hyde, Kathleen Grundy, made a mockery of her memory. Badly composed and messily typed from a worn-out ribbon on a tatty scrap of paper, it would have horrified her proud, meticulous mother. It looked for all the world as if it had been written by an ill-educated, unworldly old lady whose health was failing. Such a pathetic creature would be the very opposite of fit, healthy Mrs Grundy. Mrs Woodruff, still reeling from the shock of her mother's death ten days earlier, could not – indeed would not – believe her eyes. The will read:

> All my estate, money and house to my doctor. My family are not in need and I want to reward him for all the care he has given me and the people of Hyde. He is sensible enough to handle any problems this may give him. My doctor is Dr HF Shipman.

Kathleen Grundy was a woman of class, in every sense of the word. She was a wealthy woman from a good family who had worn a chain of office; she could have considered herself superior but kept her feet firmly on the ground. Consequently she was loved in Gee Cross, the pretty little village where she had lived all of her 81 years, as well as throughout Hyde, the adjoining old mill town where she worked so tirelessly for charity. Her sudden death on 24 June 1998 devastated all who knew her.

She was born Kathleen Platt in Hyde on 2 July 1916. The First World War had sunk to its lowest level the day before, with the beginning of the first Battle of the Somme. More than 620,000 Allied troops were to be sacrificed for the sake of five miles of mud in the following four months. But Hyde was booming. Its cotton mills, hat and glove factories, engineering works and manufacturing plants were all at full steam.

That success did not stop at the dirty old town's borders. It ran like an intravenous drip straight into Gee Cross, a tiny but thriving village sitting on the edge of Hyde. The town's well-to-do had made their homes in its old, stone-built cottages and the better-off workers settled in the new red-brick terraces. They were all well served by a pub, a couple of shops and even an undertaker's, Armitage's. They were also well served by Mother Nature, as the village rose up through steep, leafy streets to the local beauty spot of Werneth Low. There, on a clear day, you can see the whole of Manchester, a blue-grey pile shrouded in smog in those days, and beyond to the flat, pale green plains of Cheshire.

Young Kath and her brother Eric had a secure and happy childhood in this peaceful village. The little Platts wanted for nothing, but they were not spoilt. Although money was no problem for the family, it was the product of sheer hard graft and their immediate environment served as a constant reminder of this. The family ran a painting and decorating business from the yard next door to their terraced home on Stockport Road. As a result of this, and the droning of the mills below, their feet stayed on the ground. Kath was never afraid to get her hands dirty when necessary – a trait later treasured by her charity shop colleagues.

Throughout the 20s and even the 30s, the Platts continued to prosper and, as their riches grew, they bought two more houses next door to their own. Kath Grundy still owned the centre of the three houses when she died, renting it to Geoff Ridgway, who regarded her as a friend more than a landlady. 'She was lovely,' he said soon after her death. 'She had no airs and graces, though she could have. She had a good sense of humour and was always happy to talk for a while – unless she was rushing off to watch the tennis at Wimbledon.'

Little Kath Platt grew up into a smart, well-presented young lady. Hers was not what locals would call 'a chocolate-box face' but she had strong, handsome features that were a perfect countenance for her fierce brain. Most importantly, her smile, a frequent sign of her ready wit, was confident and bright and lit up her eyes. She won the heart of Manchester University lecturer John Grundy, who had also once been her schoolteacher.

Kath became Mrs Grundy in 1941. The couple set up home in Bruntwood, a pretty stone-built house on Joel Lane, the best part of Gee Cross. She worked as a secretary but gave it up when their only child, Angela, was born in 1945. Still she preferred to remain busy. She juggled motherhood, housework and helping Eric and their mother run the family business with her charity work through the Women's Royal Voluntary Service. In the meantime John became the councillor for Werneth, and then an alderman. When he became the

Mayor of Hyde for 1962–63, Kath became his Mayoress. It was a job she loved, to which she was brilliantly suited, and she equalled her husband's commitment to the town's top job. It was she who founded the popular and successful Penny A Week scheme, in which workers gave a penny of their weekly wage to a fund to help old folk. The couple made such a mark on the town that Tameside Council named a tower block John Grundy House.

John died suddenly in 1968 while holidaying alone in the Lake District. The couple loved the Lakes for its scenic walks and had bought a flat there, but Kath was at home with her mother-in-law when John died. He had collapsed with a heart attack almost at the summit of a mountain on one of his rambles and was found by a distraught walker. Mrs Grundy and Angela were told of their loss in a telephone call. They scattered John's ashes in the Lake District and Mrs Grundy, with no yearning to visit without her John, later sold the flat. She never remarried.

But despite the loss of her partner of 27 years, Mrs Grundy was not ready to hide away in widow's weeds. She embarked on a short political career as councillor for Werneth, the post once held by her husband. But when Hyde Town Council was merged with the other towns to form Tameside Council in 1972, she stepped down. She was devoted to Hyde and its people, not politics and power. 'She didn't want to be part of that,' her daughter Angela later recalled.

Mrs Grundy also threw herself into charity work, a mission that was to last her 30 years of widowhood. She devoted six days a week and many an evening to her good works. She was a stalwart of Age Concern and a familiar face in the charity's Hyde store, on the town's main drag, Market Street, where she worked Tuesdays,

Thursdays and often Saturdays as well. She also did the shop's accounts and paid in the takings at a local bank. She was a member of the Mayor of Hyde Committee, the Mayor of Hyde Trust Fund and the Mayoresses' Committee, a group of current and former Mayoresses who held fundraising events and distributed the money to charity. She and her good friend May Clark, another former Mayoress, looked forward to their monthly nights out with the group. She also had a strong interest in health issues. In the late 1970s she fundraised for a new orthopaedic unit at Hyde Hospital and just before she died she was a member of the Community Health Council. She would attend its meetings on many an evening, often working alongside local GPs – including Dr Shipman. In the May before she died, Mrs Grundy suggested her part of the Mayoresses' Fund be donated to Dr Shipman's surgery appeal fund but the committee decided against it and she had to tell him the £200 she had hoped to give was not available. The money went to Tameside's new Willow Wood Hospice instead. Mrs Grundy also gave advice to other pensioners on any minor financial problems they had. Gee Cross villager Phyllis Howsam recalled how she always had everyone and their problems in mind: 'There was never a day I saw her when she would not ask how my husband was. He was ill and she always remembered. She was so caring.'

But Mrs Grundy was best known at Werneth House, a local community centre where she served lunches to the elderly on Mondays, Wednesdays and Fridays – even though, at 81, she had years on them. She was great company and fun to be around, both at the lunches and on the days out that were often organised by the committee. On Mrs Grundy's last trip, to Bakewell, she was in her usual high spirits. Two days later, she was dead.

In what little spare time she had, Mrs Grundy was a big sports fan, especially when it came to the tennis at Wimbledon. She also had green fingers and took great care over the good-sized garden at Loughrigg Cottage. The manicured lawns, framed by a riot of colourful flowers, were the pride of a very smart street. Right up to her death she did all her own cleaning and gardening, even trying to cut down some big bushes on the Sunday before she died. The garden also featured a Victorian-style lamppost, which she used as a signal that all was well to her old friend, taxi driver John Shaw. She was John's favourite fare and he was devastated when she died, having long held suspicions about Dr Shipman. At the end of one of her many evenings out, for instance the Mayoresses' Ball with Mrs Clark, she would put the lamp on to show John that all was well – that is, if he didn't come inside to check for her instead.

Family and friends were also essential to Mrs Grundy, who was as kind-hearted as she was intelligent. She was the last remaining Platt – her brother Eric had died in a horrific accident on the Denton roundabout in 1992. He was crushed when a lorry shed its load of tyres on to his car, leaving the sister to whom he had remained close his share of their parents' fortune. His death was the talk of the village as they rallied round in sympathy for Kath Grundy.

Mrs Grundy was consoled by the fact her daughter Angela had made her proud, so proud it almost made her heart burst. She had done well at Manchester High School for Girls and, after getting her degree at Manchester University, trained as a solicitor. Angela made a good match with David Woodruff, a local man who was also the son of a wealthy businessman. Their long and happy marriage had produced two sons, Richard and Matthew, to whom Mrs Grundy was devoted. She stayed with Angela for a few weeks after each of the boys were born, in 1974 and 1975. They, too, were a source of pride. Just before their grandma died, they proved their mettle: Richard won a first-class degree and Matthew got a Japanese government-sponsored job teaching English. Mrs Grundy, described by Angela as 'a great talker', told everyone she met in the days before she died of her grandsons' achievements. 'She loved them to pieces and they loved her to pieces, too,' Angela later recalled with emotion in the witness box at Shipman's trial. The family had moved to Harbury, a picture-perfect village in Leamington Spa, but mother and daughter spoke on the telephone almost every night.

The pair were like two peas in a pod and just as close. Both were tall and elegant, with the same strong, sculpted, handsome features. Angela looked just like a younger version of her mother. Both were smart and successful but, while they did not suffer fools gladly, they were still kind, and had no snobbish airs about them. Mrs Grundy loved her frequent visits to the Woodruff family's happy home. Angela would in turn come back home for days at a time, taking her mother for treasured trips out.

All of this was recorded faithfully in Mrs Grundy's daily diary – the diary with which this meticulous woman was to undo her killer from beyond the grave.

But, for now, all grieving Angela Woodruff had was a tatty document that made a mockery not only of her mother's memory but also of their close and loving bond.

Because it was that, not the money, that hurt her so badly. Having inherited more than £1m from David's father Cyril, she was a woman of great wealth and did not need the £386,402 inheritance from her mother –

just as the new will said. Her legal firm was successful, her husband was a much-lauded physicist at Warwick University and their home was beautiful. Here she sat in a majestic residence with a huge garden, roses growing up its old stone walls and around its mullioned windows. How could she want for more? But she was in need – emotionally.

The estate included her mother's former home, 316-year-old Loughrigg Cottage, which was now worth about £140,000. Of course, her mother had died there, but she had lived there too, and happily. That cottage held all of Angela's memories of the mother she had so recently and unexpectedly lost. After her mother's sudden death, visits to the house, with everything still in place, became so distressing that David had to clear it out for her. The estate also included Geoff Ridgway's home, a small but beautifully maintained terraced house next door to where her grandparents had built up their family business. Widowed Mr Ridgway loved the home he had shared with his wife for years and was hoping Angela would keep it on. He liked that family, and liked dealing with them. The house was neat and homely, its front wall whitewashed clean to show off the original leaded windows and front door, with its stained-glass panel intact. The rest of Mrs Grundy's estate was made up of proceeds from the sale of the Platts' business assets and of Mrs Grundy's flat in the Lakes, investment accounts and shares, as well as personal trinkets that would mean the world to Angela and her bereaved young sons.

This will was obviously a fake, and a bad one at that. But how could somebody be so cruel, she wondered. And why? Was somebody trying to frame Dr Shipman?

Angela's concern for the good doctor mirrored the feeling that had been held by the Hyde community for years. Dr Shipman – Dr Death as he was known to the home helps who lost countless old dears in the GP's care – was the victim of coincidence and a talent for treating old ladies not expected to last long anyway. Surely he couldn't . . . But Mrs Woodruff, her hands shaking as she gripped the fake will that bequeathed everything to the man who meant little to Kath Grundy, was about to prove otherwise.

Mrs Grundy had died suddenly and unexpectedly in the living room of her cottage on the morning of 24 June 1998. The last person to see her alive was Dr Shipman, who called at 8.30 a.m. to take a blood sample. It is a sign of her popularity that she was found dead within a few hours, at 11.55 a.m. Her friends from Werneth House, John Green and Ronald Pickford, called when she failed to turn up to serve lunches as expected. They found the front door closed but not locked and, on entering the cottage, they were devastated to discover her body lying on the settee, fully dressed as if waiting to go out. The distraught pair called Dr Shipman out. After a cursory examination, he pronounced her dead and the news was broken to Mrs Grundy's daughter, Mrs Woodruff. A week later, true tribute was paid to Mrs Grundy when dozens of mourners attended Hyde Chapel as she was buried near to her beloved parents.

Mrs Woodruff returned home to Warwickshire. But the slow, painful grieving process was rudely interrupted by a strange phone call from Hyde-based solicitors Hamilton Ward on 14 July. They claimed to have a copy of Mrs Grundy's will. This came as a tremendous shock to grieving Mrs Woodruff – her own legal firm had had a copy of her mother's will for years and there was a copy of it in her mother's locked document chest. The new will had been signed on 9 June – two weeks before Mrs Grundy was found dead. It had arrived at the Hamilton Ward office on 24 June, the day of her death, followed by a letter on 30 June informing them she had passed away. According to this will, Mrs Grundy had left everything to Dr Shipman. There was silence as Mrs Woodruff tried to collect her thoughts. The businesslike voice of solicitor Brian Burgess continued to explain that the firm had been trying to contact her for ten days, finally getting through to one of Mrs Grundy's neighbours, who had gone into the now empty Loughrigg Cottage to turn the lights on for the evening. She had given them Mrs Woodruff's number. The story was getting stranger and stranger and Mrs Woodruff was by now almost reeling with shock. But this was nothing compared to how she would actually feel on seeing the second will.

'You only have to look at it once and you start thinking it's like something off a John Bull printing press,' Detective Superintendent Bernard Postles, called in to lead the inquiry into Mrs Grundy's death, commented later. 'You don't have to have twenty years as a detective to know it's a fake.'

He was disgusted by the forger's efforts to besmirch the reputation of Mrs Grundy, causing so much distress to her grieving daughter: 'It conjures up an image of an old person who is not very well educated or worldly-wise and is not very mobile. It looks like a one-fingered effort at typing. As soon as Mrs Woodruff saw a copy of the will she felt very uneasy and confused. Her first thought was, is someone trying to frame the doctor?'

The two letters, one with the will and one informing Hamilton Ward of Mrs Grundy's death, were just as badly written. The first, on a scrappy bit of paper, noted in bad English: 'If he dies or refuses to take it, it will go to my daughter.' Yet again, this was out of character for such a proud and meticulous woman. The second, on the same scrappy paper and in the same scruffy typewriting, said: 'I understand she lodged a will with you as I as a friend typed it out for her.' Mysteriously, it was signed 'S. Smith' but had no contact address. No such friend was known by her family or any of her many other friends, nor had any such individual turned up at Mrs Grundy's funeral.

Mr Burgess, himself worried by the strange, tatty-looking will, agreed to fax it to Mrs Woodruff. She got it the same day that her son Matthew flew out to his new life in Japan. Although still grieving for her mother, as soon as she saw the will she raced up to Hyde to investigate. The devoted daughter's sad, strange journey back home was the beginning of an amazing quest that would finally expose a sickening mystery that had gone years without being detected.

Mrs Woodruff was to call upon all her professional experience and investigative skills as a solicitor of some 25 years' standing as she dug out every piece of information – checking over official documents, carefully questioning vital witnesses, gently quizzing distraught friends, and reading over her mother's diary. Without her sharp mind, incisive judgement and bravery the truth might never have been known. Her quest also helped her deal with the emotional crescendo that was building up as she grew closer and closer to the truth of her mother's death.

She began with a step-by-step investigation of the second will. Mrs Woodruff knew her mother's signature well, and the one on the will looked too big: not right at all. She called at the bank to see paying-in slips she had filled in and signed regularly for Age Concern. They further confirmed her suspicions. Not only was the will out of character but also someone else had clearly signed it. And she realised, ominously, that the will also specified cremation – certain to erase any evidence of how Mrs Grundy died. But the devoted daughter had decided to have her mother buried at Hyde Chapel, near her beloved parents and brother.

Mrs Woodruff was shaking when she next called on the two witnesses to the new will, Claire Hutchinson and Paul Spencer, on 19 July, a quiet Sunday afternoon. By now the loss of her mother and the confusion over the will was taking its toll on Mrs Woodruff. As she carefully questioned Mrs Hutchinson about the will and her mother, whose photo she had taken along for identification, she broke down in tears. The young mum was horrified. Yes, she recalled, Dr Shipman had asked her to witness a signature while she waited for an appointment on 9 June. She had signed a piece of paper, which had been folded to hide the details, in the GP's room. And there was an elderly lady there, although she did not recognise her from the rather old snapshot Mrs Woodruff had in her trembling hand. Mrs Hutchinson had assumed it was the lady's will and even thought that she may have seen 'last will and testament' poking out of the top of the folded paper. 'That's why I thought it was OK to sign,' she explained. By now Mrs Woodruff was so upset and Mrs Hutchinson was so distraught at the result of her kind deed that Mr Hutchinson asked Angela and David to leave. Mrs Woodruff later admitted under cross-examination by Nicola Davies QC at Shipman's trial: 'They were very helpful, very co-operative and she invited us in, but I was very distraught so in that way it was difficult.' But under re-examination by Richard Henriques QC, she was asked if she had been overbearing and replied shortly: 'Certainly not; I was shaking.'

The Woodruffs also called on Paul Spencer, a young shopkeeper who lived in a tiny cottage just off Hyde's main street, just yards from his pet shop Monkey Business. Mrs Woodruff's heart was thumping as she knocked on the door and prepared to raise the questions she barely dared ask. Mr Spencer also recalled Dr Shipman asking him and another patient, there with her baby, to witness an old lady's signature. He remembered seeing her signature, 'K Grundy', on the folded piece of paper but had no idea it was a will. Mrs Woodruff was certain that whatever her mother had signed, it would not have been another will. Especially that will.

She was finding it hard to remain calm as she traced her mother's last days. She steeled herself for the next step, visiting her mother's friends, who were also still in the midst of their grief. Taking care not to distress or worry them, she gently questioned them about how she was in her last days. She was fine, they said, 'like a March hare' on the lunch club trip to Bakewell two days before her death. That vitality had made her death so much more of a shock. The night before she died she had spent the evening at her old friend Mrs Clark's house. They had chatted and she had been in good spirits, telling Mrs Clark how she was expecting a visit from Dr Shipman for a simple blood test the next morning – the day she died. Perched like a little bird in the witness box, Mrs Clark, 91, later recalled: 'She thought it was very good of him to go along to her house and save her going to the surgery.'

Mrs Woodruff's painstaking investigation began to build a terrible picture. It grew worse when Mr Green and Mr Pickford told her how Dr Shipman, having pronounced Mrs Grundy dead on that terrible June morning, suggested they call her solicitors, 'Hamilton

Ward'. They had done so but the firm had said it did not represent her, having only just received a will from her. Hamilton Ward then suggested calling Mrs Grundy's daughter and, when this proved difficult, the heartbroken friends called in the police. PCs Phillips and Fitzgerald had also spoken to Dr Shipman, who told them he would assign her death to natural causes. Her death certificate was duly signed with the cause as old age – only given when the patient is moribund and several organs are failing, making it difficult to find one specific cause.

By now Mrs Woodruff was beginning to suspect Dr Shipman. She turned to her mother's diaries, in which Mrs Grundy had always carefully noted the events of the day. The sight of her mother's neat handwriting filled her eyes with tears, but she read on, determined to get to the bottom of the mystery. Whenever Mrs Grundy had visited the doctor, she had given the time and the treatment he had prescribed in the diary. According to her journal, she had not been ill at all prior to her death. The diaries were to prove essential to the murder team as they tackled and brought down every argument in Dr Shipman's arrogant defence. They found it ironic and almost heartening that Mrs Grundy's meticulous nature had given rise to a vital tool with which to trap Dr Shipman, as well as providing evidence against his badly forged will. Mrs Grundy noted in her journal how she had visited the surgery and agreed to Dr Shipman's request to take part in an age survey for Manchester University. 'June 9 1998, Dr Shipman, 4 p.m., blood taken for survey on ageing, ears syringed,' it read. She had also told her daughter about the survey in one of their many long phone calls. A copy of the survey was to go to her solicitor – that is, Angela – the diary went on. But no such papers were ever received. The police later found there was no such survey – the cold-hearted killer had invented it as a way of getting Mrs Grundy's signature.

A terrible scenario was building up, gradually eroding Mrs Woodruff's first conviction that Dr Shipman was being framed. It made her question her belief – and that of the Hyde community – that a trusted family doctor would never use his power to kill for money. Had someone tried to frame Hyde's most dedicated GP? Not at all. For behind the carefully conjured image of a caring, hard-working GP, family man and community spirit hid a heartless killer, buoyed by arrogance and now filled with greed. Such was his greed that he tried to take all of Mrs Grundy's £386,402 estate. Such was his arrogance that he didn't bother to make a professional job of the document. Worse still, he claimed that Hyde's tireless charity worker was a junkie.

'IBS [irritable bowel syndrome] again. Odd. Pupils small. Constipated. Query drug abuse? Query at her age? Query codeine? Wait and see.' Dr Shipman had scribbled his 'concerns' about Mrs Grundy on her medical notes, following a visit to the surgery on 12 October 1996. He couldn't wait to show the police his dutiful notemaking after he was arrested for her murder on 7 September 1998. But the detectives' investigations showed that she could not have had an appointment that day – she was spending time with her daughter, who had travelled up from Leamington Spa for one of her many visits. It was written, as ever, in her diary.

The now-bereaved daughter also remembered the trip fondly. She had come up for a Manchester University class of 1966 reunion. She had spent the weekend at various events, including a garden party followed by dinner on the Saturday. On the Sunday, she and her mother had lunch and then made their way back to Harbury, from where they would travel to France to visit Richard, who was then living there. Not once did Mrs Grundy mention visiting Dr Shipman. 'She was a great talker and she would have mentioned it to me,' Mrs Woodruff later explained in the witness box.

Two more of Dr Shipman's entries, dated 15 July 1997 and 26 November the same year, suggested the same thing: '. . . pupils small, dry mouth, denies taking any other drug . . .' and '. . . really difficult as she denies everything. She is not at risk, ie she is not IV [intra-venous] user.'

Mrs Woodruff had felt sorry for the GP she thought was being framed, but the sympathy was misplaced. All along he had been planning her mother's murder – concocting an age survey simply to get her signature, rewriting medical records to make her look addicted to the poison that killed her, forging her will and finally making a home visit appointment to get a blood sample. No sample ever arrived at the lab. It had been an appointment made to kill her.

Dr Shipman had been at it for years. He had already got away with killing fourteen 'silly old ladies' – possibly many, many more. Might as well get some cash this time. As usual, no one would bother. But this time he had reckoned without the efforts of a heartbroken daughter, helped from beyond the grave by her meticulous mother. Mrs Grundy had mattered too much to too many people, and she had left her mark too indelibly on this world – enough to undo the man who killed her. Mrs Woodruff, in shock and distress, began to realise that her worst fears were justified – it was Dr Shipman.

On 24 July 1998, Mrs Woodruff walked into Warwickshire Police HQ and told them of her findings, triggering an investigation that was soon to prove what nobody had wanted to believe. DS Postles later paid tribute to the love of a daughter for her mother: 'Without Mrs Woodruff we would not be sitting here today. She didn't want to believe it, like everybody. A family doctor appeared to have forged a patient's will and murdered her for her money. It was unthinkable.'

2 A GP Blows the Whistle

But Angela Woodruff was not the first to realise that 'the best doctor in Hyde' was not all that he seemed.

Unknown to all but a few, another Hyde GP, Dr Linda Reynolds, had already seen through Shipman's charade. Courageously she risked her career and her home to expose him and save his vulnerable patients, but her efforts were to no avail. Despite her investigation, which involved sifting through death-rate figures and gathering information from sources throughout the community, the police were unable to find any evidence to support her claims, and they told her, in March 1998, that they were unable to proceed against Shipman. Tragically, three more women were yet to die at Dr Shipman's hands.

Dr Reynolds was bitterly disappointed by her pointless ordeal, forced to stand by helplessly as Shipman continued to practice unhindered. Winnie Mellor, Joan Melia and Kathleen Grundy all lost their lives in the five months that followed. But finally Dr Reynolds' gentle intelligence beat Shipman's vicious cunning: without her efforts, Mrs Grundy probably would not have been exhumed. Dr Shipman might have been quizzed about the forging of the will, but it is unlikely that the multiple murder of his patients would have come to light.

Tragically the doctor, whose selfless care for the people of Hyde was the very opposite of Shipman's appalling abuse of power, was given little more time to do her work. In the summer of 1999 Dr Reynolds discovered that she was dying of cancer.

Dr Reynolds decided to speak out to make sure her story, which would also be her epitaph, was told properly. Sitting in the spacious but homely living room of her brick-built Victorian house on a peaceful, tree-lined street in Stockport, she spoke with candour and surprisingly little bitterness about the wasted effort that marked the start of her painful last journey. Her husband, Nigel, sat by her side, a constant source of love and support to the woman he loved and whom he now faced losing to terminal cancer. He had given her the strength to do what she must – by offering to move away, to give everything up, if she ended up being blackballed by the General Medical Council and losing her job. 'Nigel is a great one for crossing bridges,' Dr Reynolds explained.

'You had no choice; you had to do it,' he protested. 'I just had to help you.'

Together they told her tale.

The police investigation was launched one cold March morning in 1998 following a nervous telephone call from Dr Reynolds to Coroner John Pollard. Shaking as she gripped the receiver, Dr Reynolds told Mr Pollard: 'I feel concerned about a colleague in Hyde and so do other people.' Not once did she mention murder, but as the sinister saga unfolded, Mr Pollard understood. Dr Reynolds believed Dr Shipman was killing his patients.

Dr Reynolds arrived in Hyde in 1995, having moved there from Stockport, where she had worked for nineteen years. She became the fifth partner at the

Brooke Group surgery, which worked closely with Dr Shipman's single-handed practice, just across the road. After a couple of years, her 'fresh' eye spotted something untoward about the town's most popular doctor. His death rate was far too high and the surgery was receiving far too much 'ash cash' from him – that is, money for co-signing the death certificates of patients who are to be cremated once their bodies have been examined. The Brooke Group's five partners were signing Dr Shipman's cremation forms on a rota basis. Dr Reynolds counted their turns in January 1998 and was stunned to find they were signing one every ten days.

Dr Reynolds' partners had not realised this as they had only ever co-signed for Dr Shipman and no other doctor. He was also extremely popular with old people – and they were bound to die more often. Nor had the partners realised it was rare for a doctor to be present at so many deaths, as Shipman so often was; again, they knew that the GP was well known for spending a lot of time with his patients and thought it normal, for him if not themselves. Dr Reynolds knew better.

Night after night, for two weeks, she talked it through with Nigel, alarmed at what she had discovered. He realised almost immediately that she would have to do something and, knowing what it might cost her, that she would need all his support. He offered to give up his job – teaching at the prestigious Manchester Grammar School – their home, their friends, the whole life they had built since meeting at Manchester University in 1969, if need be. They planned an escape route, hoping they would not have to use it. 'You have no option,' he told her. 'You have to tell.'

Her partners were horrified by the suggestion, that not only could a doctor murder his patients, but also that it could happen under their very noses for years and years. But one of them, Dr Susan Booth, recalled a recent comment from local undertaker, Deborah Massey, when Dr Booth turned up at the funeral parlour to examine yet another body for Dr Shipman: 'You're in here a lot.' Miss Massey confessed that she had been worried for some time about Dr Shipman's death rates, especially considering that so many of the deaths were of women living alone, and that they had been found by the GP when he had no easy access to their homes. She was so worried, in fact, that she had examined all his patients for wounds as she embalmed them.

Miss Massey had discussed her fears with taxi driver, John Shaw, who ran a special service for Hyde's old people. He too was 'on to him', as he recounted later. John lost twenty-four customers to Dr Shipman in seven years. Every time he got the bad news that one of his old ladies had been found dead, sitting in her chair, he would ask: 'Who was the doctor?' And every time he got the same answer: 'Shipman.'

It was the answer he was always expecting, the answer that almost drove him out of his mind with grief and guilt. But he was not ready to say it out loud, other than to his frightened wife, Kath, who urged him to keep quiet: 'They'll put you away.' He agreed only that it was a little suspicious. Miss Massey, who knew Dr Shipman as Uncle Fred, the family friend whose children she had gone to school with, happily complied.

Dr Reynolds and Dr Booth decided to meet Miss Massey, the latest to run the famous family business, Massey and Son. One quiet Monday lunchtime, on a wet February day, they gathered in Miss Massey's office at the back of her Mottram Road funeral parlour. It was an apt setting for such a sombre meeting but by the end of their twenty-minute discussion, piecing together their terrible jigsaw, the three women were heady with excitement.

'We were all very anxious by the time we had finished,' Dr Reynolds recalled. 'We were all convinced something was going on. You suddenly build up this picture from a few fragments of information, everyone putting their piece in. We were shocked and amazed at what we were coming out with, what had been happening in our midst. It was also a relief to find others felt the same. All these other people with different angles and clues.'

But the findings were mainly anecdotal, and Miss Massey was still too upset to take it any further. Still in shock, she was understandably not ready to tell the police that Uncle Fred might be a mass murderer.

The Brooke Group partners decided to test their case further by comparing the number of cremation forms they had signed for Dr Shipman with those he had signed for them in the previous year. Dr Jeremy Dirkes collated the figures and brought them to their regular group meeting over a drink at The Plough, in Heaton Moor, the following week. There was silence as the five doctors pondered the stark statistics staring back at them: Dr Shipman, with his patient list of 3,000, had sent 16 forms; they with their 10,000-strong patient list, had sent only 15. His death rate was at least three times theirs.

'We were all stunned and shocked,' Dr Reynolds recalled. 'This was something very, very serious; no longer amusing tittle-tattle. It had been going on a long, long time and was hidden by what seemed to be normal behaviour.'

Dr Reynolds and her partners felt clearly that something had to be done.

Unlike her partners, who had worked with Dr Shipman for years, Dr Reynolds had little loyalty to him. He had seemed warm and friendly at their first meeting, as he proudly took her for a tour of his surgery when she was a newcomer to Hyde. After that he was rather rude. When Dr Reynolds found him standing in their waiting room one day, she asked him if he was being seen to. 'Yes,' he snapped, then turned on his heel, arms folded, leaving his back to her.

When she argued a point with him at a meeting some time later, he liked it even less. 'He was arguing with another woman at the meeting but had it all wrong because he had not been listening properly,' she recalled. 'I told him so. He didn't like that at all.'

Dr Reynolds' partners did not like him any more than she did – he tended to be 'prickly' and unsociable – but they were too shocked and upset to make a formal complaint straight away. The Medical Defence Union also urged caution when she telephoned them for advice the following day.

Dr Reynolds understood their reticence: 'Doctors don't expect other doctors to kill their patients. It was unthinkable.'

Nigel explained it further: 'It's like the Holocaust. If someone said they were burning Jews on the other side of Stockport, you would not believe it, would you? That is why Nazis got away with it. Then, when the smell starts, people cling to excuses. They do not want to believe it.'

Dr Reynolds was also spurred on by her memory of another GP, Dr Soe Myint, who had sexually assaulted his patients. For years, she had known of his attacks on women patients, who went to her for treatment to get away from him. She had tried to persuade them to tell the police, even offering to go with them, but they had refused. It finally came to court and he was imprisoned in 1997. 'I swore never again,' she said, shuddering at the recollection. 'And this time it was more serious. Those other women could do something, but Dr Shipman's patients couldn't. He had killed them.'

One morning, Dr Reynolds went to work early. Sitting in her consulting room, she picked up the telephone and dialled Mr Pollard's number. It was one of the hardest moments in her career but she steeled herself. Her story sounded crazy but she had to stop the killing. She remembered how Mr Pollard put her at her ease: 'Afterwards I felt very encouraged. I felt he was taking me seriously. He is very approachable and said, 'As far as I am concerned, if nothing comes of this, we have never spoken.'' Her ten-minute phone call finally brought her relief after weeks of worry.

A detective was despatched to her surgery that same day and arrived at lunchtime. He listened calmly as Dr Reynolds recounted her amazing story, just yards away from the killer across the road who was sitting in his consultation room, separated from them by a slow, steady ribbon of midday traffic on Hyde's main road, Market Street. She explained all the background carefully – how she had considered the various death-rate figures and spoken to other people in the community. She also gave him the Brooke Group's cremation form records book going back to 1993. It gave him dozens of bereaved families to choose from. But they were families he would never be able to approach, such was the lack of evidence and the need to be discreet. He left, promising to investigate the matter thoroughly but covertly.

It was a daunting task that befell the lone officer. There was no incident room and no support from any other officer, all of whom were kept in the dark for such a covert operation. And Dr Shipman was aided by a number of 'lucky' breaks.

Firstly, the officer asked the local registrar to supply the death certificates of all Dr Shipman's patients who had died in the previous six months. He received nineteen. Unknown to him, there were eleven more which had been missed by the registrar.

The officer then took the certificates to Dr Alan Banks, the assistant director of primary care at the West Pennine Health Authority, to compare the patients' causes of death with their medical records. There were no discrepancies between the causes of death and medical histories. Of course, we now know that Dr Shipman had amended the records of his murder victims in order to cover his tracks, should such an investigation take place; but, back then, according to Greater Manchester Police, there was no reason to suspect that this was what he had been doing. Cunning as ever, Dr Shipman was untouchable.

The officer also spoke with Miss Massey. Their discussion took him still further from the truth. She did not make any allegations and put it all down to gossip and chitchat.

It is understood that the officer did not check Dr Shipman's criminal record, which would have revealed the GP's forgery of prescriptions to feed his addiction to the painkiller pethidine back in 1976. The fact that this was not done was later to upset Dr Reynolds. Following his 1976 conviction Dr Shipman removed himself from the Controlled Drugs Register, which allows and records doctors' use of medications such as pethidine and morphine. However – assuming, correctly, that he was out of sight and out of mind – Dr Shipman had been stockpiling morphine for future use as a murder weapon. But still the police officer had had no firm suggestion that Dr Shipman was poisoning his patients. Without taking the massive step of exhuming bodies, which would have required far more evidence to obtain a warrant from Mr Pollard, the enquiry was bound to fail.

It was also inappropriate for the officer to approach grieving families with such scant information. It would have been tantamount to accusing Dr Shipman of wrongdoing and would have breached the confidentiality of the enquiry.

Assistant chief constable, Vincent Sweeney, later defended his officer's actions: 'The system of justice in this country requires police officers to clarify facts and establish whether there is evidence to support accusations against individuals.

'Without evidence, there can be no criminal investigation.'

Two weeks later, the officer returned to Dr Reynolds' surgery with the news that he had been unable to find any evidence of wrongdoing by Dr Shipman. 'He said that Dr Shipman was a well-loved doctor, very concerned for his patients, with no motive to harm them,' Dr Reynolds recalled.

Dr Reynolds told the officer that the bodies of two Shipman patients were at Massey's funeral parlour and suggested that he ask for post mortems on them, but, again, there was not enough evidence to do that. She also warned him that Dr Shipman seemed to know about his secret investigation.

Dr Reynolds recalled how she felt feeling wounded and powerless, unable to do anything but still certain that Shipman had murdered his patients. 'I felt quite bad. I had accused another doctor – albeit old-fashioned but concerned for the community – of killing his patients. I was dragging this man's reputation in the mud.'

After that, only two cremation forms arrived at the Brooke Surgery between April and August, after which Dr Reynolds stopped her wary monitoring of them and went on holiday. Those two were both genuine deaths of people who had been terminally ill. She clung to one last, vain hope – that she had stopped the killings.

'I was convinced he knew,' she explained. 'I hoped that, because he had had this shot across his bows, he had got the message and stopped. It was the best hope I had in the circumstances. But he could not control himself.'

That summer, she and Nigel took the break in America they were, by then, desperate for. There they escaped from the weeks fraught with worry and bitter disappointment, and inadvertently missed the story, in the *Manchester Evening News*, that Dr Shipman was under investigation yet again. He had killed another patient, former Hyde Mayoress, Kathleen Grundy, and this time forged his victim's will in an arrogantly crude attempt to take her estate. When Dr Reynolds returned from her holiday, she heard the news that had torn Hyde apart and hit the national headlines. By now, Dr Shipman was behind bars on remand, awaiting trial.

She had arrived back at work rested, and ready to go on working as best she could alongside a man who she was convinced had decimated the town's elderly population. But she was immediately taken into a back room by one of the partners, who whispered, 'Have you heard? They have arrested Fred!'

Dr Reynolds was astounded, and almost faint with relief. 'I thought: there *was* something wrong. I was right,' she recalled. 'I finally felt exonerated.'

Nigel, too, felt relief that it was all over, and he was proud of his wife's efforts, which were something for which they could now be thankful. He reminded her: 'If you had not done something, you would have felt terrible when he was arrested.'

But the couple had no criticism for those who did not come forward. In fact they had sympathy for Miss Massey and Dr Reynolds' partners, who had all felt worried and helpless for so long. Their fears were justified – the man they knew so well, trusted so much, had been killing vulnerable people. But Dr Reynolds was irritated by the gossips who talked of how they had known all along. 'It's all right them saying now that they knew, but they didn't do anything, did they?' she said, understandably a little bitter.

But the modest GP did not think she been particularly heroic – risking her career and indeed her whole life to bring him to justice.

Mr Pollard did not agree. He thought that she had shown great courage and paid tribute to that, as he discussed the case later at his Stockport office: 'The GP was extremely brave in coming forward. We had to treat her report in a careful and subtle way because she really was laying her reputation on the line by saying something was wrong. If it hadn't been, she would have looked extremely foolish. She had put her career in jeopardy by speaking out, but she was only doing what she thought right.'

It had worried him too: the 'niggling feeling' that a doctor would not have come to him, taking such a courageous step, without good reason. 'Something must be wrong,' he had thought. 'This is not just a gut feeling.'

But Dr Reynolds insisted: 'No. I had a duty. I had to do it, and brave is when you have a choice and do it anyway. I had no choice.'

Nigel agreed, but added: 'What she did was against her nature; she is not an interventionist. I have utter respect and admiration for my wife and I know what this cost her.'

Dr Reynolds' courage was rewarded with the terrible news that she was running out of time. In the summer of 1999 she was diagnosed with terminal cancer. The news devastated the couple and their two children, Caroline, 21, and William, 18. At first it seemed that she was so ill, she would not live to see the outcome of Shipman's trial. When she was given more time, she saw it as just one last chance in a life that had fallen so short of them. Even though she would not live to see William go to Cambridge, on his return from volunteer work in Ecuador, or Caroline get her German and Business Studies degree from Birmingham University, she grabbed at the hope that she would see justice served in the case of the GP who had caused her and all of Hyde such pain. She deserved at least that.

It all seemed so unfair. Dr Reynolds was a good, caring doctor. She had risked everything to save her town's vulnerable citizens from a sneaking killer. In the end, it was all for nothing. And, having struggled to come to terms with that test, she found that she had no time left with her family, all still young, and with so many adventures ahead of them – adventures she would not see.

'I just hope I live to see the conclusion of all this,' she said stoically during the trial. 'And I hope he stays in prison for the rest of his life.'

Dr Reynolds had immense sympathy for the people left behind, no doubt thinking of her own situation: 'Hyde is a close-knit community and it has been very shocking for relatives. I have great sympathy for them, as well as for the ones who were suspicious, but there was not sufficient evidence. They have to live never knowing whether they would have had more time with their parent, whether they were robbed or not, which is very sad.'

And she was heartened by the tough response of the witnesses, many of whom were elderly, who courageously lined up to win justice for their mothers, sisters, friends, and dance partners. 'The elderly ladies tend to be very supportive of each other and would want to see justice for each other,' Dr Reynolds said. 'And they know the difference between right and wrong.' This was the community she knew and loved so well: 'I had a 90-year-old patient who joked, "You are a terrible doctor; if I had Dr Shipman I would not have all this pain now". Hyde people are decent and they're appreciative. I have a big box of cards from them from when I retired. There's a lot of opportunity to care for them, and to be of use.'

Dr Reynolds is the very antithesis of Shipman, and it is our tragedy as well as hers that she was given little more time than him to do her work.

'I loved my job: being part of a community; looking after generations of the same family; the intellectual stimulation of making a diagnosis; just being able to help people, be kind to them,' she said sadly. 'I would have liked ten more years to look after people of Hyde – I was just getting started with them.'

3 The Police Investigation

'You've got a tiger by the tail here, mister,' Chief Superintendent Alan Boardman finally answered after a shocked silence.

He could barely believe the case Detective Superintendent Bernard Postles was outlining to him – a doctor killing his patient, a defenceless old lady, for her money. Putting her to sleep, like a vet would do to an old dog.

Det Supt Postles was later to embellish the phrase – 'I've got a pride of tigers by the tail here' – when he realised with horror that Dr Harold Frederick Shipman might be Britain's biggest ever serial killer.

He had taken on the case after Angela Woodruff gave the findings of her own investigation into her mother Kathleen Grundy's death to her local police in Warwickshire. They had passed them on to Stalybridge CID, whose DI Stan Egerton phoned Det Supt Postles in a state of great excitement. 'I want to tell you a story. Grab a chair, sit down and hold on to the fucking sides,' he bellowed. Egerton, an old-school copper about to retire after 30 years in the force, was well known for his excitable ways and colourful language, designed to give him maximum impact. But this time, he needn't have bothered. He couldn't have made the story any more shocking.

Det Supt Postles immediately began his own investigation, double checking Mrs Woodruff's findings and adding his own, and found he agreed with the devastated daughter's conclusion – Dr Shipman had forged Mrs Grundy's will then murdered her, expecting the evidence to be destroyed with the cremation requested on the fake document. There was only one way to prove it – exhume Mrs Grundy's body from her grave at Hyde Chapel.

It was a 'mammoth step', Det Supt Postles later said, one never taken before by Greater Manchester Police and rarely ever taken by any police force in Britain. He remembered the enormity of it: 'We did not have one officer who had ever taken part in an exhumation. We asked the National Crime Squad for advice and found we had all the right things in place.' It was the stuff of horror movies and pulp fiction, not day-to-day detective work. But it was a step that was to be repeated eleven more times, making it a record for South Manchester and District Coroner John Pollard – one he is not proud of.

Mr Pollard is a sensitive and gentle man, well known for his kindness at inquests where families relive the loss of their loved ones. But he is fiercely intelligent and firm, too, where necessary. He insisted Det Supt Postles supply him with as much evidence as possible before he would give the warrant for Mrs Grundy's exhumation. Det Supt Postles was only too happy to oblige, still in shock at what he was purporting himself. Raising the dead was not something he was comfortable with and he would only do it if he were absolutely certain it was necessary.

Mrs Grundy was exhumed from her plot at Hyde Chapel on 1 August; exactly a month after dozens of mourners had stood there at her funeral. The detectives, scenes of crime officers, gravediggers, stonemasons, lighting technicians and workers from a specialist exhumations company gathered quietly in the darkness of the early hours, silently contemplating what they were about to do. The generator began to buzz and the arc lights sparked into life, throwing eerie shadows around the ancient graveyard. Their terrible task began in earnest. As the hours passed, the noise and lights woke nearby residents, who fearfully tweaked aside their curtains and peered out of their windows. No one but Angela Woodruff had any idea of the police's plans and the villagers of Gee Cross were shocked to be woken by scrapings and knockings coming from the graveyard at the foot of old Hyde Chapel. They soon realised it was official and above board, thanks to the patrolling uniformed officers, the rumble of the generator and the clinical white tent erected to protect the scene from prying eyes, but it was shocking and upsetting all the same. They also soon realised who it was – Kathleen Grundy. Many had stood at that very spot only four weeks before. They were devastated; already heartbroken by her sudden death, now finding she could not rest in peace. Why? Before morning had broken, unable to sleep, many villagers had come to the same conclusion – Dr Death. Dr Shipman was the last to see Kath Grundy alive. Her daughter, Angela Woodruff, had been in the village only a couple of weeks before, asking some strange questions about it all. And Hyde had been rife with the gossip for years, although the residents had never taken such talk very seriously: 'He's a lovely doctor but you don't last.'

That morning, Gee Cross was buzzing with stories of the terrible fate endured by Kath Grundy in death and, it seemed, in life. Meanwhile, Mrs Grundy's finger and palm prints were taken to be checked against any found on the fake will and letters. None were ever found from her, although Dr Shipman had left a solitary print from his left hand little finger on the bottom left-hand corner of the will, showing how he had gingerly handled the incriminating piece of paper.

At 8.30 a.m. Dr John Rutherford carried out his post mortem on Mrs Grundy's body in the mortuary at Tameside General Hospital. Mrs Grundy's shroud and jewellery, carefully chosen by her grieving family as they said what they thought was their final goodbye to her, were removed. It was a painfully emotional reminder of how she had come to be lying on his slab; a heartbreaking process that would be repeated eleven more times in just over four months. With each woman, just ripped from what should have been her last resting place, came a host of artefacts bearing testimony to her life – Catholic crosses, favourite pieces of jewellery and trinkets, photographs and mementoes. All reminding the staff of the lives that were cut short, the horror that was unfolding before their eyes.

Mrs Grundy's body, having been dead for five weeks and buried in a cold damp grave for four of them, was an upsetting sight too. With each body, it would be different, depending on the length of time it had been buried and the type of soil it had been in. This even changed within cemeteries as well as between them.

Dr Rutherford took a sample of muscle from her left thigh, to be tested for any poison that had flowed through the veins before coming to rest in that, the most stable tissue in the body, plus a sample from her liver. He also took a hair sample to give Mrs Grundy's drug history, shown in telltale rings along the length of each strand. The muscle and liver samples were sent to toxicologist Julie Evans, based at the Forensic Science Unit in Chorley, while the hair was sent to Professor

Hans Sachs, at Munich University. Both in Germany and the USA, the hair test is common – it is used to check potential employees for drug use. It would take some time for Professor Sachs to return his test results but Ms Evans reported back two weeks later – Mrs Grundy had died from a fatal dose of morphine.

Det Supt Postles was shocked. Shipman had used the one poison that lasts forever. A doctor would know that – opiates had been found in Egyptian mummies. Was Shipman utterly stupid or so arrogant he thought he would never be caught? 'I was surprised,' Postles later recalled. 'I anticipated that I would have had difficulty if he gave them something in way of poison lost in background substance, for example insulin, which is naturally secreted by the body. It was an unexpected bonus once I had checked that Kathleen Grundy did not take it herself.'

It had been the same with his half-baked forgery of Mrs Grundy's will. Shipman knew she was meticulous, knew she had family and thought the world of them, yet he produced a tatty will bequeathing everything to him. It was pure arrogance to imagine he would get away with it. Shipman's arrogance was to undo him in more ways than one.

'There are some parts of this I cannot understand,' Det Supt Postles later explained. 'Supposedly he has got a cold, calculating mind; he made appointments, prepared for the will – and then this thing turns up. 'You only have to look at it once and you start thinking it's like something off a John Bull printing press. You don't have to have twenty years as a detective to know it's a fake.

'Maybe he thought he was being clever – an old lady, nobody around her: "Look at it; it's a bit tacky." But everyone knew she was as sharp as a tack. Maybe it was his arrogance: "If everybody is daft enough to believe the doctor . . ."'

Knowing of Dr Reynolds' findings and the previous failed investigation into Dr Shipman, DS Postles realised at the start that there was more to the case than Mrs Grundy's death. But without the evidence gained from her exhumation, there was little point investigating the others. Now he decided to step up the investigation, bringing in Detective Chief Inspector Mike Williams as second-in-command of a 50-strong murder squad. With 24 of his 30 years as a policeman spent in CID, DCI Williams had the experience required for such a huge case. Having policed Manchester's notorious drugs wars in Moss Side for years, there was no disputing his skills. He had cracked big drugs cases, such as Operations China and Balboa, as well as investigating the murders of Nicky Murphy, 12-year-old Susanne Rarity and Steven Hughes. In addition, DI Egerton, who was to run the incident room until his retirement in December, had worked on the Moors Murders. But it was the younger officers who were to make their mark on this case with a brilliant interview technique that tripped up their smug suspect Shipman. DS Postles, of course, also had an impressive record – 27 years in the force, 22 of them as a detective, involved in many major investigations such as the Manchester Airport disaster, in which 50 people died, and the brutal murders of Pauline Stevenson and prostitute Linda Donaldson. He and DCI Williams had first worked together in the Serious Crime Squad and had a good, solid rapport. 'We have sat opposite each other every day for twelve months,' said DCI Williams, 'and we have asked the same questions over and over, to make sure we did not have it wrong.' But they were not wrong. Every step of the investigation was to prove them right.

DS Postles and his team began to prioritise patients who had died in Shipman's care. Of course, first to be investigated would be those who had been buried – those whose bodies would give up the same physical evidence as Mrs Grundy's. Again the team had to carry out a meticulous investigation into each and every death before applying for the exhumation warrant from Mr Pollard.

All this was interspersed with various court hearings as Dr Shipman was charged and gave pleas and directions to the mounting counts of murder. DS Postles juggled a vast, complicated and spiralling timetable. When Dr Shipman was charged with Mrs Grundy's murder on 7 September 1998, Postles had already decided to investigate Winnie Mellor and Joan Melia's deaths. He applied for the warrant on the morning of the hearing. 'As he was appearing in court for remand, I was in the coroner's office,' he explained. 'At that stage, we knew we had a serial killer. We were investigating the deaths of a number of females with the same person the feature – Dr Shipman.'

And so, time and time again, they uncovered sad and sorry ends for so many of Hyde's well-known, well-loved older ladies. All had been harmlessly going about their business, often helping others through charity work or just 'running errands' for their friends and neighbours, and they were always doted on by their families. Even those who were not well enough to make their mark on the community, such as arthritic Jean Lilley and manic-depressive Bianka Pomfret, meant the world to their relatives, who took a delight in seeing them fight for some kind of meaningful life – and win. All that was taken away from so many people all over Tameside and beyond as Shipman laid that sweet and vulnerable section of the community to waste.

Joan Melia [b. 2/7/16, d. 24/6/98, exhumed 1/8/98]
The team exhumed Joan Melia from her grave at Hyde
Cemetery on 21 September 1998.

Joan was a beautiful woman, both inside and out.
She looked at least ten years younger than her 73 years
when she died on 12 June 1998 at her home in
Commercial Street, Hyde. With her trim figure, she was
still able to wear size 10 clothes and they were always
trendy and smart, with designer labels such as Jaegar
when she could afford them. She kept her home well,
too, and was always redecorating it in the latest interior
designs. She did the work herself, determined to keep
her independence.

But, more importantly, Joan had an inner beauty –
she was a kind and loving aunty and sister-in-law to a
family who still kept in touch, even after her divorce
from husband Ken. He, too, still loved her and was
devastated by her murder at the hands of Dr Shipman.
Joan's niece, Jean Pinder, wept as she explained: 'She
was a natural counsellor. If you went to her with a
problem, you came away a lot lighter.'

Determined to tell her aunty's story, Jean went on,
gently and lovingly spelling out how much she had
meant to her family before Shipman took her away
from them. She had had no children of her own but she
made up for it with her six nieces and nephews. 'She
was like a mother to every single one of us,' Jean said
proudly. 'She loved ironing my little dresses. I was the
first grandchild of the family and she spoilt me rotten.
To have known her was unbelievable. She was such a
kind person; very, very loving, with a tremendous sense
of humour.'

Joan was born Joan Taylor in Flixton on 1 May 1925.
She came to Tameside during the war and met Jean
Pinder's uncle, Ken Melia. They were married for 30

years before they split up, Joan having fallen in love with someone else. She was still seeing Derek Steele when she died, but they did not live together. It was always an on–off affair, with Joan repeatedly vowing never to see him again and then changing her mind. Derek was still the other man – Joan had really fallen in love with her independence.

After the divorce, Joan would still visit Jean's mother come rain, snow or shine, taking two buses there and two buses back. The rest of her time was taken up cleaning for an elderly friend, 'little Matty', and his brother, who were actually younger than her. During the evenings, she would go to the bingo where, having turned down her hearing aid to stop it whistling and 'showing me up', she would struggle to hear the numbers. Her stories about her hearing aid – 'that thing' – always made Jean and the family laugh. When they were together, she and Derek, who lived nearby, went out for drives. He, too, loved her dearly – and he proved it through his feisty debate with barrister for the defence Nicola Davies QC at Shipman's trial.

Joan's busy life made it such a shock when Derek found her dead, sitting in her chair in the living room. She had been to Dr Shipman's with Derek that morning, suffering a minor chest problem. After that she went to the chemist's for the antibiotics and then to the market to buy her friend a birthday card. She seemed well enough as Derek drove her and a couple of their friends home. But by 5 p.m., she was dead. Derek found her when he called round after getting no answer on the telephone.

Worse still, Joan's engagement ring was gone. It has never been found and its loss caused untold trouble between Derek and the family, who thought he had taken it in a fit of jealousy. They now believe Dr

Shipman, who had called to see her after Derek had dropped her off, took it. Jean was very upset: 'She never took that ring off, even when she was up to her elbows in wallpaper paste. She would say, "It'll wash." It was a beautiful ring.'

The following day, Jean rang Dr Shipman to discuss her aunt's sudden death. Although Aunty Joan had never been one for heeding health warnings, she had thought very highly of Dr Shipman and would have taken notice of him. He had 'tamed' her after she ignored a bad chest and ended up in hospital the year before.

'Never ever let it get this bad again, Joan,' he gently scolded. 'You ring me straight away next time. You're lucky to be alive, my dear.'

But this time Jean was shocked to find a complete change in character. Shipman was rude and abrupt, caring nothing for her grief. In blunt, harsh and no uncertain terms, he told her he could have called an ambulance but 'she would have died on the way to hospital anyway'.

Worse was to come. When the story of the police investigation into Kathleen Grundy's death broke in the *Manchester Evening News*, 'alarm bells rang'. Jean contacted the police – and had her worst misgivings confirmed.

Later, sitting in their pretty home in Shaw, Jean and her husband Graham tried to explain their feelings of guilt and anger. 'Aunty Joan's death was so sudden we couldn't believe it,' Jean said. 'We kept thinking they've made a mistake. It was worse than that.' Choking back the tears, she went on: 'What I struggle with now is that I persuaded her to go to the doctor's. I feel guilty.'

But Graham, in one of his many desperate attempts to soothe her ill-founded guilt, insisted passionately: 'But that's what you do when you are ill – go to the doctors.' He was angry, and not just about what Shipman did to Joan – he was also angry about how Shipman had treated his wife, who was fighting cancer at the time, and their whole family, now torn apart by grief. 'He hid behind a smokescreen. He was a pillar of the community; he was trusted,' he said.

Jean agreed: 'It's against everything he stands for, what he is trained to do – save lives.' But that does not stop the guilt. She is now 'punished' with visions of Shipman calling at her aunty's that afternoon. 'Aunty Joan would have felt privileged; she would have let him in with open arms, thinking how nice it was of him to want to help her.' She shuddered. 'In fact he was going to kill her. These women were vulnerable, ill, and they went to him with no qualms.'

When Joan's body was exhumed from Hyde Cemetery, Jean was having a mastectomy in Christie Hospital. 'I wanted to be there. It's bad enough to bury them once,' she said. 'She was a very proud and shy lady. Now, after she died, she was exhumed and there was a post mortem.' Joan's death also came in the same year that Jean's baby granddaughter Holly, Joan's great-great-niece, had four operations for glaucoma. It has taken a dreadful toll on a loving and close family already under siege from life's difficulties. But this has been an agony too far. 'Had she died naturally we would have accepted it, but to be taken from us so violently for no reason ... She was everything to everyone; mum, aunty, friend,' Jean wept. 'When I saw Winnie Mellor's face in the paper, I said, 'That is Aunty Joan's face'. Not the looks but the kindness that shone through. Each story we read, we say this is Aunty Joan. They were all so kind and caring, so important to their families and friends and others. How could he?

'Why?'

Winifred Mellor [b. 28/2/25, d. 11/5/98, exhumed 22/9/98]

Winnie Mellor was exhumed from Highfield Cemetery on 22 September 1998, the day after Joan Melia.

She had been a fighter in a crusade for people's rights and her caring nature sometimes made her unpopular with those who had more mercenary agendas. But feisty old Win didn't care. She wasn't a politician. She was an ordinary woman – a mother of five – with more energy and verve than most teenagers and a passion for helping people out. Her death shocked all who knew her.

Her parish priest, Father Denis Maher of St Paul's Church, said it best as he recalled her 'flying about' on her many errands and good works. 'Like most of these people, she was not sitting at home, looking into the fire,' the soft-spoken Irishman explained. 'She gave her all to life and those around her.'

It was her family who benefited most from her energy. Her daughter Susan Duggan said she was her two young sons' favourite granny 'because she could still play football'. Her son James recalled her walking to the top of Werneth Low, a hill from the top of which you can see all of Manchester, while still running around with his two teenagers. 'Not bad for 73,' he insisted in the witness box at Shipman's trial. Winnie's friends also recalled how she walked everywhere, rarely taking the bus as she went on her many errands.

Winnie had worked as a nursery nurse for children with special needs at Werneth Grange School. But as well as bringing out the best in the children, a job she was particularly skilled at, she threw herself into union activities. Her former colleague June O'Reilly recalled how her spirit made her a favourite among the staff but not the bosses: 'She brought us all together and made sure our conditions of work were good. This sometimes made her unpopular with the management but the girls loved her.'

Winnie was particularly excited about the retirement age being raised to 65 for women, the same as men. She wasn't looking forward to retirement and didn't see why women were 'put out to grass' half a decade before the men. June remembered her fighting talk fondly: 'She would say, "We've got to be equal."'

Such an aversion to retirement was typical of Winnie, who used to run the chip shop at Gee Cross with her husband Stanley. She was widowed by the time it was her turn to receive pension, but she continued to work at Cromwell School as a volunteer and later at St Paul's RC Primary School, reading stories to the children. A devout Catholic, she also gave communion to the bedridden. She had the patience of a saint, too, refusing to gossip about one of her clients known at her nursing home for her bad temper. Giving the cantankerous old lady communion was a thankless task for Winnie but all she would say was, 'Oh, she's not that bad really.'

'She was a smashing woman, outgoing with a great sense of humour,' June added. 'A lot of people miss her round here these days.'

Winnie died aged 73 at her Corona Street home on 11 May 1998, just hours after doing her shopping on Hyde market and making a few telephone calls to friends. She was found by Dr Shipman and her neighbour Gloria Ellis. He had called on Mrs Ellis for help when he could not get an answer from Mrs Mellor, who he could see sitting in her chair. Mrs Mellor's shopping was still out on the table, a sign of her busy life and lively ways. Dr Shipman told Mrs Mellor's family she had been suffering from angina for months but had refused hospital treatment, adding, 'You know what Winnie's like.' They didn't agree – mum was a strong-minded, independent woman but not fool enough to refuse help when it was needed. But her grief-stricken children did not think to question it further and accepted Dr Shipman's signature and cause on her death certificate: coronary thrombosis.

The family had no idea of the terrible truth, which was only exposed when she was exhumed from Highfield Cemetery four months later.

Bianka Pomfret [b. 5/11/48, d. 10/12/97, exhumed 23/9/98]

German-born Bianka Pomfret was removed from Hyde Cemetery on 23 September 1998, making three awful exhumations in three days for the murder squad.

Bianka was different from most of the other victims. She was younger, only 49 when she died, and suffered from severe manic depression. Some days, getting herself ready and going out was an achievement in itself. The others – such as Kathleen Grundy and Marie Quinn – were forever active in the community, working tirelessly for charity despite their advanced years. But Bianka worked hard too, to overcome her problems and try to lead a meaningful life. This was difficult. Her problems had already cost her her marriage to Adrian Pomfret who found it difficult to cope, urging her to 'pull yourself together'. It also caused a rift between Bianka and her son William, who had taken Adrian's surname. As Christmas 1997 approached, she struggled with the thought that she would spend it with other psychiatric patients instead of her family. But Adrian still visited his ex-wife and the wounded mother-and-son relationship was also gradually healing. She would pop into William's corner shop in the next street to hers and visit him and his wife Gaynor in the evenings, when their children had gone to bed and they had time to talk. She was still much loved by them and well thought of by her neighbours and friends.

Next-door neighbours Paul Graham and Jeanette Millward remembered her as a kindly old lady who was generous and friendly to their young sons, not realising she was only in her 40s.

'She was a nice person, very quiet, you didn't know she was there,' Paul said. 'She was always talking to the kids; they thought she was lovely. She brought them a stick of rock back from a day trip to Blackpool, to thank them for looking after her dog.'

He last saw Bianka the day before she died, sitting in her chair in the front room, gazing out of the window. Watching him – he thought – as he worked on his van. Now he wonders, with a shudder, if she was dead.

'That's how they found her so maybe she was dead even then,' he said, grimacing at the thought. 'It was a shock when we heard she had died. She seemed pretty well at the time.'

Paul and his family kept Mrs Pomfret's Bible, which they found left in the back yard after the house was cleared. It was inscribed, 'God loveth a cheerful giver, Corinthians II.' The church had meant everything to Bianka; it had been a much needed and fully appreciated source of love and support. At her worst, Bianka thought of throwing herself from the motorway bridge as she walked to St Paul's Church. But she always insisted to her psychiatrist Dr Alan Tate, 'I don't want to die.' Father Denis Maher, her parish priest, should have visited Bianka the day after she was found dead at her Fountain Street home on 10 December 1997. But Shipman got there first – with his own answer to her pain.

Father Maher, a deeply caring shepherd to his flock, recalled with great pain how he missed her on a promised visit and left a card. He planned to call again but this time he was too late. 'The Sunday before she died, she was at Mass. I could see her following me with her eyes. There was always a sadness about her, in her eyes; her eyes were always following me, pleading. That day, she waited for me and asked me to visit again. I said I would on Wednesday or Thursday but on Tuesday, she was found dead.' He was devastated and shocked that she had died – she didn't seem unwell and was coping with her depression quite well. 'I was terribly upset,' he said. 'She did suffer from depression but she was coming out, getting herself ready. She always looked smart. I was always glad to see her at Mass.'

Dr Shipman signed Bianka's death certificate, giving the cause as a clot in the heart and heart disease, with secondary causes smoking and manic depression. She was buried on a rain-sodden day at Hyde Cemetery, her plot marked with a black marble gravestone inscribed, 'She will be loved and missed forever.' Less than a year later, the pot plants and flowers were removed from the grave, still carefully tended by her son William and his family, and the digger moved in.

Ivy Lomas [b. 31/8/33, d. 29/5/97, exhumed 12/10/98] Ivy Lomas, exhumed from Hyde Cemetery on 12 October, was the only one of Shipman's fifteen victims to die in the surgery. When the police called before tracing her next-of-kin, the cold-hearted GP told them: 'See that chair? We're going to put a plaque over that saying, "Permanently reserved for Ivy Lomas."' She was a 'mitherer', as they say in Hyde, and she irritated him with her constant calls.

When the police investigated Ivy's death, they realised with horror how audacious Shipman's killing spree had become. Detective Superintendent Postles recalled the moment he and his team uncovered the horrific case: 'We got to the point where this fellow was not only doing it in their homes but in the surgery as well, when there were people knocking about.' The surgery was always busy – full of patients from his large and impressive list, all knowing they could have as much time as they liked. Dr Shipman was so kind and patient. He had enough time to see to them – and kill Ivy Lomas in cold blood. He saw to three patients after injecting Ivy with the lethal dose of morphine and leaving her to die in the treatment room.

Sadly, Shipman's cold response to Ivy's death was not unusual. Most people found her opinionated and argumentative. She had fallen out with many in her time, including next-door neighbour Christopher Mather. Their relationship was so acrimonious that they had started court proceedings four months before she died. But by the time she died on 29 May 1997, the two households had patched it up. Despite her funny ways, those who knew her better agreed she was just good at hiding her big heart and was difficult only because she had led such a difficult life. Ivy, the widow of engineer Ronald Lomas, had devoted her life to bringing up her son Jackie. He was seriously psychiatrically ill and spent most of his time in a residential unit, Wickham House. But Ivy had brought him up to make the most of his life. Jackie would do odd jobs for his mother's neighbours at her request. Underneath it all she was kind-hearted and her son was a credit to her.

A neighbour, whose wife went to bingo with Mrs Lomas, spoke with a candour he believed she would have appreciated: 'Yes, she was a nuisance but she was all right underneath. We had quite a few set-tos but you just said, "Aw, shut up, Ivy". She would say her piece and then forget it. She was a good mother to her lad Jackie, too.'

Another neighbour, who had known Ivy since childhood, agreed, keen to set the record straight after realising what Ivy suffered in her last moments. 'Ivy could come across badly sometimes, a bit rough, but that was just her way,' she insisted. 'She was always very good to me. If she ever got flowers, she would come straight across to me with them because she knew I liked them and she didn't. Jackie was a lovely, helpful lad to me, too.'

Jackie was living at home when his mother died. He had returned from Wickham House and taken to his bed. Mrs Lomas, herself on anti-depressants because of the stress of looking after him, duly organised his new routine. She discussed the matter with her daughter Carol Dalpiaz, just before Carol went to work at 7.30 a.m. Jackie had been ill for years and the two women were terribly worried about him yet again, lying beneath the sheets and refusing to move or even open his eyes. After that, Mrs Lomas walked over to Brindle House, where his social workers were based, to discuss the situation. Then she took a taxi to Wickham House to collect his belongings. By now she was so exhausted that she had to ask her friend Charles Hill to carry the pitiful heap of big black bin liners for her. No wonder Mrs Lomas was forever at the doctor's: she needed someone to look after her, too.

Jackie was devastated when his beloved mother, his closest friend and fiercest protector, died. That day, Dr Shipman left Mrs Lomas in the treatment room for 30 minutes and told staff he had had trouble with the ECG, the heart-monitoring machine. He dealt with three more patients before he returned to her and found her collapsed. He came back out agitated and flushed, leading the distressed patients and receptionists to believe he was distraught. But he did not ask for the emergency services or for any help with resuscitation and she died in the surgery. Dr Shipman signed her death certificate and gave the cause as coronary thrombosis, heart disease and smoking.

Jackie was heartbroken. Now her murder has been revealed, he is inconsolable. He and Carol are still too devastated to talk.

Marie Quinn [b. 10/8/30, d. 24/11/97, exhumed 13/10/98]
Marie Quinn was exhumed from her plot at Hyde Cemetery, just yards from her Peel Street home, on 13 October 1998.

She was as good as any angel, according to those who knew her. She was a strong woman and a devout Catholic, but her religion was not just pious posturing – her tireless charity work reached all corners of Greater Manchester and beyond. Her parish priest, again Father Denis Maher at St Paul's, could not make it plain enough: 'If Marie isn't in Heaven, there's not much hope for me.'

He and Marie were very close; she called him 'one of my spiritual sons'. She first met Father Maher when he arrived at the parish just over three years ago and soon 'adopted' him along with other priests she felt close to, such as Rev. Donald Smith in Japan, who helped her son John settle there as a teacher. Father Maher, unable to hide the pain as he recalled the life force that has gone, explained: 'She was a dynamo, a live wire. She amazed me. If Marie happened to be going round a corner and you met her, she was like a whirlwind passing you. She was always on her way to her next appointment; she always had a destination.' The destination was usually somewhere where she could help others. Father Maher went on: 'She was a spiritual person, which is different from religious. Church was a big part of her life but it didn't end there – that was the beginning. She went out and lived what she did here.'

That was proved at her funeral at St Paul's Church, Hyde, which was meticulously planned by her devastated only son John and packed with mourners from voluntary groups from all over Manchester. Mrs Quinn's neighbours were there too, paying tribute to their good friend. Lorraine Leighton, who used to live next door, laughed as she remembered Marie outrunning her, such was her energy and verve: 'When we were going to Hyde, she would already be on her way back. My kids thought she was great. She would often ask if we wanted anything from the shops; she was always offering to help someone. She was a lovely woman and very spritely. It was a terrible shock when she died and worse when we found out she had been exhumed.'

Margaret Dmytriw, 76, whose sister Ellen Hanratty was Mrs Quinn's best friend, was heartbroken that such a good-hearted woman should have her life snatched from her: 'Marie was such a lovely lady, a good, God-fearing woman who would help anyone who needed it. Even her cat was a neglected one she had took in off the street.'

Mrs Hanratty, who accompanied Mrs Quinn on a pilgrimage to Bosnia a year before she died, learned of her friend's exhumation while recovering from a heart attack in Tameside General Hospital. Mrs Quinn had organised the trip to the Bosnian town of Madjurgorje, which had been featured on the BBC's *Everyman* programme and in the *Manchester Evening News*. Her undying faith was shown in an interview with the

Manchester Evening News, telling how she saw the Light of Lights, a sign from the Virgin Mary. 'It was absolutely beautiful,' she recalled. 'You can't stare at the sun normally but when it started spinning you could look directly at it and see all the colours coming from it.' She also brought back a candle for Father Maher, 'to prove you are always in my prayers'. Their friendship was a happy one but, after her death, it led to the traumatic job of Father Maher attending her exhumation. 'John asked me to go; he felt comforted knowing I would be there,' Father Maher said. 'It was hard for him to know what was happening while being so far away. Somebody dies and then it's their funeral. There's a finality; you are saying goodbye and there's healing in that. Now we have to go back and do that. It was terribly upsetting.'

Caring as she was, he added, the 67-year-old retired food processor was no fool: 'Up-front was Marie. She had no hesitation in telling you what she thought and did not suffer fools gladly. She was strong-willed. She would have had a lot to say about this case, had she been here.'

He last saw her on the Sunday before she died. The following Sunday, when he announced her death, he looked over to her usual place in church. 'I said, "That's where she was last Sunday". She always knelt in the same place. I can still remember her there.'

Irene Turner [b. 11/2/29, d. 11/7/96, exhumed 10/11/98]
Irene Turner was exhumed from Hyde Cemetery on 10 November 1998. She was 'a bandbox', as they say locally, never a hair out of place and never out without her make-up on. So it was a sickening irony that the proud grandmother-of-four – described as 'exquisite' by

her family – should have her body removed from its final resting place.

Mrs Turner was found dead at her home in St Paul's Hill Road on 11 July 1996. She had just returned from a holiday and was suffering from a slight cold and an upset stomach, so she took to her bed. But she was on good form, chatting away to her friend Michael Woodruff about her holiday exploits. Being poorly did not dim Mrs Turner's spirits. She had fought and beaten breast cancer three years before. Now she took her tablets and got on with her life.

Mr Woodruff, who later married Mrs Turner's daughter Carol, had taken her a meat and potato pie for lunch but, such was her pride, she refused it. 'She didn't want to be seen eating a pie when the doctor called, in bed, in her nightdress,' Mr Woodruff explained in the witness box. 'She looked as bright as a button.'

Within hours she was dead.

Neighbour Sheila Ward found her, after Dr Shipman had carefully set her up to make the devastating discovery. He had rushed over to her house, asking for her help. 'Can you go over and pack a bag for Irene?' he said. 'She's got to go to hospital. But, er, leave her a few minutes, while she sorts herself out.' He then dashed off, 'to do a few tests'.

When Mrs Ward finally got to Irene, she was dead.

It was a shock to everyone. Mrs Turner was a fit and healthy woman, hiding her 67 years with her lively ways as well as her care over her appearance. One neighbour described her as 'Marina', the vampish character from *Last of the Summer Wine*. She went out a lot in order to forget her difficult times, such as when her second husband Frank died shortly after their wedding reception in 1988. But Mrs Turner was well respected and loved, as shown by her carefully tended grave, headed with a brown marble headstone. It might have been removed in a macabre but necessary desecration of her grave, but its inscription still tells her true story – 'A dear wife, mum and nana, always in our hearts and sadly missed.'

Jean Lilley [b. 15/10/38, d. 25/4/97, exhumed 13/10/98] Jean Lilley, exhumed on 13 October 1998, had not enjoyed the best of health in all her 58 years. But despite suffering chronic arthritis, she had made the best of her life as a loving wife and mother.

However, because of Dr Shipman, she missed out on being a granny – a role she would have loved most of all. When Jean died, her daughter Odette Wilson was six months pregnant with Holly, who would have been Jean and her husband Albert's first grandchild. The day she died, she was looking forward to the weekend when she and Albert would forgo one of their regular trips to Blackpool in favour of a shopping trip for baby clothes. A former neighbour, shocked that Jean's sudden death had been a murder at the hands of the doctor who had so often helped her, said: 'Jean was a lovely woman and a nice neighbour. She was quite quiet because she was ill with the arthritis. It is so sad, such a shame she died and missed their first grandchild Holly.'

Mrs Lilley was found dead at her Jackson Street flat on 25 April 1997. She had moved here because she could no longer manage the stairs at her former home, a council house on Stansfield Street. Her bereft husband Albert is left, like Jean Pinder, with the awful knowledge he talked Jean into inviting her killer over. She had a cold and Albert, concerned it should not get any worse, told Jean to call out Dr Shipman as he left for work as a long-distance lorry driver at 5 a.m. Mrs

Lilley was the only victim living with a husband, but Mr Lilley's job gave Shipman every opportunity to mark her out as a possible target. Shipman's own father had been a lorry driver, but he had been present when his wife, Shipman's mother Vera, died after a long battle with lung cancer in 1964. Albert had no such chance to say goodbye. He has now moved back to their old street to be near Odette, who took over their former home.

The police found that, with Mrs Lilley's death, Shipman's behaviour had been particularly odd. Mrs Lilley's best friend and neighbour, Elizabeth Morgan, had spotted that Dr Shipman's car had been parked outside for 40 minutes and called to see if she was all right. As she arrived at the door of her flat, she saw the GP walking out of the block's main door. She walked in, shouting their favourite phrase, 'It's only me, missus.' There was no reply. Mrs Morgan was horrified to find Mrs Lilley sitting motionless on the sofa, her lips cold and blue. The distraught neighbour ran back and shouted to the doctor, but he simply glanced through the open window of his car and drove away. Later, in the witness box, Mrs Morgan explained how they had spent the morning 'chatting over a cuppa', as usual, before the doctor arrived. 'I left her laughing,' she recalled.

She called the paramedics, whose efforts were to no avail. When Dr Shipman came back, she broke down in tears. The callous GP had no comfort: 'There's no point in crying; she has gone now.' She was hurt and angered but still had no idea of the full, horrible truth. Shipman signed Mrs Lilley's death certificate, giving the cause as heart failure, heart disease and hypertension, with secondary causes inflammation of the lung and hypercholesterol anaemia.

Muriel Grimshaw [b. 21/10/20, d. 14/7/97, exhumed 8/12/98]

Muriel Grimshaw was exhumed from Highfield Cemetery, Bredbury, on 8 December 1998.

A good, God-fearing woman with few health problems, she had been to church with her daughter Anne Jones just the day before her death, at her Berkeley Crescent home, on 14 July 1997. Mrs Jones had found her in good spirits and perfectly well. Mrs Grimshaw was an infrequent visitor to her GP Dr Shipman's surgery, despite suffering a little from blood pressure problems and arthritis. She was a timid patient and she would tell her daughter of any health problems she was suffering and let her decide if she needed the doctor. Once, just two months before her death, Mrs Jones arranged a home visit for her mother. Dr Shipman sped to the pensioner's house so fast that he arrived before Mrs Jones had phoned to tell her that he was on his way.

That Sunday, the close mother and daughter made arrangements to meet up later in the week. Mrs Jones told the jury: 'She waved me off at the doorstep in really good spirits because we had made arrangements and she had something to look forward to.' In fact, she did not.

Mrs Grimshaw's body was found on Tuesday 15 July. Again police found that Shipman had behaved rather oddly, 'out of order' according to one officer – and according to the law. Shipman had decided to record her death as 14 July – the day before she was found. Deaths are always recorded at the time and date a body is found, but Shipman was very certain: 14 July. Police investigations later showed he had visited Mrs Grimshaw that day and recorded it on his practice computer – yet he failed to tell that to her devastated daughter.

Mrs Jones had discovered her mother's body after being called out by Mrs Grimshaw's friend Barbara Ryan, who had come for one of their usual twice-weekly shopping trips and got no answer. When the pair let themselves in with Mrs Jones's key, an eerie scene met them. The interior doors were all open and the television was still on, echoing through the house. Mrs Jones thought it strange – her mother always listened to the radio in the morning. She watched the television in the evenings and always unplugged it, fearing it would start a fire if there happened to be a thunderstorm. Then she found her mother's cold, lifeless body, lying on the bed, a drink of orange juice by her bedside. The distraught women called out Dr Shipman, who solemnly diagnosed a stroke and duly signed her death certificate, changing the details as he saw fit.

The truth was revealed to Mrs Jones, still too devastated to give a tribute to her mother, when Mrs Grimshaw's body was exhumed eighteen months later.

Three other women were also exhumed – Alice Kitchen, Sarah Ashworth and Elizabeth Mellor – but Dr Rutherford was unable to find any evidence of morphine toxicity. Their families have faced further torment following the pain of having the bodies exhumed, with no definite answer to how they died, and no good reason for having them disturbed from their peaceful sleep.

Alice Kitchen [b. Jan. 1924, d. 17/6/94, exhumed 11/11/98]
Mrs Kitchen, known to her friends by her middle name Christine, was the mother of eight children, one of them Hyde Councillor Joe Kitchen. She had a hard life. Now her death has ripped apart her family.

'She was a very caring, loveable person,' Joe said. 'She would always help her fellow neighbours even though she didn't have much herself. She hadn't had an easy life but she was still so caring and loving.' His words played down just how hard a life it had been and hid a terrible split that has torn apart his feuding family even further.

Mrs Kitchen was born Alice Christine Harney, one of thirteen children, in the Republic of Ireland in January 1924. She married council worker Edward Kitchen with whom she had four sons and four daughters, but the marriage was not a peaceful one. The marriage was turbulent and Christine sent her oldest daughters Philomena and Christine to stay with her sisters in Ireland. It was no escape for the girls, then aged five and six. Philomena was abused by her aunt and, as soon as she was able, she took a job caring for disabled children in Dublin. Forgoing nights out with the girls, the determined teenager saved her wages for the fare back to Hyde. She was hoping and praying for a happy reunion but Mrs Kitchen felt so guilty at what she had done that she felt uncomfortable with her prodigal daughter's presence.

'I stayed with mother for a little while but we were never really close. I think I reminded her of the past and she wanted to shut that out,' Philomena explained sadly. She kept an open mind and heart, hoping her mother would grow closer to her, especially when her three children were born. The old lady tried but failed. But Joe grew up with a sense of responsibility, which took him into civic life, and he grew warmer towards his estranged sister. The other siblings did not. Their relationship with her was always awkward and her presence always unwelcome. It was to turn even colder, with even Joe shunning Philomena, when their mother was exhumed.

Mrs Kitchen died a widow, aged 70, at her home in Kirkstone Road, Hyde, which she shared with her son Michael, on 17 June 1994. Dr Shipman – whose patients included Mrs Kitchen's four sons and four daughters – signed her death certificate, giving the cause as a stroke. The much-loved grandmother of 21 was buried at Hyde Cemetery in a plot marked with a black marble headstone, inscribed 'loyalty, devotion, endurance and beyond reproach'. Philomena was devastated that she had lost the battle to win her mother over before it was too late. But she still had Joe, who would happily invite her in for a cup of tea whenever she called over. All that was to change.

When the police exhumed Mrs Kitchen's body on 11 November, Philomena asked her parish priest, Father Denis Maher, to attend her reinterment. This caused consternation among her brothers and sisters, who had asked their own priest, Father Peter Hibbert, to attend. In the end, fourteen members of the family gathered for the service with both priests in attendance, giving their services simultaneously. Councillor Kitchen was, as ever, diplomatic when he said, 'It has been a very uncertain time for all the family. It is all very upsetting.' There was one thing, though, that they all agreed on: 'We all loved her very much.'

Sarah Ashworth [b. 13/9/18, d. 17/4/93, exhumed 7/12/98]
Sarah Ashworth, known as Sally, had by contrast led a charmed life, ending her days in a beautiful big house, Bella Vista, on leafy Bowlacre Road, just a few yards from her son's home.

Mrs Ashworth was born Sarah Thomas in Bangor on 13 September 1918. She married Frank Ashworth, a successful businessman whose work saw them both company directors, and the couple had two sons. Mrs Ashworth was a widow, living alone, when she died at her home on 17 April 1993. Her son John signed the death certificate along with Dr Shipman, who gave the cause of death as heart failure and heart disease with secondary hypertension. Police, believing she was another of the GP's many victims, exhumed her from Dukinfield Cemetery on 7 December 1998. But they were unable to find any morphine in her body. It is thought Mrs Ashworth and Mrs Kitchen had been buried for too long to give up the evidence required. Mrs Ashworth was buried in 1993, Mrs Kitchen in 1994, and the earliest death proved to be a Shipman murder, following exhumation, was Irene Turner's in July 1996.

However, Mrs Ashworth's death was still to play a major part in the Shipman case. Police found that he had been stockpiling morphine from patients who died without using all their medication, from those he continued to prescribe after their death and from those he prescribed even though they did not need the painkilling drug. Mrs Ashworth was one of those listed in Volume 8 of the prosecution's evidence, fought over so vehemently – to no avail – by the defence in legal arguments prior to the trial's first day. Defending barrister Nicola Davies QC told Mr Justice Forbes that Shipman had collected it for his own use. The prosecution proved it was for something even more sinister – murder.

Elizabeth Mellor [b. 18/12/19, d. 30/11/94, exhumed 9/12/98]
Lizzie Mellor died on 30 November 1994. She was 'a plucky devil', bravely fighting back from the stroke she had suffered the year before. Even though she had been ill, everyone was shocked at the news she had been

found dead, sitting in her chair at her Sidley Place council flat. They thought she was on her way back up and were pleased, knowing how it drove Lizzie mad not to be out in the garden she kept so beautiful for all her neighbours. She was so determined to keep on going that she insisted on doing all her own ironing, even though this task now had to be completed while sitting down in the kitchen.

Lizzie was a true Hydonian, born and bred, as was her husband Sam. Sam, a bricklayer by trade, was well known in the area for his gentle ways and wealth of knowledge on local history. When he retired he would go to the primary school next door to the couple's home, to give the children talks on how things used to be. He was a good speaker and the children loved his visits. Lizzie, lively and good-natured, was his perfect partner. The couple had a daughter, Shirley, and Lizzie worked as a cleaner before retiring. She was a widow when she died, aged 75.

Her friend and neighbour Joyce Harrison found her when she went upstairs for one of their many chats. Lizzie looked as if she was sleeping, with her book open on her lap. But when Joyce touched her gently to wake her, she was cold. Her old friend was devastated. 'We would spend hours talking about everything and anything. She was very easy to talk to and a good laugh,' she recalled. 'I would hate to think anything had happened to her.'

Lizzie was exhumed from Hyde Cemetery on 9 December 1998, the last of the twelve women to be torn from their graves in a murder investigation that devastated the whole community. But, again, no morphine was found and Shipman was not charged with her murder.

* * *

Detective Superintendent Postles and DCI Williams worked hard to organise the exhumations, making sure that they were carried out with as much dignity and sensitivity as possible. In addition, they were racing against time as the nights drew in, leaving less time between exhumation and reinterment, and it grew closer and closer to Christmas. They were ever mindful of all the women's anniversaries and birthdays, as well as the festive season, which would hurt the families enough without the worry of whether their mother, sister or aunt was 'next'. And each one would prove a complicated process, following an in-depth and painstaking investigation into the death, to gather the evidence needed to convince Mr Pollard and the families that it was necessary.

Each and every time, in order to keep security as tight as possible, dozens of officers and other workers – stonemasons, gravediggers, lighting technicians and a specialist exhumation company – were drafted in at the very last minute. When a stonemason brought his friend along, the two leading officers considered introducing ID cards for all involved. 'It seemed like everyone but the station cat was there,' Det Supt Postles recalled with a little irritation. Pathologist Dr John Rutherford was kept on standby at the Tameside General Hospital morgue, so he could do his post mortem that morning and have the body reinterred in the afternoon.

Again, at the last minute, distraught families were approached and asked if they would allow it, even though ultimately the decision rested with Mr Pollard. Many people, having seen the press coverage, at first refused and the officers had to be mindful of the grief the investigation had unleashed, tearing divisions within some families. But in the end all of them agreed. They were given the option of attending the reinterment but only one family – the Kitchens – were able to face such an ordeal. Often they sent their parish priest to watch over their loved one. Father Denis Maher attended three and found each one to be among the worst experiences in his many years as a cleric. 'It was terrible,' he recalled softly. 'I was not alone in being conscious what a violation was being carried out, although the police were very sensitive.' He added, with anger growing in his voice, 'If Dr Shipman could have been there that morning, if he could see what had to be done because of him, that almost would have been sufficient punishment for him. He would know, "I caused this."'

The exhumations had to be carried out by night, adding to the eeriness of the officers' work and upsetting the cemeteries' neighbours. June Wilson, whose terrace backs on to Hyde Cemetery, was terrified the first night. When she woke to the sound of generators tearing into the graveyard silence, she thought aliens had landed. 'When we realised what was really happening it was even worse,' she recalled. 'I knew Winnie Mellor and Marie Quinn very well, so to think what they were going through was heartbreaking. You just lie there – you can't sleep – thinking about them. They led such good lives and then ended this way.' Mrs Wilson thought it unnecessary that the exhumations were done by night. But DS Postles and DCI Williams had carefully considered the best way to carry out the task for all concerned, especially the families. They had to protect the families' loved ones, keep security tight, keep prying eyes at a distance and have the whole process done within a matter of hours. And they had to protect the rest of the community, already shaken by the case, from a task so macabre that darkness could not have made it any worse. 'A cemetery is a working environment. In addition to funerals being held there, people were coming to put flowers on graves. The last thing they want to see is what we were doing,' DS Postles explained.

Throughout those dark winter months, DS Postles had to make sure his team were coping with their terrible job of repeatedly disturbing the dead. His concern for them turned to immense pride, for his worry was not necessary. 'There was a spiritual aspect and we were uncomfortable with what we were doing,' he said. 'Words like stress are used a lot. Confidential counselling is provided by our occupational health department and I asked to be told if as many as five or six of my officers had requested it. We wanted to know so we could change the way we were working if necessary. It wasn't.'

The teams also began to investigate the deaths of patients who were cremated. Even though there would be no bodies to give them physical evidence of Dr Shipman's killing spree, there were signs of his guilt that could not be ignored. He had changed their medical records to make them look more ill than they were. He gave them conditions they did not have, fictitious ailments that he would later blame for their deaths. He had lied about them calling him out, lied about them feeling unwell and lied about his arriving to find he was too late. And he had pretended to call and cancel ambulances for women he knew would never survive his lethal dose. Each and every time, Dr Shipman had played out a cold-hearted charade.

DS Postles also found that his team members were getting 'pushed on' by the publicity in the press and on television and radio. Fearful families were contacting them, asking them to investigate the deaths of their own relatives, so many of which were so similar to those in the reports. The detectives had to respond swiftly to make sure they got there before the media, to ask their questions of a source unadulterated by the drama of having a reporter on their doorstep.

The team was to add another six women to their roll call of victims, which was now being referred to as 'Shipman's list' in the pubs and shops of Hyde.

Marie West [b. 22/12/13, d. 6/3/95]

Maria West died at the hands of Dr Shipman while her best friend waited next door in the kitchen. Dr Shipman had no idea that Marion Hadfield was there, waiting good as gold for the doctor to finish his very important work.

Mrs Hadfield had been having a cup of tea with her old friend when Mrs West told her that Dr Shipman would be calling on her that day. Mrs Hadfield thought she had better leave Mrs West to her appointment, but first she visited the bathroom. As she returned through the kitchen to the lounge, she heard a man's voice. Typical of a generation who easily deferred to the doctor, she decided it was best to keep out of the way. It took just those few moments for Dr Shipman to murder Mrs West. After a few minutes of silence, as Mrs Hadfield wondered if Dr Shipman had left, he walked in – and looked at her in shock.

'I didn't know anyone was here,' he said, floundering for his next sentence. 'I was just going upstairs to see if her son was in. She has collapsed on me.'

Mrs Hadfield was distraught; Marie had been perfectly well a few minutes earlier. She ran to her friend, who just looked as though she was sleeping. 'Can't you do something?' she begged the GP.

She looked in horror as the GP, now back to his old arrogant self, lifted her dead friend's eyelid and said peremptorily, 'See – no life there.'

Despite her horror, she knew little of the true scale of his cruelty.

When, during his first police interview, he was asked whether he had tried to revive his patients, Dr Shipman replied of one case: 'The lady was obviously dead, but there's a routine you go through; if nothing else it impresses the relatives.' But sometimes he didn't even bother to do that. As DCI Williams said, 'He knows how they have died – he has killed them. He doesn't even put on that show for the relatives. He is that arrogant.'

Marie, as she preferred to be known, was a 'one-off' and a true Hydonian, according to her friend, taxi driver John Shaw. She had run a children's clothes shop in Newton and was well known throughout the town. She was a good woman who had made the most of her 81 years. But it had not all been easy. She had lost her daughter Jacqueline to cancer eight years earlier. Now widowed, devoted grandmother Marie threw herself into watching her surviving loved ones – her son Christopher and his family in Stalybridge – grow.

She had been born Maria Howcroft in Hyde, where she lived all her life, just a few days before Christmas 1913. She went on to marry mechanic John West and they had two children, Jacqueline and Christopher. John Shaw, who had gone to school with Jacqueline, wondered if her husband, former Stockport policeman Bill Price, ever had any suspicions about his mother-in-law's sudden death. It seems that, at the time, he did not. Despite his close call, all went smoothly from then on for Dr Shipman. He signed Marie's death certificate, giving the date as 6 March 1995 and the cause as a stroke. She was cremated at Dukinfield Crematorium on 14 March 1995. It was another three years before the truth was finally revealed.

Lizzie Adams [b. 5/2/20, d. 28/2/97]

Lizzie Adams had just celebrated her 77th birthday when she died at her Coronation Avenue home in February 1997. But age was no matter to her – the former dance teacher was fit and well with plenty of life and energy left in her. In fact, she had only retired from her teaching the year before and still 'cut a rug' with her dance partner Bill Catlow several times a week. Both nimble and slight, she with her dark curls and he with his white straight hair, they made a couple of star quality.

Born on 5 February 1920 in Hyde, Lizzie Simpson stayed in the town and became a machinist. She met and married Edmund Adams, by whom she had two daughters, and they settled at Coronation Avenue. Edmund died after he retired from his job as an engineering labourer and Lizzie found solace in her family and dancing.

She had just returned from a trip to Malta with Bill and the over 50s club and returned looking relaxed and well, despite suffering a little cough from the Sahara dust that had blown around the resort. Two days before Lizzie's death, her two daughters, Doreen Thorley and Sonia Jones, called to see her and suggested antibiotics would help get rid of the bug that had left her slightly under the weather but still in high spirits. The following day she enjoyed an all-day shopping trip with Doreen in Stockport, stopping only for a spot of lunch.

On the day she died, 28 February 1997, Lizzie was hanging out the washing when she got a call from Doreen. She suggested Lizzie change her tablets, as they were not agreeing with her. Just like Jean Lilley's husband Albert and Joan Melia's niece Jean Pinder, Doreen persuaded her mother to invite the killer into her home – a visit from Dr Shipman was arranged.

Lizzie died as her devoted dance partner Bill called to see how she was at 2 p.m. – to find Dr Shipman examining her display cabinet of porcelain figurines. Lizzie sat motionless in her favourite chair in the next-door room. Her legs were crossed, she was fully clothed and she was still warm. Bill took her hand – and could still feel her pulse. He begged Dr Shipman to help but the hard-hearted GP told him it was his own pulse he could feel. She was dead, he insisted; he would have to cancel the ambulance. He left the room to use the telephone while Bill cradled his dance partner for the last time.

Doreen was summoned from work and collapsed when the bad news was broken. She and Sonia were never happy with the circumstances of their mother's death. She had been so well, the iron was still on and a meal was cooking on the stove. The little tie at the top of her pretty blouse was still done up, yet Dr Shipman had told them she had been fighting for breath. But, grief-stricken, they accepted his diagnosis and he signed her death certificate, giving the cause as pneumonia. Eighteen months later, Sonia, shocked to read of the investigation into Dr Shipman in the *Manchester Evening News*, contacted the Greater Manchester Ambulance Service to make sure the GP had called an ambulance for her mother. She was devastated to find it had all been a sham.

Laura Kathleen Wagstaff [b. 8/1/16, d. 9/12/97]
It was not unusual for Dr Shipman to get Christmas presents from his devoted patients, but the bottle of gin from Ann Royle, which she took to the surgery on 9 December 1997, gave rise to a sickening twist in his killing spree.

Dr Shipman mistook Mrs Wagstaff for Mrs Royle, whose daughter Angela was married to Mrs Wagstaff's son Peter. He had planned to thank Mrs Royle for her lovely present with a lethal injection of morphine – but he showed his 'gratitude' to the wrong woman. Having killed Mrs Wagstaff, Dr Shipman walked over to Dowson Primary School, where Angela Wagstaff worked, and told her that her mother had died. He left her distraught, being comforted by her heartbroken colleagues.

There began an hour-long ordeal for Angela and Peter Wagstaff as confusion took hold. Sobbing, Angela decided she had to go to her mother. But she and her friend Margaret Nathaniel were unable to get into her car because the alarm was broken. Instead they sprinted to Mrs Royle's nearby home. Gasping for breath, Angela knocked on her mother's door, expecting Dr Shipman to be there. There was no answer. She tore open the letterbox and looked through – to see her mother walking down the hall towards her. Angela was hysterical with shock. 'Mum,' she screamed. Minutes later she rang her husband, who was driving home from work to comfort her. 'She's here, she's here, she's alive, she's OK,' she cried. Then suddenly it dawned on the couple. Maybe it was Peter's mother instead. Peter Wagstaff rang the surgery and Dr Shipman, then aware of his terrible mistake, broke the news. Yes, it was his mother. Mr Wagstaff pulled over and stopped the car, unable to drive with the shock of this revelation.

Dr Shipman had realised his mistake when he told receptionist Carol Chapman what had happened. She knew the family well and knew that the kind old dear who had popped in with the Christmas bottle and asked what she should get the 'girls' behind the counter was Mrs Royle and not Mrs Wagstaff. When she explained, he replied, 'Oh shit.' Later he apologised to the family for the confusion but suggested Angela had been too distraught to understand what he had said. 'We both apologised to each other in a way,' she later recalled in the witness box.

Mrs Wagstaff and Mrs Royle meant the world to their families. Peter and Angela Wagstaff were close to both their mothers, such wonderful and well-loved grandmothers to their daughter, and all three households were within minutes of each other and the school where Angela worked.

Kathleen, as she preferred to be known, was a Geordie, born Laura Kathleen Powell in Middlesbrough just eight days into 1916. Later she married garage manager George Laughton Wagstaff and they had two sons, Peter and John. When Kathleen was widowed, she threw herself into her family. Her death was a shock to them – she was fit and well as far as they were concerned – and they quizzed Dr Shipman about it. He assured them he had done all he could, having found her in a declining condition. He told them he had been called out by pager, during his rounds on the nearby Wych Fold estate, after Mrs Wagstaff had called the surgery saying she was seriously ill. He found her looking grey, with blue-ish lips. He helped her from the front door back upstairs into the flat and then called an ambulance, after which he went to his car for his equipment. When he returned, she was dead. Dr Shipman signed Mrs Wagstaff's death certificate, giving coronary thrombosis and heart disease as the causes.

But in fact she had been her normal, cheerful self, according to local gardener Andrew Hallas. The kindly, thoughtful widow had brought him a cup of tea and later he saw her go out to Hyde. Mrs Wagstaff's next-door neighbour, Margaret Walker, had heard her say, 'Fancy seeing you here' when the doctor called later that day. But 45 minutes later, Mrs Wagstaff was dead. Investigations by the police showed there had been no call from Mrs Wagstaff to the surgery, nor any pager message to Dr Shipman, nor any call to the ambulance service for that address.

There was only one reason for Dr Shipman's visit to Mrs Wagstaff's home – to kill her, or rather, the woman he thought she was.

Norah Nuttall [b. 6/12/33, d. 26/1/98]

Norah Nuttall was another old Hydonian who had never shaken off the label of her maiden name, Mansfield. They were a well-known family in Gee Cross, where Norah was born and bred, and she and her sister Elizabeth Oldham were known as 'the Mansfield girls'. Their father Walter was much respected – even feared. Walter, who owned the farm at the top of the village and later the Hare and Hounds, was a big man who ran a strict regime. No young blood would dare put his arm round his girl if Walter was about. Even after she had married builder's labourer John Lord Nuttall – even at her death – Norah was still referred to as Norah Mansfield.

People believed Norah was the victim of her obesity when she died at her Baron Road terrace, which she shared with her son Anthony, on 26 January 1998. But taxi driver John Shaw, who often took her shopping and was a friend of Anthony, knew otherwise. He had been suspicious of Shipman for years but dared not tell anyone for fear of being charged with slander or even declared mentally ill. He was heartbroken to hear how Anthony, who had gone out to a nearby field to see some ponies for half an hour, returned to find Dr Shipman walking out of the front door. His mother had been to the surgery with a wheezy cough earlier that day, but she did not seem that poorly. 'She's took a turn for the worse,' the GP said, adding that he had called an ambulance. Anthony rushed in and grabbed his mother's cold hand – she was dead. As Anthony sobbed over his mother's corpse, Dr Shipman called to cancel the ambulance.

The police investigation revealed that it was another of Shipman's sick charades – there was no call to order or cancel an ambulance from that address. The GP had been play-acting as devastated Anthony Nuttall wept for his dead mother. John Shaw shuddered as he recalled: 'When I heard what had happened, I wanted to say something to him – but you can't say that, can you? Anthony thought so highly of Shipman; he wanted to give him a keepsake of his mother's. He was going to give him a ring. He went to her jewellery box – it was missing. I couldn't say to him what I wanted to say to him.'

Pamela Hillier [b. 9/12/29, d. 9/2/98]

Pamela Hillier was a strong independent woman and the heart of her close-knit family. She spent every Sunday with her daughter and son-in-law, Jacqueline and Martin Gee, and their two girls, her treasured granddaughters. She also spent many weekdays with Jacqueline, and they talked on the phone all the time.

Following the death of her husband Cyril, Pamela became a stalwart of Mottram Church. She attended every Sunday, helped make coffee and tea after the service and raised funds for its repair as a fully active member of the Friends society. She would think nothing of walking her dogs two or three times every day, she still drove and she still worked at a solicitor's, alongside Martin, when the staff were off on holiday. The week before she died, Mrs Hillier had even stripped the wallpaper from two rooms and moved all the furniture, all on her own, in preparation for decorating at her smart Stalybridge townhouse. It was her new start as she prepared to face the first anniversary of Cyril's death – Valentine's Day. All the family were a little sad that week but, as usual, she was determined to cope.

Mrs Hillier had also bumped her knee after tripping on some loose carpet, but it was a minor injury. 'It's just a little sore,' she assured Jacqueline. It was 9 February 1998 and her daughter had called in to walk the dogs and invite her to stay at their Glossop home. Mrs Hillier said she would have her knee seen to by her GP, Dr Shipman, who would making a home visit that afternoon. After that, Jacqueline could pick her up. But when Jacqueline rang her later, there was no reply. She and her two young daughters tried several times. They then rang Mrs Hillier's next-door neighbours, the Ellwoods, and asked them to make sure she was all right. The distraught couple found their friend and fellow church stalwart dead.

'She was a lovely woman with a strong independent streak and a kind heart,' they recalled later. 'She would do anything to help you; such a good neighbour. She will be missed by the Friends of the church, too. We were terribly shocked by her death. It was so unexpected.'

Mr Ellwood found Mrs Hillier lying on her back, on the floor, in a three-foot gap at the foot of her bed. There was a bottle of tablets on the counterpane. He rang Jacqueline and asked her to come over. Mrs Ellwood also called out an ambulance and Dr Shipman while her husband tried to revive their friend. Paramedic Stephen Morris lifted her on to the bed and took over Mr Ellwood's attempts at resuscitation. He soon realised there was little point; she had been dead for some time. When Jacqueline was told, she became so distraught that the paramedics decided to stay. 'I thought she would be my next patient,' Mr Morris recalled in the witness box.

When Dr Shipman arrived, he pushed past Mr Ellwood at the front door and dashed upstairs. The neighbour later heard one paramedic suggest they call the police: 'It's a sudden death at home.' The GP snapped back: 'I don't see there's any need for that.'

Shipman also talked Mrs Hillier's family out of having a post mortem.

Mrs Hillier meant the world to her family. Born Pamela Marguerite Willington in Mitcham, Surrey, on 9 December 1929, she was smart, worked hard and trained as a secretary. She and financial advisor Cyril had a long, happy marriage until he succumbed to a lengthy illness on 14 February 1997. She stayed on at their townhouse, on the same street where the artist Lowry had once lived, and spent more time with their old friends the Ellwoods. It was through them that she joined the Mottram Church congregation, always sitting in the same pew as them and beginning to make new friends.

Mrs Hillier's son Keith, who dashed over from Loughborough the day after her death, quizzed Shipman at length about her death and demanded a post mortem. But Dr Shipman took the conversation 'in circles', saying her blood pressure was high enough to kill her but not high enough to warrant her GP's concern, and told him how unpleasant such a procedure would be. Too upset to continue arguing, Keith gave up. Dr Shipman signed her death certificate, giving the cause as a stroke, and no doubt breathed a sigh of relief when Mrs Hillier was cremated at Dukinfield Crematorium a few days later. He didn't know that, just a few months later, the truth would finally be out.

Maureen Ward [b. 14/8/40, d. 18/2/98]

When Dr Harold Shipman murdered college lecturer Maureen Ward, he was returning to the scene of a previous killing – the home she had shared so happily with her mother. Irish-born widow Muriel Ward died on 24 October 1995 as Dr Shipman was examining her in the living room of their Ogden Court flat. At the time, Maureen was brewing up in the kitchen.

On 18 February 1998, Shipman returned and murdered Maureen, Muriel's only daughter, in exactly the same way and in the same flat. Muriel's death, at 87, was signed as heart failure by Shipman. Two years after co-signing her mother's death certificate, Maureen was dead too – killed by brain and breast cancer according to the same cold-hearted GP.

Police have not been able to charge him with the first murder since he killed the only witness – Maureen – two years later.

Maureen had been a life force at the sheltered accommodation where she had made her home. She was still young – only 57 when she died – with plenty to live for, having successfully fought off breast and skin cancer. She was only too happy to run errands for her elderly neighbours and loved nothing more than sunbathing in the communal gardens, chatting with the women as they all relaxed. She had recently retired from her post at Tameside College and was planning to move to Southport, to be closer to her old friend Christine Whitworth. That was after the holiday of a lifetime, a cruise in the Caribbean with her friend and neighbour Mary France. Taxi driver John Shaw, a friend of Maureen's, had been due to drive her to the airport on the Saturday following her death. 'She was fine, looking forward to her holidays and going to live in Southport,' he recalls. 'I imagine she told Shipman she was going.'

Indeed she had. The day before she died, Maureen called at the surgery to see Dr Shipman and, as he saw the smiling spinster out, he remarked to receptionist Carol Chapman, 'Maureen's moving to Southport and she's going on a cruise.' She was to do no such thing.

The following day, Maureen's body was discovered lying on her bed, just a few hours after she was seen shopping in Hyde, doing her washing and carrying a bin liner full of washing to the laundry for Mrs France. A tin of cat food with the fork still in it stood on the kitchen counter. Dr Shipman had called for the warden, Christine Simpson, saying Maureen had left the door 'on the snip' for him but when he went in, she was dead. Mrs Simpson was perturbed – the door had a release button, for reasons of security, which Maureen could have used instead. And she was horrified when Dr Shipman added, 'She did have a brain tumour you know.' She and the neighbours had no idea – because it was not true.

Police investigations revealed that Dr Shipman had tampered with Miss Ward's medical records, to make it look as if she had a brain tumour. But she had been given the all-clear from both her cancers by two different consultants and, in any case, a brain tumour does not kill quickly and suddenly, as Dr Shipman would have it.

Mrs Simpson was already devastated by the death of a tenant who was also her friend, and the revelation that Maureen had been murdered only added to the pain.

It was more difficult to prove murder in the cases of the cremated bodies, but the diligent and hard-working murder squad did it by painstakingly probing every aspect of Dr Shipman's life.

On 7 September 1998, they searched his modest semi in the leafy enclave of Roe Cross Green, Mottram. Dr Shipman's wife Primrose and their two youngest sons David and Sam stood by as the detectives systematically took apart their family home. One officer was impressed by how the family coped. 'They were very helpful and quite pleasant, considering,' he recalled. 'One of the lads even showed us where to find things. He was a nice lad, very polite.' But he added that 'the house was filthy, with clothes strewn all over and food left lying around the kitchen. It was not how you would expect a doctor's house to be.'

The officers took away a jewellery box filled with tiny rings, old-fashioned brooches and necklaces. When asked who owned this jewellery box, Primrose replied, 'Me'. The officers were surprised. As one explained, 'Her fingers were like Cumberland sausages; we couldn't believe she had ever worn such tiny rings.' The jewellery was photographed and put into a catalogue for relatives to look at, but no one ever spotted the trinkets that had gone missing when their loved one was found dead.

The team also found boxes and carrier bags in the garage, each stuffed with old medical records and labelled with the word 'dead' in red letters. Dr Shipman had chosen to keep his old records, instead of giving them to West Pennine Health Authority for storage. However, as per his contract with West Pennine, he was expected to keep them safe, for obvious reasons of confidentiality. The 150 records stuffed haphazardly into boxes and bags were testament to his lax attitude – and some were testament to his murderous intentions.

The team employed a nurse from Merseyside, who spread all the records on her kitchen table and got to work, deciphering the doctor's typical scrawl and putting them into chronological order. Dr John Grenville, a GP from Derby, was also called on as an expert witness and was shocked by what he found in the notes. He was amazed that Dr Shipman had left Ivy Lomas, apparently dying of a heart attack, while he attended the colds and sniffles of three other patients and he did not bother sending Joan Melia to hospital because she would probably die on the way there.

On 14 August 1998, detectives searched Dr Shipman's three-storey surgery on Market Street, Hyde, as the GP and his then-loyal staff stood by. Dr Shipman, still playing the innocent victim of a wealthy widow's misplaced loyalty, handed them a typewriter. 'I believe this is what you are looking for,' he said, the picture of co-operation but also a little defiant, knowing what effect it would have on his audience – both the police and his sympathetic employees. The officers thanked him and took it away for forensic examination. It showed the typewriter had indeed been used to type the fake will – but that did not bother Dr Shipman, for he was claiming Mrs Grundy had borrowed it. He insisted that was how she had produced her own second will. But fingerprint expert Andrew Watson found no prints from Mrs Grundy, only those of Dr Shipman and his wife Primrose.

The officers also examined more of Dr Shipman's medical notes, paper documents bound in the traditional light brown Lloyd George envelopes. They were shocked to find Dr Shipman suggesting that Mrs Grundy was addicted to codeine – a painkilling drug containing morphine. The entry for 12 October 1996 read: 'IBS [irritable bowel syndrome] again. Odd. Pupils small. Constipated. Query drug abuse? Query at her age? Query codeine? Wait and see.' Two more entries, dated 15 July and 26 November 1997, suggested the same thing.

At his first police interview, on 7 September 1998, Shipman could not wait to show these records to the officers. But their investigations later showed that Mrs Grundy could not have had an appointment on 12 October 1996 – she was spending time with her daughter, Angela Woodruff, who had travelled up from Leamington Spa for one of her many visits. The details were dutifully recorded, as always, in Kathleen Grundy's diary. And when Dr Shipman had apparently been noting his concerns on 26 November 1997, he was actually shopping in York. His credit card records showed two transactions, in the Waterstones and Signatures stores, 200 miles away. But this was yet to be uncovered and Shipman took his chance to fox the interviewing officers, Detective Sergeant John Walker and Detective Constable Mark Denham.

Arrogant and offhand, Dr Shipman used medical jargon and argued about the officers' interviewing technique in a bid to put them off. He was already irritated after being booked into Ashton police station by a mere sergeant. DCI Williams, with a typical flash of wit, said later, 'He would have liked the Chief Constable to be there.' DCI Williams and DS Postles, listening to the interview in another room, had every sympathy for their officers, who were bearing the immense pressure of being the first to tackle Shipman properly while still waiting for all the evidence required.

'Shipman was extremely difficult to deal with in that first interview,' DCI Williams recalled. 'It was a minefield for the officers, who had to establish why Kathleen Grundy had morphine in her body and understand medical issues. Shipman used medical jargon; it was quite easy for him to do that. He set out to belittle the officers: "I'm the intelligent one here." He saw it as a competition, a challenge between him and us; he had superior knowledge and intellect.' But Shipman's arrogance was about to undo him.

The computer examination unit had also attended the surgery on the day of the search and took a copy of Dr Shipman's hard disk, which held all the patients' records. This was to prove some of the most damning evidence of all, thanks to the GP's superiority complex. Dr Shipman was very proud of the computerisation of his practice. He told the officers at his first interview: 'I'm a firm believer that the concept of GP and computerisation is being held back by finance, underdevelopment and political decisions by government. That doesn't stop me computerising my practice.'

He was referring to his practice appeal fund, which raised £19,000 in six years thanks to the efforts and generosity of his devoted patients. In a sickening irony, many of Dr Shipman's victims had contributed both in life, with a few coppers in the pot pig kept on the counter, and in death, with donations made in lieu of flowers. Mrs Grundy had been considering donating her part of the Mayoress's Fund, but the committee voted against the suggestion. She told him the bad news just before she died. It was through this fund that many pieces of equipment had been bought, including the extravagant computer system.

Dr Shipman had installed six computers, all networked together for all the staff to use after putting in the password – the GP's initials 'HFS'. He had even employed a computer operator, Margaret Walker. But no one could use it like he did. He jealously guarded his leading role, often snapping at staff struggling with the system.

And only he changed patients' records shortly before they died.

That was to undo him in his second interview. Unbeknown to Shipman, the computer examination unit had uncovered the fact that he had tampered with the notes to make the women look more ill than they actually were. They had followed an audit trail, a shadow left on all computer disks, which showed when he had really created his notes, regardless of the date he had typed on the file. DS Postles expected that a computer hotshot, as Shipman portrayed himself, would know of this flaw in his plan. But no – he had changed records within minutes of 'finding' women dead, creating and deleting dozens of entries in a blizzard of activity around the time of their sudden and unexpected passing.

It made chilling reading.

Maureen Ward's medical records showed all the signs of a woman with a brain tumour. Shipman had noted that on 17 December 1997 she was suffering 'headache, it comes and goes, dull, nauseous, legs not steady, retina of eye is OK, eyesight is normal'. But the audit trail showed he had created that file on 18 February 1998 at 2.49 p.m. – 45 minutes before he found her dead.

DCI Williams spelt it out: 'Maureen Ward was found by Dr Shipman at 3.30 p.m. He was in surgery at 2.45 p.m. making that entry. Two minutes later there's an entry for the day before, suggesting secondary cancer in the brain. Two minutes after that one for 17 December. He is creating a history, so that having a look at it will show a tendency to the cause of death. He had done the dirty deed. He had called on her, goes back to the computer, then goes back to "find" the body.'

DS Postles began to see what a pathetic figure the doctor really was: 'He was like child who had done something naughty and couldn't wait for someone to find out. He had to go back and make sure she was found.'

It was the same for three other victims – Pamela Hillier, Winnie Mellor and Bianka Pomfret. All four women's medical records changed within hours of their death. Out of a list of 3,000 patients, this was no coincidence. Nor could Dr Shipman have been able to remember blood pressure readings weeks, even months, after the so-called consultation.

Detectives had also checked telephone and pager records for the surgery, the women's homes and Greater Manchester Ambulance Service. They too uncovered a web of deceit in Dr Shipman's claims that his victims had called him or he had cancelled an ambulance or his surgery staff had paged him.

When Shipman came back for his second interview, on 7 October 1998, the trap was waiting – and he marched arrogantly into it.

DS Postles and DCI Williams had introduced a new interviewing team, a move designed not only to relieve the pressures on the existing team but also to see how Dr Shipman would react to a woman. Detective Sergeant Mark Wareing and Detective Constable Marie Snitinsky made skilful work of the painstaking job ahead of them, as Postles and Williams listened in on an audio system.

'He wasn't too impressed, answering a DC, and he considered it even more demeaning answering a woman,' Postles recalled. 'It was in the inflection in his voice, in his body language, answering the male sat next to her.' But that was of no matter to DC Snitinsky, who was about to bring Britain's biggest serial killer to his knees, to the delight of her bosses.

DCI Williams remembers how he and DS Postles listened with growing excitement as the two officers went into great detail about the computerisation of the practice. They asked Dr Shipman who was responsible.

He replied that he was: 'I'm particular about that.'

It was then that the officers struck home. They asked if it had been he who had changed Winifred Mellor's records within hours of her death. Dr Shipman suddenly realised that they were aware of his cover-up and they had blown apart his cast-iron cover as the town's most marvellous doctor.

'They led him nicely up a particular path,' DCI Williams recounted. 'So then it was, "Well, explain that then." It becomes apparent it is clicking; he's less arrogant; it takes more time for him to answer. He was floundering; he didn't know a counter argument. You put the pin in the balloon.' He and DS Postles have listened to those tapes over and over. DCI Williams recalled with glee: 'There is a crucial moment where he knows the game is up. I thought he was going to cough it.'

The proud DCI added: 'It is difficult enough in any interview but that's what we are trained to do. In these circumstances they had a more difficult job because of the way he reacted to them and treated them. They were extremely skilful. They were under extraordinary pressure but they coped extremely well and did a damn good job.'

DS Postles also recalled that wonderful moment, sitting in the other room, listening to the interview: 'He had considered he had won. "I'm up to it, let's get the boxing gloves on." The officers led him along. You get to the point where he can see it coming, when you listen to the tapes.'

That night, Shipman suddenly stopped and asked for a private consultation with his solicitor. The door closed and the cold-hearted killer fell to his knees, sobbing.

After fourteen years and fifteen deaths, and possibly hundreds more, the game was finally up for Dr Death.

4 The Life and Times of Dr Harold Shipman

There were no such tears shed when Shipman's mother lost her long, agonising battle against lung cancer in 1963. Young Fred – he was then known by his middle name – went to school as if nothing had happened.

It was typical of the aloof working-class-boy-done-good not to tell his grammar school mates of his terrible loss, or of the months and months in which quiet, kindly Vera Shipman battled stoically in such terrible pain. The woman who had invested so much in her son, so that he could escape their lowly roots, had spent her last days sitting in the front room window of their well-kept council house, gazing outside in a vain bid to ignore the agony that racked her withering body. When she was finally spared, on 21 June 1963, 17-year-old Fred took his grief into the night, running for hours on end in the pelting rain until two or three in the morning. His schoolmate Mick Heath found out by accident.

'What did you do last night?' he asked as they walked to High Pavement Grammar, the prestigious Nottingham school to which they had both won scholarships.

'Oh,' replied Fred, somewhat uncomfortably, 'my mum died.'

Mick, unaware that Mrs Shipman had been ill, was shocked at the news: 'I'm so sorry – are you alright, mate?'

'Yeah, I went for a run,' came the reply. The night before had been a nasty one, Mick remembered, bucketing down with rain. Fred said he had pounded the streets for miles.

Fred's numb response the following morning was not out of character; he was rather cold at times. But the lads looked up to him. He was more mature than they were – and a talented sportsman – so his dark, solitary race in the rain seemed perfectly natural for him.

Young Fred Shipman had become a Pavior in September 1957. High Pavement Grammar was not only Nottingham's premier high school, founded in 1788, with a tradition of academic and sporting prowess. It was also a supportive and encouraging launch pad for the working-class boys clever enough to get there. Head teacher Harry Davies was a firm-but-fair Welshman with a strong sense of social justice, which he passed on to the sons of miners, lorry drivers and factory workers who flocked to him from council estates all over the city. It had an extremely high reputation in Nottingham and the Midlands and produced batteries of fine young men, who were sent off into the professions with reasonable success. The boys enjoyed the best of starts.

Mr Davies, who later became chairman of education at Nottingham University, was also from the working classes. He was of high intellectual ability, and a member of the Fabian Society. He was the socialist head of a top grammar school, eloquent but caring. When the softly spoken head teacher took Shipman's poorly schoolmate Bob Studholme home, his gentle manner put the lad's flabbergasted mum at ease. Bob explained: 'That was the kind of place Fred came through. It appreciated him; he slotted in and got attention, caused no problems and became a doctor.

We were the people Margaret Thatcher hated – clever, successful and caring. Feet in working class; head in middle class. Fred never would have worn a chain of office [like Kath Grundy]. He was in a caring profession. He would have been aware of that.'

Another friend, John Soar, agreed: 'Harry Davies was hard but fair. If you crossed the line, you knew it, but if there was a glimmer of hope he wouldn't stop giving all the encouragement he could.'

The 50s and 60s were exciting times for the young men freed from the constraints of their class, now able to pursue exciting subjects and excel at a variety of sports at their top flight school. But while his schoolmates took to their new life with gusto, Fred's was an unremarkable school career from the start. But what Fred lacked in flair, he made up for in hard work. Fred was 'a plodder', always walking to school because he could not afford a bike, carrying a big rucksack of books like a snail. According to Mick: 'We had it easy but he really worked, worked like the clappers. He was in C stream. I remember he had a long, loping stride – still does, I see – he was a plodder.' Still, Fred thrived under Harry Davies's regime at High Pavement – enough to make it to medical school – but he never shone. He remained at the back, on the edge of the 'inner circle', respected rather than popular, the only one without a nickname. 'That was his way,' according to Mick.

Only on the rugby field did he ever lose his impressive and well-known cool, turning into 'a ferocious tackler'. That, too, put his schoolmates where he wanted them – at an admiring distance. He was a determined player who never showed physical fear and he would do anything to win. He could 'clatter' people, though did not seriously injure them, and liked the rough and tumble of the game as a release from his well-ordered, scholarly life. Bob explained: 'We were all expected to behave in a proper manner. In assemblies, eight hundred boys standing up and sitting down and you could hear a pin drop. That's why these schools had sport on the timetable, letting off adolescent steam.'

Fellow cross-country runner Terry Swinn recalled Fred being obsessed with using Sloane's Liniment: 'We all used it, but he was addicted.' This, it seems, was a sign of things to come. His addiction to pethidine as a young GP cost him his job and landed him in court in 1976.

But Fred's rugby-field stardom was not to last. Well built and mature as a youngster, he was overtaken by the other boys by the fourth form. He still worked hard at keeping fit but his new-found mediocrity on the rugby field confirmed his place 'at the back'. In October 1961, he won the prize for most improved student – a backhanded compliment that was to be one of the few highlights of his school career. Only when his peers left and he stayed to resit his A levels did Fred become school captain and take on roles such as readings at the school's Unitarian church in the city centre. Even that was only after Terry Swinn had left early in the new school year, having passed his Oxbridge exam. Terry had a firm-but-fair deputy in Fred. 'Very straight up and down,' he recalls. 'If you asked him a question, he would give a straight answer.'

The lads always looked up to Fred, even after he lost his head start. He was mature, both physically and mentally, and the first to start shaving – in the first form, too. He maintained his sophisticated image by proudly sporting sideburns that were the envy of every lad in school. Bob recalled: 'In a traditional day-boy grammar school in the 50s and 60s, this got him status. He enjoyed that.'

In the sixth form, the lads, now trend-setting young men, took to the social scene with enthusiasm and verve. But Fred remained as steady and serious as ever. 'We were often flash and stupid, running round, twanging girls' suspenders and all that,' Bob recalled with a laugh, 'but Fred wouldn't take part. He would be there when we were being puerile and facile, he would grin at us, but he would be on the edge of our company. He would not have demeaned himself. If there was a dirty joke, Fred would laugh – once. He thought us immature, I'm sure that was the look on his face, but he was not looking at us in a bad way. We were not bad lads but we had some growing up to do. Fred was serious; we were stupid. We thought him old-fashioned. We were lads from a working-class background, traditional, brought up properly. We all adhered to rules – opened doors for women, called people sir. Fred was even more like that.' But he insists there was nothing sinister about it: 'Fred was a serious individual, a gentle person. Lots of guys are nice and kind but they always say he is different when he drops his trousers. Fred changed for rugby, as soon as he got his kit on. He would do all to win. He was a great guy.'

John Soar agreed: 'He didn't mix much but he didn't suck up to authority, so people admired him. We went on a field study course in sixth form, to Slapton-Lee. We went to the pub and I remember Fred's rucksack full of the empties, chinking. He wasn't a stick-in-the-mud. Fred was not in the inner circle but he was not on the outside looking in. He just did his own thing and we admired him for that.'

Back then the boys did not notice how distant Fred really was. But now Bob says: 'He was too quiet. I was an open book; he was a closed soul. We had a fabulous youth, going round to other lads' houses, eating baked beans. If we went round to any house, say the Heaths', Mrs Heath would say, "I bet you are hungry." Fred didn't come, and you didn't go to Fred's house. We didn't know his family.'

But the boys did meet Fred's sister Pauline, who was always his partner at High Pavement's dances with the local girls' school. Eight years older than Fred and somewhat taller, she and Fred made a strange couple. Again his schoolmates did not think it odd – he did not seem ill at ease with the girls; he just preferred his sister's company. They were very close. As Bob Studholme said, 'There must be a lot of people in Manchester, wondering if there has always been a question mark, who find it disturbing. But I find it hard to believe he hated women. He was not a womaniser but I have seen him in the company of women and he never disliked them. He was good looking with dark curly hair and liked socialising.'

But Mick Heath found it all rather sad: 'I remember on that rugby tour to Redcar, it was someone's birthday and we got him the Beatles' first LP. I had met the Beatles, Billy J Kramer and Gerry and the Pacemakers at the Co-op record department, where I worked on Saturdays, at a special preview. We were singing the songs; it was a time of music and spirit, a good time, a great atmosphere. But Fred wouldn't join in.'

Young Fred was never going to lighten up with the weight of his working-class parents' dreams on his shoulders.

In 1938, Harold Shipman senior and his young wife Vera were the first people to move into 163 Longmead Drive on the newly built Edwards Lane estate in Nottingham. A new house and a new start for a couple determined to rise from the Nottingham rag-trade masses they had come from. Harold, described by neighbours as 'a true gentleman', and sweet-natured Vera were devoted to one another and lived for their three children, Pauline, young Fred and Clive. But the Shipmans' pride in their polite, studious children was more than a source of happiness – it was an essential bedrock of family life. It gave the couple self-esteem and a springboard out of the working class. Harold was the son of a hosiery warehouseman, Vera the illegitimate daughter of a lace clipper. Their three offspring were hope for a better future. They were better than the other children on the street – they would beat a path off the estate that had soon become 'like the Wild West', according to next-door neighbour Ursula Oldknow. But they were not so snobbish that they didn't make friends – they soon took up with the Cutlers, who lived opposite. Hannah Cutler remembers them as 'a lovely family'. But the children never mixed with the other kids; they didn't play in the street and when they came home from school, they stayed in the house. Hannah explains: 'Harold and Vera wanted them to be different. They didn't want them to be like other kids on the estate; they wanted something better for them.'

Vera's early death, at the age of 43, devastated her devoted husband. Neighbour Ursula Oldknow has fond memories of 'old Mr Shipman', who often chatted to her mother over the fence: 'He was a true gentleman. Mr Shipman lived for his family and he was devoted to his wife, who I used to see sitting in the window in the months before she died. I suffered cancer when I was just 24, about the same time, and I knew she had had it too. It was so sad for such a lovely family. All the people round here knew was how to throw as much ale down their throats as possible, but not that family. To come out of a council estate with a doctor, a health inspector and an office worker, that's brilliant. Mr

Shipman was proud of Fred and all of them. He didn't single any of them out.' On 5 January 1985, Shipman senior died of a heart attack after collapsing in the kitchen of that same council house, where he had lived quietly for 47 years.

Fred's sister Pauline, who had been living with her father, was too upset to stay on at the family home after his death. They had remained close, going to watch Notts County together and buying the house from the council between them. She sold up and moved in with Clive, who had a big, modern house in the nearby town of Long Eaton. They too had done their parents proud. Ever-industrious, Pauline became a secretary. She also got involved in the local netball scene, rising through the ranks to become one of the main organisers in the Nottingham Netball League. According to her friend and former next-door neighbour Ursula, 'she would have done even better, had she not been a woman'. Clive, three years younger than Fred, became a health inspector and father. His semi-detached home, with its perfectly groomed garden, on a neat, modern estate, is the picture of middle-class respectability.

Luckily Fred's parents had no idea of the evil growing up in their happy, peaceful home. Both died without ever knowing their eldest son's destiny, before having to face the terrible shame of a serial killer in the family. Shipman's Uncle Reg, left to answer the inevitable questions spared his brother Harold, said quietly: 'I'm glad his dad isn't alive to see this. He was a good man, a good father. They were a well-brought-up family.' As shocked and as heartbroken as his brother would have been, he added, 'I don't know why this has happened.'

Reg Shipman last saw Fred as a small boy, aged eight. Fred, Pauline and five-year-old Clive, accompanied by their parents, had walked across town to see their cousins, a trip they would take once or twice a year. Reg recalled: 'They were nice kids. Fred was a quiet, clever little boy. They were all bright.' Fred not only murdered the sweet old ladies of Hyde and the trust that patients have in their family doctor; he also killed the respectable and hard-won hopes of his family. The Shipmans were good people who only wanted happiness and prosperity for their children, like any other mum and dad. Now they are not just like any other mum and dad – they are the couple that raised Britain's biggest serial killer.

It hadn't been easy for young Fred, carrying such big hopes on little shoulders. After passing his eleven-plus, he had to get up before seven and take two buses across town to get to the High Pavement Grammar School. It was dark when he came home and he spent his evenings poring over his books, rather than face being ridiculed by the other boys on the estate for his fancy uniform. He wouldn't even 'play out' with his one friend, Alan Goddard, the only other boy on the estate to go to the grammar school, who lived only six doors away. But Alan, an only child, spent a lot of time with Fred's family. They invited him over for Bonfire Night parties in their back garden, where they ate bonfire toffee and parkin, homemade by Mrs Shipman. Alan remembers those days fondly: 'They were a nice family. Mrs Shipman was a lovely, sweet woman. I used to go to football, Notts County, with Freddy and his dad. I support them to this day because they took me there for my first proper football match.'

Fred's path to success began at Whitemoor Primary School. He should have gone to Bestwood Primary School but, because he was bright, he was bussed three miles out to the new school on the Whitemoor council estate to study for his eleven-plus. Even then, young Fred was a serious little man. John Soar, who also went to High Pavement Grammar with him, recalled: 'Fred was old before his time. A wise head on young shoulders; always focussed on something. We were in different classes so I didn't know him that well, but we were on the stoolball team together and I remember he was very good. He was good at anything sportswise. He worked hard and played hard as I remember.'

It worked. Fred passed his eleven-plus with good results and won a scholarship, which gave him the best of starts. Without High Pavement, whose old boys include actor Peter Bowles and satirist John Bird, it is doubtful he would have made it to medical school.

Maybe young Fred had plans to 'live it up' once he secured a place at Leeds University. If he did, he didn't get the chance. Within a year of starting his degree, at the age of twenty, he had married his first girlfriend, Primrose.

The daughter of Edna Oxtoby, the landlady at his student digs in Wetherby, Primrose was only seventeen and five months pregnant when she and Fred tied the knot on Bonfire Night 1966. It was a quiet register office do, witnessed only by Mrs Oxtoby and Fred's father, at Barkston Ash, York. Primrose, a window dresser and the daughter of highways labourer George Oxtoby, came from the same working-class stock as her young husband but did not have the same high-flying prospects. But she was fiercely loyal, if sometimes aggressively so. And, according to Fred's fellow students, he took to his new life with good grace.

Their first child, Sarah, was born in March 1967. Their son Christopher followed four years later, when Fred was still just a house officer at Pontefract General Hospital. The course was a tough round of theory and practical classes, leaving the 80 students with little time or energy for socialising, let alone bringing up a young family.

The classes were concentrated, with no free periods. For the first two years it was half theory – basic sciences and lab work – and half practice – ward visits. Then the practice element increased. It was a modern medical school with a major theme in all its teachings – people. As one of Shipman's fellow students recalled: 'We learnt how to deal with people, how to treat patients with respect, to be professional and polite and understanding and honest. How to be a doctor.' It was a class that Fred ultimately failed, but one that was never tested in theory – only in practice, 30 years later.

Fred was no high-flyer, but neither was he a struggler. Both would have marked him out, which was something he appeared keen to avoid. His leap into marriage and fatherhood, long before anyone else on the course, did mark him out to some extent but no one judged him for that. Simply bad luck, his fellow undergraduates said. And he had done 'the right thing' so he was no cad, just a victim of the swinging sixties. But while the other students would pop over the road to the Victoria, the local pub, for a quiet chat over the day's work, Fred would wearily pack up his books and go home. He missed out. The work was not so heavy that the students didn't enjoy themselves, let their hair down a little. Romances blossomed from those meetings at 'the Vic' – at least two maturing into long, happy marriages. It is well known that doctors' marriages within their profession are successful because each partner understands the pressures of the job, and some of Fred's fellow graduates found this to be true.

But Fred never complained. In fact he spoke of his family in the normal proud terms of any young dad.

Maybe he was just pleased that he had the chance to study medicine. Leeds University was a friendly, open institution with a particularly modern outlook. Many students who found themselves rejected by more austere, old-fashioned establishments were given a chance here – and they were grateful. Another fellow student, also from a council estate, had 26 rejections before being accepted by Leeds. He knew that Fred would be grateful, just like he had been. 'You have to have a burning ambition, be single-minded, to become a doctor,' he explained. 'It was hard for us, both coming from council estates. He must have really wanted to be a doctor. It must have been even harder, having to resit his A-levels after his mother died. I felt very relieved when I knew I had got in at Leeds. Leeds had been very positive at the interview so I knew I stood a chance.'

He went on: 'It would have been incredibly difficult to have a baby as well as study but he took it well. It was very pressured and he must have struggled financially too, with his wife and children as well, but he never complained. Fred talked about his family a lot in very normal, proud terms.'

He was to get to know the Shipman family much better years later, when the whole brood – there were now four children – attended a class reunion. The reunions, organised by Dr Colin Wilkinson, were held at Bramcote Trust House, in Leeds, and always featured the same people. Dr Wilkinson always appreciated the effort of those who made up the 50 per cent turnout – making sense of all his hard work – but more especially those who had come from abroad. Fred Shipman, then based in Hyde, only had to travel 40 miles up the M63. Fred and Primrose attended the last two, which were five years apart.

They were fun, gossipy affairs where everyone caught up with each other's news and wished them well with their new plans. They laughed at jokes and anecdotes as only they could, all sharing the infamous black humour that sees medics through the horrors of making life-and-death decisions. Fred fitted in brilliantly. For the first time, his fellow graduates got to know him really well and found he had a healthy dose of that dark humour and a willingness to ask them how they were, not just talk about himself. And he was passionate about his work, which they admired. Fred had recently gone 'single-handed', running The Surgery, on Market Street, Hyde, alone. Chatting to another GP who had also gone single-handed, he was full of excitement. He had such plans for his practice; he would look after his patients better than a group practice such as Donneybrook House, which he had just left. The other GP agreed: 'I'm not surprised Fred was loved in Hyde; he was very caring. It's hard to work single-handed. You do that for reasons of wanting to give a better service to your patients. Speaking to Fred, as one single-handed practitioner to another, that was the sort of thing he said. He wanted to give a better service to his patients, do things his way, which he couldn't do before.' In his typical fashion, Shipman underlined his position on the subject by taking on even more work. He was the treasurer for the Small Practices Association, a support group for practices of three or fewer. His fellow graduate was impressed: 'And running an appeal for new equipment on top of that – as he did – would have been very hard.'

Primrose, meanwhile, was a confident partner to Fred at these gatherings. Many non-medic wives were intimidated by their husbands' old university friends, but not her. Again, this was a revelation – many had not met her while they were studying. But she and the children were a delight. One of the partygoers recalls inviting the Shipmans to their hotel room, as their children were a similar age to his: 'Fred spoke most, took the lead, because it was his reunion, but Primrose was also very pleasant and amiable, good at mixing and at ease. The children were very polite too, well brought up.'

Fred Shipman was a social success, now his fellow graduates had finally caught up with him. Dr Wilkinson explains: 'While everybody else had aged, Fred had not – because he had always been middle-aged. I suppose this was because he had got married so young.'

The first inkling that Shipman was not the serious, straight-backed pillar of society came in 1976 – when he was exposed as a junkie.

Shipman had struggled to pass his degree, fulfil his medical qualifications and dig a niche at his first group practice, as well as bring up a young family for ten long years. There was no support from his in-laws, who fell out with Fred and Primrose soon after Sarah's birth. It is not known why, but Edna Oxtoby has not spoken to her daughter for 30 years. The couple and their two youngsters rarely visited Harold Shipman senior and the sister he was once so close to. Ursula Oldknow recalled: 'I saw Freddy and his wife visit with the children, but not very often. I suppose they were too busy.' On completing his studies at Leeds, Fred became a house officer at Pontefract General Infirmary where he worked under general surgery consultant Mr LC Bell, aural surgery consultant Mr K Mayll and medical consultant Dr J Turner, all now dead. He was fully registered with the General Medical Council, number 1470473, on 5 August 1971. After that, still living in hospital accommodation at Friarwood Lane, Pontefract, he took a Diploma in Child Health and a Royal College Diploma in Obstetrics and Gynaecology. But it was general practice he was destined for, with devastating results.

In March 1974, Fred became a much-valued junior GP with the Todmorden Group Practice run by Dr Michael Grieve. The hard-working and enthusiastic young GP, who was 'brilliant with a needle' as well as a productive administrator, was treasured by his senior partners. He and Primrose were also well liked by the local community, spending their weekends clearing out the Rochdale Canal with a band of volunteers. But within fifteen months, he had shown his true Jekyll and Hyde nature – when he flew into a rage as his addiction to pethidine, an opium-derivative painkiller given to women in labour, was exposed.

When Fred arrived, his young family in tow, he was welcomed as a breath of fresh air. It took just a month for him to be promoted from assistant to principal GP; such was the impression he made on the partners. He had so many plans and fully backed Dr Grieve's forward-thinking ideas. And he didn't just support them in theory. In typical fashion, Fred rolled up his sleeves and worked day and night summarising the patients' notes for a new pre-computerised system. Dr Grieve appreciated the efforts of his 'young apprentice': 'Fred fitted in and was settling down, which was great. Doctors move a lot and leave practices in high dudgeon. Fred was enthusiastic and interested in next-stage development of health service.' Dr Brenda Lewin, another partner at the practice, took to him too. Dr Grieve recalled: 'Brenda liked Fred. Fred thought she was wonderful, and she did him. They had a lot in common, their ways of thinking.' And, according to Dr Grieve, the patients loved him: 'He had a lot of fans. I remember there was one girl, whose baby he delivered, who still thinks the world of him.'

Fred and Primrose made quite an impact on the Rochdale Canal Society, if only for the fact that he was a doctor. Secretary Brian Holden was ecstatic that a doctor would soil his hands on what was then a thankless task. Brian was a teacher but, like most, he regarded medicine as a higher calling. 'He would help clean out the canal and she would be making tea with the rest of the wives,' he recalled. 'I was very flattered that a member of the medical profession would get involved. I was a mere schoolteacher and doctors were held in great esteem.' The Shipmans' image as a good, solid, community-spirited couple was further enhanced when Fred bought a dinghy so they could take little Sarah, then eight years old, and four-year-old Christopher out sailing on the waterway they had worked so hard to clean up.

The only problem, as far as the practice was concerned, was Primrose. She was young and fiercely loyal to the hard-working, successful husband who had rescued her from a dull, working-class future. Her loyalty manifested itself in an ability to take offence on his behalf at the least thing. Fred seemed to be working well with his mentor Dr Grieve, although no hard-working practice made up of professional partners is without dissent on some issues. Still, if there were problems, Fred did not mention them. However, Primrose saw fit to broadcast her dislike of Dr Grieve and the way he treated her husband to the receptionists, causing no end of discomfort to them. Dr Grieve's wife overheard her and told her in no uncertain terms to shut up. She did not stop to lecture her on how the staff did not appreciate such divisive gossiping. This young, fiery, somewhat stupid woman, she decided, would never make a doctor's wife.

But Primrose's sniping paled in comparison to the problem that was festering silently behind Fred's gentle, dedicated demeanour. He had started to suffer sudden blackouts, once falling into the bath as he and Primrose were decorating. His loyal wife took to driving him to his calls and backed up his self-diagnosis that he was suffering from some kind of epilepsy. The partners, worried for him, accepted his theory and offered him any help he needed. He was OK, he assured them, and he would deal with it. Not long after, the truth was out – he had been taking pethidine.

One morning, the practice receptionist went to the local chemist's to pick up a few dressings. She telephoned first, to let him know she would be over, and arrived within a few minutes. It was enough time for the worried chemist to do what was necessary – he left the drugs book open for her to see. She was perplexed at first; why was the book open? She had not requested it. When she looked closer, she was horrified. Pages and pages of entries, all in Shipman's name, all for pethidine, a drug rarely used in day-to-day healthcare. He had taken thousands and thousands of ampoules. Former partner Dr John Dacre, whose mother-in-law recorded the incident in her diary on Thursday 25 September 1975, remembered what happened next: 'The reception-ist came hotfoot across to the surgery. I went back and saw all the entries in Shipman's name. There were thousands of ampoules. It was excessive. We never use it except for labour pains or as a painkiller before you went on to morphine. Everybody was absolutely horrified.'

Dr Dacre and Dr Lewin, who were on duty that day, discussed the matter and decided Dr Dacre should investigate further. Then they would confront Shipman on Monday morning, after his weekend shift. They did not tell Dr Grieve, the senior partner, because he would be working that shift with Fred. That upset him a great deal. When the news was broken to Dr Grieve and Fred at the practice's usual Monday morning meeting, it was a double blow for him – his young protégé was a drug addict and his partners were keeping it secret while he worked alongside him. 'I was fed up quite honestly, I knew nothing of it,' Dr Grieve recalled. 'I had been sat in surgery with him all that weekend, John Dacre had gone off investigating it all, Brenda Lewin knew, then it was sprung on me. I felt I had been kept in the dark.'

His shock was compounded by mild-mannered Fred's reaction to the accusation. No denial, no embarrassment, no remorse. He flew into a rage. But first he begged. 'He said, "I will stop – can you give me another chance?" ' Dr Grieve remembered. The partners refused and stood amazed at Shipman's explosion of fury.

Dr Dacre recalled: 'We were astounded, amazed, to find out what was going on. It was shattering. It was the first time I had seen him lose his cool. He stormed out, saying he'd resigned.'

But worse was to come. An hour later, Primrose barged into the meeting, where the shocked partners were still discussing what to do next, and declared Fred would not be resigning. 'You'll have to force him out,' she said. It took the practice six weeks to sack him from the partnership, for breaching practice rules by misusing drugs. In all that time, although not working, he was on full pay. It was a hard-faced attitude he was to show to other colleagues twenty years on, at the Donneybrook House group practice in Hyde.

In court, Shipman blamed the surgery for his crimes. He told the magistrate, a GP called Dr Goldin, how he had taken to drugs as he descended into depression caused by bad relationships with his colleagues. Dr Grieve vehemently denied this: 'He was enthusiastic and hard working and we were pleased with him. I had sympathy for him even after the case and another doctor, Brenda Lewin, always thought the world of him.' She visited him at the rehabilitation centre, The Retreat, in York, many times after the case. Dr Grieve said he would have understood the pressure Shipman was under, had he been told: 'He worked incredibly hard to summarise our notes, harder than was physically possible. Now we know why – to find out who was on pethidine. Being a doctor is a hell of a job – it's not easy. You get blamed for deaths anyway, even when you've tried to save them. That's why you get drug use with doctors and midwives, also because they have to try what they're giving their patients. We thought the world of him.'

At Halifax Magistrates' Court in 1976, Shipman was fined £600 after pleading guilty to eight drugs charges and asking for 67 other offences of obtaining drugs by deception and seven counts of forgery to be taken into consideration. When confronted by an NHS inspector and police, he had admitted he had been injecting pethidine for six months, taking more and more as he became more depressed. Sometimes he had taken some of the drug prescribed for a patient; on twenty other occasions, he took it all. And he forged the signature of a nursing home manager to do it.

His talent for forgery was to come in handy again 22 years later – when he copied the signatures of his last victim, Kathleen Grundy, and two 'witnesses' to a fake will in a bid to grab Mrs Grundy's £300,000 estate. But by then he had grown so arrogant, so lazy, that Mrs Grundy's daughter spotted it was a fake straight away. At Todmorden, his arrogance was revealed only by the number of ampoules he had stolen; hence a lapse of fifteen months before its true nature was exposed.

The court heard from two impressive character witnesses – Ken Fieldsend, the managing director of a Todmorden engineering company, and the conductor Dr Ben Horsfall. Both said they had confidence in his ability. The magistrates were also told that Shipman had been treated for his 'serious medical problem' and moved to a post in Durham, where he had no access to drugs. Dr Grieve remembered how Goldin told Fred to 'get better and out of medicine'. Now he wonders: 'What happened between that and him getting a single-handed practice? It is extremely difficult to get one of those.'

It was this ability to bounce back and his steely determination to do well that led him to start up again in Hyde, joining the Donneybrook Group Practice and then leaving it – poaching 3,000 besotted patients and assorted staff in the process. His empire building continued at his single-handed practice in Market Street before ending with his horrific killing spree.

But first he had to rest and recuperate, come to terms with yet another setback in what should have been a brilliant career. Once Shipman was treated for his addiction to pethidine, his comedown was complete when he, Primrose, 10-year-old Sarah and six-year-old Christopher moved into a council house on the Burnhill estate in Newton Aycliffe, Co Durham. Just like his parents, they were the first to move in. He had fought hard to rise from his lowly roots. Harold senior and Vera had told him time and again that he was too good for their council estate back home in Nottingham. No doubt he agreed with them. Many people who have known Shipman recall his arrogance and his intolerance of those who opposed him in any way. In his new local authority home, his early promise must have rung hollow in his ears.

Still, it was a nice estate back then. Brand new houses, built in a modern, clean-cut design among wide grass verges and privately owned bungalows with pretty gardens, surrounded by countryside. The Shipman's was a good size too – three bedrooms – and their two children fitted in with the locals quite happily. One man, whose children played with Sarah and Christopher, recalled: 'They were friendly enough; they would say hello. They were quiet and seemed just a nice, normal family. Theirs were good kids from a happy-go-lucky family.' But, he says, Fred kept his distance: 'I remember him – he had a beard I think – but I didn't know him well. I didn't even know he was a doctor. We can't believe it's the same people involved in this lot.' Even here, where Shipman lay so low and stayed for just a year, this shocking case has left its mark. And yet again, Shipman has won sympathy. Another neighbour, Margaret Norris, said: 'I cannot believe this has happened. He was a lovely man and I am still their friend. I feel so sorry for Primrose and the children.'

After a break of one year and 264 days, Shipman became a clinical medical officer for children for the South West Durham Health Authority on 12 September 1977. Just eighteen days later, he left for Hyde and joined the Donneybrook House group practice.

Shipman now realised this was his last chance to claim some of his early promise. Once in Hyde, he began rebuilding his life. He and Primrose rented a pretty, semi-detached house on Lord Derby Road for a year. The modern-style home, with its lawned gardens and nearby schools, was perfect for the children. Its wide windows let in plenty of light as it stood at the top of one of Hyde's many hills. With your back to the front door, looking out to the right, you could gaze across the town, taking in the old chimneys and dying mills, to the hills beyond. The estate was out of the way of the dirty old town, quiet and respectable. Here he had the chance to finally settle down after being given a chance by Donneybrook, whose partners knew of his past drugs problems. He knew this was his last chance.

It was not to be enough.

In 1979, Fred and Primrose finally settled when they bought their last home together, a modest semi in a leafy enclave, Roe Cross Green, Mottram, and added to their brood. David was born on 20 March of that year, and Sam was born on 4 April 1982. The boys represented a new start for Shipman: the children, polite and well-liked youngsters, provided a pathway into a community's heart once again.

Shipman threw himself into work at Donneybrook, a practice of seven doctors that had hit the headlines when it was set up in 1967. The new system, fourteen doctors in two practices serving a whole town from one building, was a major innovation back then. One founding member, Dr Bill Bennett, hardly remembers Shipman – they worked at opposite ends of the corridor for only a short while before Dr Bennett retired following a heart attack brought on by overwork. Dr Shipman worked just as hard. He was also extremely demanding of his colleagues at their monthly meetings. 'He was very assertive,' Dr Bennett recalled. 'He didn't like people opposing him very much as I remember.'

Dave Owen, chief officer of the Tameside and Glossop Community Health Council, agreed: 'Dr Shipman was very assertive at meetings and could come across as abrupt and rather arrogant. This was no major concern, though; in fact it was a bonus when it came to him negotiating services for his patients. He was very good at that.' It seems the 'ferocious tackler' was never far under Shipman's mild-mannered exterior.

One colleague who was constantly harassed by demanding Dr Shipman was practice manager Vivian Langfield. Miss Langfield, now a lay preacher, was much valued by the other doctors. Over 25 years at the practice she built up vast experience in dealing with patients and, gently spoken but firm, she had a talent for getting the best out of the receptionists, who she called 'my girls'. They worked extremely hard and Miss Langfield was horrified when Dr Shipman began snapping at them. When she defended them, he turned his attentions to her. One receptionist remembered how he would turn white with rage – just because one of them had forgotten his cup of coffee. 'I am always frightened of people who turn white, not red, with temper,' she said. 'He would be very calm, not raise his voice. He would ask her, "Who was that girl?" She'd say, "You know who it is." And he'd say, "Tell her to leave on Friday."'

Dr Shipman did not really have the right to have receptionists sacked, being one of seven partners, but Miss Langfield had no choice. He was her boss. Shipman was just as hard on his fellow doctors, once he had settled at the practice and felt he could get away with it. 'The atmosphere had been lovely when the surgery started up,' the receptionist recalled. 'But it changed after he arrived. He talked down to people. He said to one doctor who did not speak up for himself, "Oh, Derek, if you can't show an interest in the practice then leave it to those of us who can." In front of all of us, too. He was a divisive, despicable man.'

Dr John Smith, another GP at Donneybrook, found him much more approachable, but then Shipman was quite happy to show some respect to such a confident senior partner. 'He could be abrupt and arrogant and bawl out receptionists if he didn't like them. He didn't like Vivian Langfield. He bawled her out,' Dr Smith, now retired, recalled. 'We mentioned it to him at group meetings, but not forcefully. You can't talk down to a professional man.'

Once again, Shipman's arrogant and aloof nature kept people at the distance he required while he asserted himself. He did not attend the practice's 21st birthday party, thrown by its neighbour and co-pioneer, the Clarendon Group Practice, such was his problem with being a latecomer to the practice and therefore somewhat junior in its pecking order. But he was astute enough not to isolate himself completely and invited some of the doctors, including the bluff and popular Dr Smith, to his 40th birthday at York House. He also worked extremely hard and was well loved by the patients, to whom he was dedicated. 'I had no problem with him then; he was a hard worker and the patients loved him,' said John Smith. 'He had a lovely theatrical bedside manner that really worked with them.'

All went well enough for fifteen years but again Shipman was about to show his true colours. The receptionist was right; he was never a team player – a fact demonstrated by his leaving Donneybrook to set up his own single-handed practice. Shipman not only poached three receptionists and a district nurse – he also lured away 3,000 patients. 'It left a big hole in patient numbers,' Dr Smith recalled. 'Nearly decimated the practice. The receptionists and district nurse as well. The district nurse knew everyone, especially the old ladies, very well. Now they are all dead. He would not have been able to do that in a group.' Dr Smith, smarting over the way he and his colleagues had been treated, fell out with Shipman. His disgust was compounded when he realised Shipman had been lying about why he wanted to leave. 'He told me he didn't like the way the group practice was modernising,

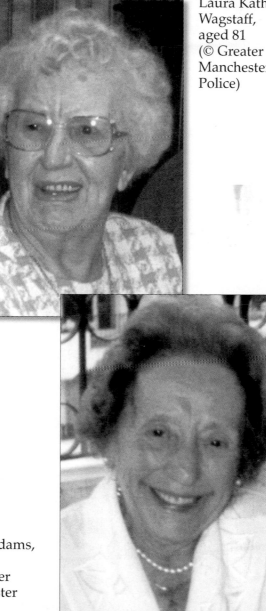

Laura Kathleen Wagstaff, aged 81 (© Greater Manchester Police)

Lizzie Adams, aged 77 (© Greater Manchester Police)

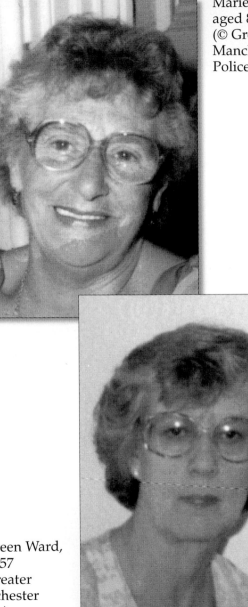

Marie West, aged 81 (© Greater Manchester Police)

Maureen Ward, aged 57 (© Greater Manchester Police)

Norah Nuttall, aged 65 (© Greater Manchester Police)

Jean Lilley (© Greater Manchester Police)

Angela Woodruff (© Greater Manchester Police)

Below Harold Shipman (© MEN)

Above Police exhume a body from Hyde cemetery as part of the ongoing Shipman investigation (© MEN)

Right The seventh exhumation (© MEN)

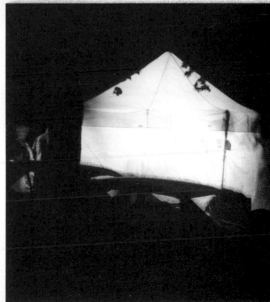

Left The former home of Dr Harold Shipman (© MEN)

Right The front page of the Manchester Evening News, Wednesday 18 August 1999 (© MEN)

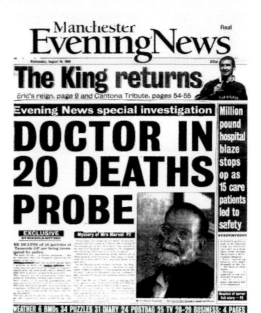

Left Shipman's childhood home (© MEN)

Right Coroner John Pollard (© Ashton Reporter)

Detective Superintendent Bernard Postles (© Greater Manchester Police)

Dr Linda Reynolds (© MEN)

getting in computers, that sort of thing,' he explained irritably. 'What's the first thing he does? Gets in a computer.'

That Dr Shipman could set up his new surgery just yards away from his former group, after stealing their patients, showed how hard faced he was. Medicine is an incestuous, gossipy profession where it helps to get on with your colleagues and peers. But Dr Shipman did not care. He had finally wrested control of his working life, happily ensconced in his own little empire – The Surgery, on Market Street. Separated by the grimy grey bus station and the tatty old bingo hall, where the old ladies of Hyde came and went on their business, The Surgery literally turned its back on Donneybrook.

Shipman's patients adored him and word soon spread – before long, there was a waiting list to join his practice. He was renowned for his tireless efforts and long hours, giving people as much time as they needed and even calling at their homes after hours for non-emergencies; 'Just to see how you are,' he would say benevolently. And he wasn't miserly with the medication, either. Shipman was one of the five highest prescribers in Tameside, which had 104 doctors. He constantly went over budget and was visited quarterly by West Pennine Health Authority's medical adviser. She found him 'strong-minded' with a robust defence of his methods – he insisted on maintaining complete control of his patients' needs and would treat them himself rather than refer them to hospital. But his arguments as to why he gave so many drugs and used so many expensive brands were always rational and she would leave, having made no headway, knowing she would have to return again the following quarter. Shipman had complete control of his practice. A happy by-product was the widespread acknowledgement of his role as local hero. 'He's the best doctor in Hyde,' his patients declared.

Shipman's devoted patients included his neighbours Alan and Jane Smith, who lived next-door-but-one at Roe Cross Green, and Alan's parents Doris and Stanley Smith, who lived in Hyde. Doris and Stanley joined the practice in 1978 after Shipman had graciously popped across to Alan's for an impromptu examination of the elderly couple. Being such a kind GP, he gave them a flu injection there and then. Stanley died a year before Shipman's arrest. When Doris heard the GP had been charged with murder, her first thought was 'poor Dr Shipman'. She insisted: 'He is absolutely marvellous; I can't speak well enough of him. He is so patient and has got time for you. I can't believe it.'

Alan agreed: 'He is a very caring, conscientious doctor. I know a lot of doctors put a lot of hours in but he does more than most. He is a very dedicated doctor.'

Dr Shipman has helped both Alan and Jane through breakdowns. With Alan, he immediately prescribed eight weeks sick leave. 'No drugs, they won't help,' he said. 'Rest is what you need.' He was right. With Jane, he did much more. She became ill following the death of her father and one evening was so distraught that Fred and Primrose insisted on driving her and Alan to Tameside General Hospital. 'I'll never forget what they both did for me that night,' said Jane, who has sat through nearly every court hearing with Primrose. 'He is a wonderful man.'

Another patient, Brian Dean, even attended the surgery while Shipman was being investigated over his mother Joan's death. Stalybridge businessman Brian was devastated when Joan died in January 1998 and Elaine, his partner of ten years, left him. Joan, a glamorous social butterfly, had filled his life with music and laughter. He remembered that when he was a child their home was always packed with actors and musicians. Joan herself had appeared in *Coronation Street* and John Savident, big-mouthed butcher Fred Elliot in the show, was an orator at her funeral. But she did not approve of Elaine and, because of this, her relationship with Brian had grown cooler. So, Brian turned to Dr Shipman for help and the two discussed the stress they were both suffering.

'I've been expecting you,' said Dr Shipman, calm and confident as ever, as Brian walked into his treatment room. 'What do you need, one month off or will you do what I do – work?'

He went on, without distress or self-pity, winning Brian's confidence: 'You know about Kathleen Grundy? She was a very self-willed person, determined; you couldn't persuade her. I've known her twenty or more years; we were on committees together.'

Brian, surprised at how freely and easily the GP could discuss the police investigation of him, decided he must be an innocent man. Now better and no longer in need of the doctor's self-serving support, Brian added: 'It was only later, when I thought about things he had said and things going missing from my mother's house, that I had my doubts.'

Many patients rallied to Shipman's defence when the news broke about the investigation. One recalled injuring his knee in a squash game. Shipman examined it and, before prescribing anything, drew a diagram of it to explain his choice of treatment. 'He delivered my kids too. He was wonderful,' the patient said. Cards from well-wishers flooded the surgery and Shipman's loyal receptionists pinned them up for all to see. 'It looked like Christmas,' one passer-by recalled. The flood only subsided several weeks after his arrest, as the murder list grew.

Another fan was Jenny Unsworth, a warden at Chartist House, a tower block of sheltered accommodation for old folk. She met Dr Shipman when he first moved to Hyde and found him charming. 'He always called me Jenny,' she recalled with a smile. 'You can only speak as you find and I found him nothing but a gentleman.' She was impressed by the time he took with his patients and compared him with the other GPs who had patients with her: 'Some doctors have written out the prescription before you've sat down. Not him. Some doctors can't even say good morning to you but he would stop and explain to us if someone was ill, so we could explain it to them. That's rare. We recommended him to people who came to us from other areas but there was a waiting list.'

Jenny Unsworth babysat for the Shipmans on their first New Year's Eve at Lord Derby Road. Fred had promised to take Primrose to a party in Leeds and when their childminder let them down, he rang Jenny in desperation. She found Sarah and Christopher very well behaved and polite. They went to bed with no fuss, leaving her to tuck into sandwiches and coffee provided by a grateful Primrose. 'I remember hearing popping noises from behind the settee,' she recalled. 'I had a peep and saw bottles of homebrewed beer. He was very down to earth.' A few days later, Dr Shipman and Christopher brought her a beautiful big plant to say thank you. But, she recalled, 'I wasn't green-fingered and it died.'

Jenny was interviewed at length by the police about the deaths of her residents in Shipman's care, particularly Moira Fox and Ronnie Davenport, known fondly as the Bishop. Ronnie was eccentric and believed he was a bishop, even dressing the part with a hat he had made himself and a ladies' skirt. But he was gentle and well spoken and still quite young when Jenny found him dead in his chair six years ago. Jenny recalled: 'Ronnie had been ill but we didn't expect him to die.' She called out Dr Shipman, who telephoned Ronnie's mother and asked her to come over. Unaware of the tragedy, Mrs Davenport said she would come after her game of whist. So unexpected was his death that she insisted she was 'off out', forcing Dr Shipman to tell her the bad news over the phone. Jenny recalled: 'He said, "No, dear, you have to come here." He was very upset telling her over the phone.'

Moira Fox, another eccentric, died ten years ago, while Dr Shipman was with the Donneybrook practice. Tall, slim and well educated, Miss Fox's end was a tragic relief. Jenny said: 'She had been through every doctor in town. She would come down here; we could tell it was her through the glass in the door because she wore a big hat. She would ask for my husband Ralph to go up, then ask him, "Will you look at my piles?" ' She added: 'When you are in this job, death is traumatic but you can accept it as a blessing – they are not suffering anymore. With the elderly, you expect it. We have lots of deaths.'

Mary Burgess, whose daughter Jennifer was one of the receptionists who had left Donneybrook to go with Dr Shipman, also babysat for him. Dr Shipman asked her out of kindness, to get her out of the house when her first husband died. By that time, Sam was one. Mary and Primrose, then working as a registered childminder, became firm friends. 'The babysitting really helped me,' she said. 'I could talk to them both at any time; they were wonderful. Primrose was bubbly then, we used to have a laugh. The children were lovely, very bright.' Later, Fred helped Primrose do the catering at Jennifer's wedding. 'I can still see them, buttering bread,' Mary recalled. 'Fred is not one of those snooty doctors; I can't do with them, especially when you are not well. He would help anyone if he could. He was human, not stiff and starchy, "I'm a doctor, hands off." He was like an old-fashioned family doctor but not godlike, like they could be.'

Mary, a tough-talking woman who, in her own words, will 'stand no messing', appreciated Dr Shipman's straightforward ways and swears she will never truly accept another GP. She explained: 'Dr Shipman was a quiet man but he would say to me, "Mary, let me talk, I'm the doctor." He would listen to you and took time with you. The other doctors round here don't have that. They may be very good but I have yet to meet better than Dr Shipman.' She added: 'If he came back this afternoon, I would be there on his doorstep. Dr Shipman was wonderful with my second husband, who has been very ill with heart problems. We also found out he had two ulcers and it had also brought his eczema out. When Fred saw him, he just said, "When were you last well, lad?" He tried everything, then sent him to a specialist.' The case has left her heartbroken and she clings to the belief that the women were killed by a rogue batch of drugs: 'I will never be able to believe he did it. Kathleen Grundy was the same way, she was no fool, and she would ask questions. No way would she fall for anything. He has been wonderful to me – and others. I am heartbroken.'

But some patients despised him. Mother-of-two Lorraine Leighton was a nervous 17-year-old when she went to see him at her Bredbury surgery, where he was working as a locum. Embarrassed by her problem – a lump in her breast – she had ignored it for months but, when her mother and sister begged her to 'get it seen to', she made an appointment. As she shyly explained her concerns, Dr Shipman made her feel like a fool. 'He made comments about my breasts, their size,' Lorraine, now 35, recalled. 'I fled.' She left it months before going back to the surgery when another doctor booked her in to have it removed. Luckily it was a benign cyst. But Lorraine will never forgive Shipman: 'It might not have been benign. I could have been another of his victims, couldn't I? I think he does have a problem with women. He was very arrogant and dismissive of me. It was terrible.'

Lorraine's friend, a barmaid called Eve, agreed. When she went to Dr Shipman over problems with her nerves, he barked at her to pull herself together. 'Go home and look after your kids,' he snapped. When her husband went for the same reason a few weeks later, he got a sick note for two weeks. 'Has he got a problem with women?' Eve fumed as she served the regulars at her bar. 'I'll say.'

Another patient also found Shipman's bedside manner lacking. He was a cyclist taking part in a charity bike ride organised by the Shipmans' local, the Dog and Partridge, in Stalybridge, and a college friend of Sarah Shipman, who also worked in the kitchens there. One Sunday, as the team tried a practice run, the lad fell off his bike and suffered a bad graze to his knee. Dr Shipman, whose daughter called him out to help, scrubbed away the dirt and loose skin with a viciously heavy hand. 'He was awful,' the cyclist recalled. 'I almost cried, he was so rough. It was bloody painful.'

But for most, Shipman's dedication to his patients was unquestionable. It was sealed with a highly successful appeal fund for medical equipment at his surgery, of which he was particularly proud. It raised £19,199.86 in six years, proving his patients' devotion to him and, they thought, his to them.

Shipman ran the appeal fund with his district nurse Gillian Morgan and his friend and patient Les Fallows. Les would run raffles and social nights throughout the year. Dr Shipman and Primrose would always turn up but it was more through duty than the love of a good night out. When enough money had built up, Les would ask Dr Shipman and Gillian what new pieces of machinery they needed. They raised enough for nebulizers, blood pressure monitors, even an electrocardiogram (ECG) machine and a sonic foetal heart detector. Some of the generous donations had come from the women who died at Shipman's hands.

Les remembered exactly how he came to run the appeal. It came about after he had offered Dr Shipman a donation when he first went solo, to thank him for helping his extremely sick wife.

'I'm retired, not too bad off – is there anything I can get you?' he asked the GP.

Dr Shipman could not believe his luck. 'Oh, it's funny you should say that,' he answered carefully. 'I was talking to my wife and we decided to start an appeal fund. The only person we could think of to run it was you. Will you?'

Les, a retired detective with time on his hands, was only too pleased. 'I would love to,' came the reply.

Les came to terms with the shocking turn of events a long time ago, thanks to his years in the police force, but he is saddened that he and so many others have been let down by the man they were devoted to. 'I was so shocked to hear of the charges,' he recalled. 'I trusted him. It's like Dr Jekyll and Mr Hyde.'

Les was not just Shipman's appeal manager; he was also his friend. He and Dr Shipman shared a love of sport, especially rugby. He often took him, Sam or David to watch Sale Rugby Club on his season ticket, or he would give Sam and David his Manchester United tickets if he were away. 'I remember when I was in the force, I was busy working, just like Fred,' he explained. 'When you're working, you don't see too much of your kids. I felt a bit sorry for the lads in that respect.' But like many men, enthusing about sport was the limit of their friendship. Ask Les about Shipman's finer feelings and his brow furrows: 'I just found him a quiet man who just liked to talk about sport rather than discuss any deeper issues.' The closest the pair came to emotion was when they cheered on Shipman's youngest, Sam, who had followed his father's footsteps on to the rugby pitch. The talented youngster played prop forward for Ashton Rugby Club and Lancashire's youth teams, alongside Billy Beaumont's son. All of this has been denied him in the past eighteen months. 'Sam is a smashing lad,' Les said sadly. 'I feel sorry for him and the other children, they're nice kids, and Shipman is an unusual name.'

The children were an essential part of Shipman's careful image building, a pathway deep into the community's heart and an excuse to spend more and more time working instead of at home.

He was a parent governor at Longdendale High School, which Sarah and Christopher attended, and gave talks on family planning to the older girl students.

He became involved in Ashton Rugby Club with Sam and was eventually elected chairman of the junior committee. According to secretary Neil Mather, the club members had no idea a serial killer was in their midst, even after the police had launched their investigation. Just days before his arrest, Shipman attended a club meeting. Nobody mentioned the matter. Neil explained: 'We couldn't believe it. He was such a normal bloke. When we heard about Kathleen

Grundy, we thought, poor old duck, she's left him her money.' It took a long time for some people to believe it even after Shipman was arrested and, again, he has elicited some sympathy. 'The boys have coped well with it all, it just seems exciting to them, having a serial killer at the club,' Neil explained, relieved they have not been traumatised. 'But we all feel very sorry for Sam. He's a nice guy.'

Shipman also joined St John Ambulance, where he taught dozens of young members. One of them, Steven Hartley, was so shocked that he saw no irony when he said: 'Poor Fred. He taught me everything I know.'

It was through this organisation that he taught first aid to registered child minders, turning on the charm for the dozen or so women who came for free weekly lessons at Roughtown Community Centre in Mossley. Dr Shipman, as he had them call him, was 'a ladies' man' – charming but a little arrogant, revelling in the esteem afforded by his pupils. He taught them in a fun, light-hearted way, which helped them remember their lessons better. But he also had a tendency to belittle people who gave the wrong answers, often after persuading them to speak up. One of them, Janet Redfern, recalled with disdain: 'His attitude was just below arrogance. He was superior – "I know I'm better than you but I won't rub your noses in it. I will let you know that so you like me a lot." But he wasn't offensive and we did learn a lot.'

His methods worked – many of the women liked his way so much, they asked if they could join his practice. Shipman loved it. 'He said he had a very busy practice,' Janet said. 'He was showing off.' Ominously, Shipman also claimed to be allergic to bee stings and told them he had to have a syringe of antidote in his car at all times. 'We didn't actually see it, though,' Janet recalled.

Janet, who now runs the Tipperary Tearooms in Stalybridge, does not care that Shipman duped her and the other women. 'I feel part of history,' she mused at the counter of her busy cafe. 'I say to people, "Don't ask me to do first aid – I've been taught by a murderer." But I do feel so sorry for the families. I lost my dad through no foul means and that was painful enough. To find out they have been killed must be horrendous.' The case has been the talk of the Tipperary and Janet remembered the moment she saw Shipman on the front of the *Manchester Evening News*: 'At first I didn't register who it was, then I saw his picture and recognised him. He didn't seem that kind of person. Still doesn't. I thought he did it for the money, then they started piling all these bodies up and I wondered if he was a psychopath or not. They said Crippen was a nice bloke.' She added: 'He deserves all that is coming to him, but I feel like that about anybody, like Myra Hindley. It doesn't matter how repentant you are in years to come: you did it; face the consequences.'

Shipman's work was also a rich source of respectability. He took on lots of roles in the hope of gaining *gravitas*. He was treasurer of the Small Practitioners' Association, a national support group for surgeries with three doctors or less, and a member of the Tameside Local Medical Committee, whose secretary Dr Kailash Chand described him as 'no diplomat but a good doctor'. He added: 'I would have been his patient happily.'

All Shipman's hard work at the surgery and at various community venues throughout Tameside kept him away from home.

The Shipman children were a credit to Fred and Primrose. As well as going to college, Sarah and Christopher worked part time at the Dog and Partridge,

Stalybridge. The pair were bright and mature with no qualms about hard work. Their parents often enjoyed their Sunday lunch there. There were no fancy restaurants for Dr and Mrs Shipman, just a plain pub lunch every now and then. Former owner Gino Sassanelli remembered: 'They were a brilliant family. Mrs Shipman was a big lady but she had a heart of gold. The kids were good kids, bright, hardworking. Sarah was a very confident girl, good looking. Chris was brainier.'

Blonde, blue-eyed Sarah, popular with the pupils at Tameside College, seemed especially suited to the catering industry. She has gone on to run a hotel down south with her partner, no doubt taking after her mother, whose culinary skills are fondly remembered by the family's friends and even mere acquaintances.

Primrose often did the catering for Donneybrook's Christmas parties and made a grand job of the food at the wedding of Shipman's receptionist Jennifer. Another receptionist recalled: 'She was very good at it. It was her thing.'

Primrose also ran a sandwich shop in Hollingworth, after a stint as a childminder registered with Tameside Council. Mary Burgess recalled: 'She was good with children, a lovely girl.'

Their son Christopher, more like his father, went on to university. The younger two, 20-year-old David and 17-year-old Sam, who was still at West Hill High School for boys in Stalybridge when his father was arrested, have yet to make their way in a world that knows their father as Britain's biggest serial killer. Again they are hailed as good, polite, friendly young men. Police officers searching the house during the murder investigation were impressed by how helpful the boys were. As Les Fallows says, they are 'both smashing lads'.

All four children have stood by their mother as she watched her husband's every court hearing bar two, day in day out. Young rugby prop Sam must have aged another twenty years as he shielded Primrose from the press pack that chased them down the street as the trial began in Preston in October 1999. But those court hearings also showed a strange side to the Shipman family. Primrose would often giggle at something while waiting for her husband to be brought into the dock. Sometimes the children would join in, such as when Sam's mobile phone went off suddenly at Tameside Magistrates' Court. Other times, they would throw an odd smile at the press pack.

A receptionist from Donneybrook remembered Shipman being very hard on his two youngest sons, who sometimes called at the surgery for a lift home with him. They would sit doing their homework in his room and then troop out, 'heads down, in tears,' behind him when he was ready to go. But Sarah, confident enough to answer her father's barked demands, got on well with him. The receptionist recalled that Shipman had a bad relationship with his own father: 'I remember we heard his father had died and one of the girls said, "I am sorry about your father, Dr Shipman," and he said, "Are you? I'm not." '

Primrose, for all her talents in the kitchen, was no perfect little homemaker. The Shipman house was described as 'filthy' by the police officers who searched it. Many of the family's friends agree. A schoolfriend of Sam's said: 'There were clothes strewn all over and it was dirty and smelled a bit. Dr Shipman seemed really nice but Mrs Shipman was moody.'

Les Fallows said: 'I live alone but their house was messier than mine, more like a man-alone's house. I suppose that's families for you.'

Dr Wally Ashworth, Shipman's GP and friend of many years, was less diplomatic: 'Your feet stuck to the carpet, it was so filthy.'

Dr Ashworth believed the killings were a result of Shipman's control-obsessed personality: 'He was a little man with a big woman. He was dominated at home; then he came to work. He was controlling and a perfectionist, a bloody hard worker but not very intelligent. I have seen other doctors with God complexes and I think that's what Shipman had.'

Dr Ashworth added rather sadly: 'I should have known.' But he is being far too hard on himself. He was not the only one taken in by Shipman's carefully contrived image – dedicated doctor, loving family man and community spirit. That is why he got away with such a horrific crime, over and over again, for years and years. Even as the home helps called him Dr Death as a joke.

As one home help put it: 'This is not like the Moors Murders – people were filled with hate talking about him and her; she was such a cold female. But somehow they still can't feel hatred for Shipman.'

5 Life After the Charges

When Fred Shipman was arrested on 7 September 1998, it came as a total and utter shock to him. Arriving at Ashton Police Station at 8.30 that morning, he greeted the *Manchester Evening News* photographer Chris Gleave with open arms. As Chris snapped shot after shot, his film whirring through his camera, the GP faced him up, shrugged and held out his hands, saying sarcastically, 'Have you got enough?'

Dr Shipman and his solicitor Ann Ball had arrived in her car. His wife Primrose and their youngest son Sam followed ten minutes later in the family's big red people carrier, ready to take him home after he had 'helped police with their enquiries'. As Dr Shipman and Ms Ball walked across the car park, they suddenly took a detour away from the entrance of the police station. He wasn't ready so they took a twenty-minute walk through the terraced streets at the back of the station. Past the primary school, getting ready for a day of stories, painting and play. Past the builder's yard, slowly grinding into life. Past the tiny red-brick houses, their families rousing themselves for work. Unbeknown to Dr Shipman, these were his last ever steps as a free man.

Chris Gleave had driven ahead and jumped out, camera at the ready. Walking backwards, he took snap after snap of Shipman. I chased up from behind, asking for any comment, giving him what would be his last chance to claim innocence. Ms Ball scolded me: 'He has nothing to say, leave us alone.' The pair walked for twenty minutes. Ms Ball, tall, slim and straight backed, talked calmly and confidently to the slightly shorter Dr Shipman, who had his hands jammed in his pockets. Both of them looked ahead as they strolled along, preparing for the interview, his second in the two months since the investigation had started.

All that time he had continued to practise alone at his Market Street surgery, the waiting room as hectic as ever. Patients queued beneath a huge array of good luck cards pinned to the wall. The receptionists had put them up with pride, apparently still not questioning why, time after time, Dr Shipman's women patients passed away within hours, sometimes minutes, of seeing him. As the patients left, filled with the new siege mentality of the practice, they snapped at the dozens of reporters who descended on Hyde: 'He is a marvellous doctor, why don't you leave him alone?' All around the town, Dr Shipman's friends lined up to defend him, the neighbouring newsagent certain 'it's sour grapes on the part of Mrs Grundy's daughter'.

Dr Shipman made the most of his supportive surroundings with a few well-chosen monologues performed for the right audience. He broke down as he told patient Lesley Pullford how he would scold Mrs Grundy, if she came back from the dead: 'If I could bring her back and sit her in that chair, I would say, "Look at all the trouble it has caused. I was going to say I did not want the money but, because of all this trouble, I will have it," ' he railed. The shocked but sympathetic patient thought how their roles had suddenly reversed.

He also tearfully told district nurse Marion Gilchrist how unfair it was, that he should become embroiled in a nasty row over a will. With that, he added a brazen black joke: 'The only thing I did wrong was not having her cremated. If I had had her cremated, I wouldn't be having all this trouble.'

It was during this time, no doubt fuelled by the blind support of so many, that Dr Shipman gave his first police interview on 14 August. He had answered the Home Office drugs inspector easily. He was on his own territory, the surgery, where the spectators who watched him welcome the officers into his consulting room were on his side. And he knew he had taken himself off the Controlled Drugs Register after his court case in 1976, hence out of the mindset of the officers who policed it. That night he had gone home, in his eyes and those of his loyal family and staff, victorious. On 7 September, he expected more of the same. He was mistaken.

Dr Shipman and Ms Ball walked into the police station at 9 a.m. He was arrested immediately, for the murder of 81-year-old former Mayoress Kathleen Grundy. He would not be leaving the station for home but for a prison cell. The GP's shock was compounded by his disgust at being booked in by a mere sergeant. Being fingerprinted and photographed was bad enough, but for it to be done by a sergeant just like any grubby little crook was unbearable. Detective Superintendent Postles and Detective Chief Inspector Williams, aware of his arrogance, knew the effect this would have. 'He would have liked the Chief Constable to be there,' DCI Williams joked later. 'He had been watching too many films.'

As Dr Shipman's fingers were pressed on to the moist, inky pad he joked with the officer to be careful with his little finger, in which he suffered RSI. 'Repetitive strain injury,' he explained. No doubt from his busy hours at the keyboard, changing the medical records of the women he had left dead, it was remarked later.

Meanwhile Primrose and Sam waited outside the low-rise police station, its boxy, modern structure embellished by an incongruous old-fashioned blue police lamp, a few sparse trees between the car park and the constant queue of traffic on Manchester Road and, as was often the case, wooden boarding on a kicked-in glass door panel. When mother and son followed Shipman's last free footsteps into the police station, they found that their tense and tedious drive through the rush-hour traffic had been a wasted journey.

Dr Shipman regained his composure for that first interview, responding arrogantly and condescendingly to Detective Sergeant John Walker and Detective Constable Mark Denham. He enjoyed the challenge of competing with the detectives and, so he thought, winning. But when he realised he had been caught out, in his second interview on 5 October, he fell to his knees and sobbed. He broke down again in the dock at Tameside Magistrates' Court two days later. As three new charges were read out to him, that he murdered Bianka Pomfret, Winnie Mellor and Joan Melia, he crumpled. His shoulders drooped forward, his head bowed and he shook, his mouth gaping slightly with an unheard cry. When he was asked did he understand the charges, he shook his head and wiped away his tears, shrinking into the dock. The highly esteemed family doctor had turned into a tiny old man with a snowy beard and beady pale blue eyes, dressed in a tatty black jumper, looking two decades older than his 52 years. Primrose watched from the public gallery, helpless and downcast. Dr Shipman sank to his lowest point as she and dozens of reporters looked on. It was never to happen again.

From then on, helped by tranquillisers and his will not just to survive but also to master his circumstances, Dr Shipman grew stronger. He was remanded to Walton Prison in Liverpool; such was the concern for his safety at Strangeways, where there could be inmates and even wardens with relatives who had died in his care. But later he was moved to the Manchester jail where he took to prison life 'like a natural', according to a hospital wing nurse. Father Denis Maher, the priest at St Paul's Church who lost three parishioners to Dr Shipman, was disgusted to learn how he strode the corridors 'like he owns the place'. Father Maher has no redeeming words for Shipman: 'Such an arrogant man. He took the lives of these women, ruined their families' lives and for what? In the end, it was money.'

Shipman's fightback was no surprise to those who knew the GP. All his life he had battled to get where he wanted and then, again and again, to crawl back from adversity often of his own making. In the corridors, cells and recreation wings of Strangeways, he was as manipulative and calculating as he had been in the streets, homes and community centres of Tameside – as ever, playing the part of the dedicated, caring doctor.

He would counsel inmates who no other prisoner would even speak to, such as Aaron Nicholls, who set fire to his 12-year-old girlfriend Lauren Carhart. When asked why he was helping a callous child murderer, Shipman replied, 'We're all in here for something.' More importantly, by helping Nicholls he was maintaining his self-made mantle as prison witchdoctor. His revered position as Britain's biggest serial killer, added to his penchant for looking after his fellow cons, had created a Florence Nightingale-cum-Hannibal Lecter persona that served him well, placing him safely at the heights of the prisoners' hierarchy. Yet again he was keeping people at a safe, admiring distance.

Shipman cemented his position of power when he saved the life of his cellmate Tony Fleming. That even impressed the warders. Tony, who was serving a short sentence for theft, tried to hang himself with Shipman's shoelaces. Shipman cut him down. 'Now I know he is no killer,' the ex-con said. 'If he enjoyed killing, he would have let me hang.'

Tony had waited till the early hours before silently slipping Shipman's shoelace from his shoe, tying it round his neck then to the bunk and plunging to the ground. His desperate gasps woke the GP who immediately leapt into action, holding his hefty cellmate up while shouting for help. The next Tony knew, he was being carried away on a stretcher. 'I heard the guards talking about it,' he recalled. 'They said he saved my life.'

Afterwards, when Tony returned bruised and shaken to their cell, Shipman quipped, 'Next time, use someone else's shoelaces. Mine are ruined.' A shot of black humour was just what Tony needed at that desperate time. He and Harold, as Tony knew him, began to bond. Shipman sat for hours listening to him, how he missed his home, his friends, his freedom and, most of all, his wife. 'We are a team,' he explained. 'We are both disabled, me mentally and her physically, so we help each other.' But Shipman rarely broke down himself.

Tony spent ten weeks with Shipman. When he was released in July 1999, he had a sheaf of letters from Primrose and others, which Shipman had given him to sell to the newspapers. 'You need the money, lad,' he had said. It is little wonder Shipman was happy to give the letters away. Many of them were the mundane witterings of well-meaning friends who did not know what to say. And Primrose's were so badly composed, they were almost illiterate as well as dull. 'My dearest Fred,' she wrote on 2 March 1999, 'only 216 day to go, good idea, keep my maths going. I have done everything this morning when I should have done the paper work, sorted the clean sock [*sic*], made bed . . .' She went on in the same unreadable fashion, describing how she had listened to a piece about the secrets of a long marriage on *Woman's Hour* and commenting on the judge, Mr Justice Forbes: 'The judge seems more lively and with it, not sitting there like a piece of lard.'

After that, Tony got more letters – this time from Shipman himself.

In them he discussed his trial and how impressed he was by his solicitor Ms Ball, 'she of the steel-tipped heels and intimidating nature'. Prisoner CJ8198 was clearly enjoying the notoriety and attention: 'You can tell I'm involved. Never thought court would be interesting. I know I'm involved but it's more. Fascinated to see the QCs set out their wares with booby traps hidden. No applause which I feel would help the audience.'

Travelling to Preston every day made a pleasant change for Shipman. His usual routine was much more boring. Too clever for normal lessons and even the prison's weekly quiz, he became an assistant to the teachers who taught English and art to the prisoners from 9.30 to 11.30 every morning. He also challenged the wardens to a game of Scrabble. The rest of the time, he led the dullest of prison life and carried out the lowliest of tasks – mopping out his cell first thing, followed by breakfast duty. He was locked up in his cell again between lunch and dinner but at least this was broken by Primrose's faithful daily visit at 2 p.m. sharp. After dinner, at 6.30 p.m., he would be locked up for the night. Then he would write letters, surrounded by pictures of the family he had left behind – Primrose and Sarah on a trip to Buckingham Palace, young Sam in his school uniform.

He and Tony also played Monopoly – two games every night without fail. But Shipman hated losing. 'He was a cheating sod,' Tony recalled with a laugh. 'If we bought property, we put the money in the middle of the board – and then he would slip it in to his bank. We used to have a laugh about it. He was determined to beat me and I didn't want to spoil his moment of glory.'

'I miss him, you know,' Tony added pitifully, sitting in the lounge of his Bolton council-owned mews. 'Harold would sit there and listen to all my problems, take it all in. He was very caring. He was also a very intelligent, very interesting bloke. I can't understand what is happening. He's so clever; he would not make mistakes like forging a will like that. I will never, ever believe he killed those women. He saved my life – that's the man he is.'

Meanwhile, on the outside, those who had known Dr Shipman were stunned by the news that he had been arrested for the murder of vulnerable old ladies. Such a quiet, gentle man, carrying himself with such dignity all his life, carefully plodding on, so devoted to his chosen caring profession. Consequently their shock was – and still is – almost matched by their sympathy for him. They refused to believe he was a monster, first clinging to the hope that it was euthanasia then, on realising all his victims were women and there was a will involved, turning to the belief that he had had a breakdown.

One of his fellow graduates, sitting in his own single-handed surgery, turning his ink pen over and over in his hands, thought for a long time before saying, 'I'm very saddened by the news; it's tragic. I have no reason to suspect he would do something like that. He is a very caring man.' He had recognised Dr Shipman in the paper straight away, having spent some time with him at a recent Leeds University reunion. 'I felt really sad because in that particular picture he looked so downcast,' he added. 'I just felt sorry for him and didn't believe he had done it.'

Another who studied at Leeds with him, Dr Colin Wilkinson, agreed: 'Something has gone terribly wrong. He is not a monster.'

The Old Paviors, too, will not condemn the man. To them he is still their old friend, the serious young man they all looked up to, who walked to school like a snail yet tore up the rugby pitch like a tiger.

Alan Goddard, watching the news with his wife one evening after work, could not believe the slow-motion film of Fred Shipman being led away in handcuffs. 'I didn't recognise his picture, but he looks a lot like his dad,' he recalled with a shudder at his pristine, expensively decorated semi on a modern estate in Nottingham. 'His mother was such a nice, kind person. The family were close. This would have hurt them so much.'

John Soar believed Fred must have been mentally ill: 'I feel sorry for him and his family, as well as his victims. I was very sad to hear about Fred – such a waste of talent. If I was asked why Fred Shipman would be in newspapers at 53, I would say because he was an exemplary GP doing something for his community, not this.'

Terry Swinn agreed: 'You need strength of character to become a doctor, put in the graft. I liked him. I'm perplexed, as everyone else is. He is not the first man that would come to mind in this sort of circumstance.'

Bob Studholme is sympathetic too, although he says 'he has rather let the side down', bringing infamy to such a great school as High Pavement. 'We were all so surprised, slightly lost by it,' he said. 'It's not the sort of thing he should have done. I saw another friend at a rugby match after the news broke and I asked him, "Is it him?" He said, "Yes, I'm afraid it is." '

He believed Fred's reserved ways, his struggle to get the grades he needed for medicine, especially after his mother died, and the shotgun wedding as a student, pushed him too far. 'I was shocked to hear he did no more sport at university,' Bob explained at his warm and cosy family home, busy with books, records and the debris of his children's hobbies. 'I found that phenomenal, incredible, impossible. At least once a year I would think, where is Fred Shipman? He was a sportsman yet never appeared on the rugby scene. He never came back to school reunions or Nottingham. He left High Pavement and I never heard of him since.'

Bob, whose colourful personality and years of teaching have made him an entertaining raconteur, expanded his theory: 'He needed to work hard to get qualifications and he would take everything seriously. If he got married, he would be serious about that marriage, serious about his children. His focus was taken away from sport, concentrating on family and getting qualified. Fred was always controlled. We would be fighting in Marks & Spencer; Fred would have thought that was abominable. That would have furrowed Fred's brow. Fred would focus on marriage and the offspring.' While Fred's old schoolmates stayed in touch with each other, Fred disappeared. The next they knew of him was when he appeared on television, arrested for killing old ladies by the dozen.

According to Bob, 'If I saw him now I would say, "Hi Fred, how are you?" Then I would ask him about it man to man – "What the bloody hell have you done?" '

He explained further: 'Doctors have to have a degree of detachment. Life is full of people who die; you can't win them all. We have to respect that aspect. We all have a bill to pay in life. A sportsman's is physical, and mental too. GPs have in particular. I think there but for the grace of God go I. It's not malice that led Fred to his actions, there's a kink that's allowed that, perhaps overwork. People setting him up, going to him when things go wrong. That happens to me as a senior teacher. If I saw him now I would feel sorry for him. I feel sorry for people who lost people because of Fred but, because of my age and experience with the human race, I'm able to see both sides.'

Bob went on: 'All of us are only one inch from this. Women with small children under threat are capable of killing. It's nothing to be ashamed of. We have such a veneer in our civilised society, but it's not that thick. A little bit of jungle juice . . . The Germans have a saying – let the pig out. It means letting off steam, getting rid of frustration. Like he did on the rugby pitch. Maybe that was it. He didn't permit himself to let go; now he has in the worst possible way.'

Even people who did not grow up with him, who had little time to grow close to Dr Shipman, feel unabashed sympathy for him. His neighbour from the Burnhill council estate in County Durham, Margaret Norris, knew him for just a year before he moved to Hyde. Yet she was close to tears as she stood on her doorstep and said: 'I cannot believe this has happened. He was a lovely man and I am still their friend. I feel so sorry for Primrose and the children.' And at Lord Derby Road, where again the family lived for just twelve months, loyalty reigned yet again. The neighbours are so attached to Fred and Primrose they remain steadfastly silent, even though his victims were plucked from their community, several of them from the streets nearby. They are well aware of the devastation he has caused, yet one woman would only say: 'I am still their friend.'

Dr Michael Grieve, who enjoyed no such loyalty from his protégé the young Fred Shipman, also refused to condemn him. Shipman blamed him and the other partners at Todmorden for his drug addiction. But Dr Grieve had only sympathy for Shipman. 'Being a doctor is a hell of a job,' he said. 'You get blamed for deaths anyway. I wonder what drove him to this.'

There are even those in Hyde, a town devastated by the GP's evil work, who insist on his innocence. Mary Burgess, the friend and patient whose loneliness Dr Shipman cured with a prescription for babysitting, swore she would never truly accept another GP. She is a tough, old Hydonian but she was so hurt by the media coverage of the case that she could not watch the television news for weeks, for fear of seeing the footage of him in handcuffs that left her in tears. Warden Jenny Unsworth, whose residents Dr Shipman tended, coped much better with the shocking news that he was suspected of mass murder. But she was still infuriated by the gossip surrounding the case, both in Hyde where 'people want their twopenn'orth' and beyond. She recalled how she scolded a stranger on holiday: 'We were on a coach tour when a lady in front had the Sunday paper with Dr Shipman's picture on. She turned to her friend and said, "It's awful, fancy having a doctor like this, horrible man." I tapped her on shoulder and said, "No he is not."'

But for the most part, the community of Hyde has been left stunned and angered by Shipman's killing spree. Hyde is a battered and beleaguered old town. Nestling in a smoky hollow by a grimy girdle of grey-green Pennines, it is dying year by year. Its factories are closing down, its once busy mills are quiet and its smoking chimneys no longer paint streaks against the leaden sky. It is a dying town best known for death and that is unfair to its people, the good, solid, down-to-earth folk who remain loyal to their town even as it fades away. Hyde was best known for the horrific Moors Murders, which sickened the whole country and beyond in the mid 60s. Now it is also known as the home of Britain's biggest serial killer.

Dr Shipman murdered at least fifteen old ladies, putting them to sleep like a vet would a dog. But Coroner John Pollard said the figure could be 1000, most of them Hydonians as it is the town where Shipman practised the longest. Consequently there is not a person in Hyde untouched by this case.

There are many people directly affected, devastated, having learned their mother, aunty, sister, friend or grandma did not die naturally and peacefully as they imagined. They wonder to this day, did she realise she was dying, did she know she was being murdered, did she beg for help as she faded away? The answer is, thankfully, probably not. Marion Hadfield was standing in the kitchen when Dr Shipman murdered her best friend Marie West in the living room next door and she didn't hear a sound. Maureen Ward was brewing up when Dr Shipman killed her mother Muriel, known to her friends as Molly. There was no violence, no threats, no begging for mercy, for Maureen remained his patient – until the day he quietly and callously picked her off, too.

Other people in Hyde have friends who have lost loved ones to Dr Shipman and, try as they might, they cannot imagine what they are going through. Their support has been strong and unwavering, but blind. Few know what it is like to have their mother murdered. And even fewer, just fifteen families, can understand losing her to Britain's biggest serial killer.

There are those who have lost loved ones in Dr Shipman's care but have not had the closure that comes with him being charged, convicted and sentenced.

Irene Phelps, who lost her two brothers to Shipman, broke down in tears as she recounted her grief at her sheltered-housing flat. When she read the *Manchester Evening News* court report telling of Shipman's 'taste for murder', she put the paper on the floor and stamped on Shipman's photograph, calling him names and sobbing for her dead brothers.

The pair, Ken and Sid Smith, and their next-door neighbours, married couple Tommy and Elsie Cheetham, all died within eight months of each other, all after visits from Dr Shipman. At the time, no one suspected the GP. But Ken, the third of the four old folk to die, said with chilling foresight: 'Don't let that man near me – he is the angel of death.' Shortly after that, he was dead.

Irene tearfully explained: 'He didn't know it, he just didn't like him, but he was right.'

Sid died first at the Garden Street council house that had been the brothers' home for 60 years. They, their brother Cyril and only sister Irene had moved there with their parents in 1936. Soon after, Tommy Cheetham and his family moved in. He was like another brother to the Smiths and stayed next door when he married Elsie. 'It was like *Coronation Street*,' Irene explained wistfully. 'Everyone going in and out of each other's back doors.'

Sid died in the lounge on 30 August 1996 as Ken made him and Dr Shipman a cup of tea in the kitchen.

Sid was well known in Hyde for his twice-daily shopping trips, all noted carefully in his diary. His last was on the day he died.

Afterwards, Dr Shipman walked into the kitchen and broke the shocking news to Ken, then left him grief-stricken; Sid still sat in his favourite chair. 'The undertakers walked in and started talking to Sid, thinking he was asleep,' Irene's daughter Sheila Marshall later recalled. 'They were disgusted he had been left that way. Ken was in a real state.'

Ken was still grieving for Sid when Tommy died. Sid had cared for him so well, running the house while he rested his leg ulcer and watched the horse racing with Tommy. Now he had lost them both. Elsie, who had taken over Sid's role, was also devastated. But her ordeal was far from over.

It was she who found Ken dead, sitting in his chair, on 17 December 1996. The window cleaner had spotted him sitting motionless and asked her to see if he was all right. She walked in through the back door, as usual unlocked, and was unable to revive him.

It was her turn to die next.

Irene and her family were sad to see 'the end of an era' at Garden Street. But until the police called to say they were investigating the four deaths, they had no idea of the horror behind it. Irene's son Stephen Phelps, a nurse, explained: 'It was too unbelievable.'

Irene, who lost her surviving brother Cyril and husband Frank the year she discovered her brothers had been murdered, has been left distraught and angry. The 77-year-old clenched her pale fists helplessly as she said: 'We were such a close family and the Cheethams were lovely. How dare Shipman take all that away from us and leave Ken and Elsie alone in their last months? If I could get near him I would cause him some damage, that I would.'

Other families facing the same uncertainty include the large family Kitchen. Hyde councillor Joe Kitchen and his brothers and sisters have been ripped apart by the distress and uncertainty of their mother Alice's death. Mrs Kitchen, known by her middle name Christine, was exhumed but no morphine was found in her body, the evidence probably lost in the four years she had been buried. Now her eight sons and daughters and twenty-one grandchildren are split, confused and angered by their emotional limbo.

But Brian Dean, who suffered a breakdown when his mother, actress Joan Dean, died in February 1998, has come to terms with his loss and confusion much better. Joan was a lively social butterfly who left Brian with too many happy memories for him to remember her with heartache. 'Mother was a very, very touchy-touchy huggy-huggy person,' he recalled. 'The house was always full of theatrical people. She loved playing charades, dressing up and entertaining. She always had lots of friends. I couldn't believe her death was being investigated and I still don't know what really happened. I probably never will.' But having hit the bottom, he decided to come back up and not worry any more. 'Mother wouldn't have wanted that,' he declared with more than a little relief.

Other people who lost loved ones in Shipman's care are now racked with guilt. They had felt uneasy but said nothing. Now they spend sleepless nights wondering if, had they spoken out, they could they have saved the lives of all those old ladies. Father Denis Maher has been counselling one woman, who lost her mother five years ago. Other parishioners feel guilty because they cannot forgive Shipman, as the Bible says they should. The priest, angry and upset that his flock is so ravaged by a horror not of their making, said:

'They say to me, "How can I come to church when I can't forgive him?" The lady who lost her mother feels so terribly guilty as well as constantly bereaved. But I have told her that no one could believe such a thing of a doctor. The only one who should feel guilty is Dr Shipman.'

Taxi driver John Shaw, who lost 24 customers to Dr Shipman, knows all too well how they feel. He almost went out of his mind with grief and guilt as he counted them, one after the other, for seven years. 'I knew for years that something was wrong with Shipman,' he recalled. 'I kept losing my customers and it was always him who was the doctor. At first I thought he was unlucky or incompetent, then I realised it was something more sinister. I felt guilty, like an accomplice. I could have saved them. But I couldn't tell anyone. Who would believe it? They would have put me away.'

John and his wife Kath began to keep a list of the patients who were dying suddenly in Dr Shipman's care. It rose to a staggering 24. The hard-hearted and brazen GP, dedicated only to his secret reign of death, was unaware that one man was 'on to him'.

John and Kath Shaw knew Shipman's victims well and they considered each and every one of them a friend rather than a customer. John had run his one-man business, Case Cars, for eleven years, serving a select bunch of the old folk in Hyde. The strapping, gently spoken six-footer became a familiar and welcome face to them – taking them on their regular weekly trips, to see their families or meet their friends at local dances and bingo halls. He would also run errands for them and when he took them home, he would pop in to check all was safe and well inside for them. Strong, independent Kath Grundy preferred to do that for herself but John would wait for her sign – lighting the old-fashioned lamp in her garden – before driving off. A true gent – but he was unable to save her or the others from the sneaking killer who struck from behind a carefully constructed veneer of respectability.

Driving the Miss Daisys of Hyde was a job John loved but when he retired in September 1999, it was 'a relief'. Thanks to Dr Shipman, his journeys became a constant reminder of lost friends, helpless women who went unknowingly to their deaths when they answered the door to the doctor. Each one a new shock, a new heartbreak for John. He explained: 'For instance, I used to take one lady from Baron Road to see her two daughters on Tuesdays and Saturdays. On Tuesdays I would go past Norah Nuttall's house, then Flo Lewis's, then Ada Hilton's. On Saturdays I'd go past Norah's again – she lived on Baron Road – then Mrs Adams's. It was extremely distressing.'

John and Kath have another reminder of the torment they suffered as their list grew year by year – Dinky, Rena Sparks's cat. They adopted Dinky after Rena suddenly passed away in December 1992. Years later they put the proud pensioner who 'always kept her house and herself right' at the top of their list. The roll-call also included Irish-born widow Muriel 'Molly' Ward – and, two years later, Molly's daughter Maureen. And there was former shopkeeper Maria West, who died at her cottage on 6 March 1995. Norah Nuttall was obese and no one was surprised when she died suddenly of heart failure, according to the death certificate signed by Shipman. But John knew better. The final name on John's list is the one that causes him most pain – Kathleen Grundy. 'She was special,' he said. 'Such a lovely woman and a good friend. I could have saved her if I had spoken up.'

But his wife Kath, who had spent those years terrified for her husband's well-being, had begged him to keep quiet. Now her faith in doctors has been destroyed: 'I shall never trust them again.'

Finally, after seven long, heartbreaking years, John contacted the police, who were then investigating Mrs Grundy's death – and nineteen others. 'I told an officer, who I know, all about it, and I was right – I couldn't have spoken out any earlier,' he said. 'The policeman said he would have thought I was somebody with a grudge against Shipman. He told me, "He's the next thing to God, a doctor, as far as you and me are concerned."'

That trust, which should, indeed must, exist between patient and doctor, has been destroyed in Hyde and beyond, thanks to Dr Shipman. Some of Shipman's patients, whose medication has been dropped by the new locum, now wonder if they were to have been next. They will never find out – luckily for them – but even they will suffer as the guilt that comes with survival takes its toll.

Many people will never forget being woken by the bright white lights and the groaning generators of an exhumation. June O'Reilly, who lives just yards from Hyde Cemetery, recalls: 'It was dreadful, so eerie. It was even worse when we realised what was happening. We knew Marie Quinn and Winnie Mellor, both such lovely ladies, and couldn't bear to think what was happening to them.'

Father Denis Maher has seen the worst of it. He has attended exhumations and counselled grieving relatives and friends. He himself was heartbroken when Shipman was charged with murdering three of his congregation – 49-year-old Bianka Pomfret, 73-year-old Winifred Mellor and 67-year-old Marie Quinn. 'I miss them,' he confessed readily in the cold, spare consulting room at his church home. Surrounded by a few practical sticks of furniture and mournful pictures of icons, he sat with his hands clasped before him, looking down as he collected his thoughts; he looked desolate. He takes only a little comfort in his belief that the three women have gone to a better place. But he fired up with a passion when he finally spoke: 'All these people were not sitting at home, looking into the fire. Winnie Mellor was always flying about. If you met Marie coming round a corner she was like a whirlwind passing you. There was always a sadness about Bianka – she suffered from depression – but she was a lovely woman, who got herself ready and came to church. I was always glad to see her at Mass. These were popular, strong women, women who got things done.' But he had no such kind words for Dr Shipman: 'He is the closest thing to evil I have ever come across.'

Coroner John Pollard, not one given to dramatic statements, agreed. 'I think he is a genuinely evil man,' he said bluntly at his office in Stockport, 'because he has taken some of the most vulnerable people in society and exercised the power and privilege of his position and totally twisted it and used it in the worst possible way – to kill them. To my mind that is evil.' According to Mr Pollard, there could be 1000 victims – or more. Again it is shocking, coming from such a sensible, intelligent man: 'The official figure is the figure proved in court but it is possible there are other deaths which have not been reported or come to light, and this could be as many as 1000.'

Mr Pollard is used to the grief and distress that comes with death, having been the South Manchester and Districts Coroner for almost five years. He sees his difficult role as an essential one; to obtain justice and win peace for lost loved ones. But this case – and 'the perverted pleasure he derived' – has torn apart not only families but also a whole community. 'It has really disturbed the whole community,' he said. 'There's never been a case like this. He is now biggest serial killer in country. I always feel angry whenever anybody does anything which potentially destroys or affects adversely the community. One of my loves in this country is the tight-knit communities we have. A big city like Manchester breaks down into small communities with the local councillors, doctors and priests. If any breach that trust, it can break the whole community.' He said it was worse because Shipman's victims were generally elderly and always vulnerable in the trust they had, and needed to have, in others. 'The older you get, the more you tend to rely on other people, especially three people – your priest, your solicitor and your doctor. If any of these three breaches that trust, it can have a devastating effect. This was a terrible breach of faith.'

He just hoped some good would come of the case, although not a knee-jerk reaction condemning all GPs to unnecessary draconian measures. 'The law should evolve, not rapidly change,' he explained. 'Doctors are unaccountable and have to be by the very nature of their job, but 99.9 per cent are good honest people.' But he did want to see the end of the single-handed practice. Mr Pollard would also like to see more deaths being reported to the Coroner: 'I have done since this case broke, if only to confirm the doctor's view. People don't know the procedure and maybe one of the few benefits of this case will be an education of the general public on what the Coroner does and how he can help resolve problems and establish the true cause of death.'

And he was fortified by the way the community had fought back: 'There have been a lot of very brave people. The GP who rang me in the first place was very brave. Mrs Grundy's daughter Angela Woodruff has also been very brave. She knew what it would involve when she took the matter to police. Then there are all the relatives and friends who gave statements and have gone to court, which is a hard thing to do. They are all to be commended for doing that because it ensured justice was done.'

Mr Pollard added: 'I feel sorry for the Hyde community. For over thirty years they have had to cope with that soubriquet, the Moors Murders. If you asked what people knew about Hyde, you would almost invariably get the response, "Is that where Hindley and Brady are from?" That's just disappearing thirty years on. Now the town of Hyde is rapidly becoming famous again as the place where Dr Shipman practised. In fact it is a very pleasant little town with nice people living there.'

June O'Reilly, youthful for middle age, smartly turned out and quick to put the record straight, is a typical Hydonian. She was born and bred there and, like all Hydonians, she is heartbroken to see her hometown so devastated. 'Hyde was best known for the Moors Murders, now this,' she said in the brightly decorated kitchen of her traditional red-brick terraced home. 'It's a lovely old town and it doesn't deserve that.'

Father Denis Maher, who is now faced with rebuilding the town's very soul, agreed: 'We are facing unanswered questions, living in limbo, because of this man. And you know what else this town is known for, don't you? The Moors Murders.

'People are very upset. Our parish is suffering sorrow and shock and sadness. There's not a lot of healing.'

6 The Case for the Prosecution

The Hyde community was finally able to heal itself with a moving performance in the witness box. Testimony after testimony from a 'small army' of sons, daughters, friends and neighbours, as prosecutor Richard Henriques QC described them, brought Shipman to justice.

They were ordinary people, and most of them had never seen in the inside of a court in their lives. Each one of them took the box with trepidation, some so frail they had to be helped up the steps then sit down, a hand resting on the top of the box in a bid to lean forward and impress their words upon the jury. These witnesses were even more dwarfed by Preston Crown Court's stately, old Courtroom One than those who could stand. It was a beautiful room, its dark wood panels rising to an ornate stained glass ceiling, the portraits of old judges with grave expressions looking down on the proceedings. But it was not a comfortable room, and nor was it meant to be. Still, the courage and determination of those witnesses as they recounted their final moments with loved ones focussed the attention of the jury. They could not have failed to find Shipman guilty.

The sun shone from the brightest of blue skies on the day Shipman's trial finally started. It had been a long time coming for Henriques' small army, and they knew it was to take many more weeks before it was over. By the time the trial came to an end, the season had changed. The wild, wintry squalls of January had blown away the clear, crisp sunshine of that first autumn day, 5 October 1999.

Even then the sunlight seemed unable to brighten the grey pallor of Preston, the Lancashire town that was to host the trial of Britain's biggest ever serial killer. It was an apt venue, a town not unlike Hyde; bigger but still old-fashioned, with the same well-loved old market, the same bland indoor shopping centre, the same bargain stores and parched pea stalls, all favoured by the old folk who seemed to dominate the population.

Small groups of the town's pensioners stopped to stare at the swarm of cameramen and photographers who buzzed around the old courthouse. They tutted, their arms folded, shopping bags at their feet, as the paparazzi ran after Shipman's wife Primrose, who arrived smiling her usual strange, incongruous smile. Then they moved on, along with the young mums with trolleys and excitable kids bunking off from school who had joined them. They had seen it before, when Preston Crown Court played host to the trial of child killers Robert Thompson and Jon Venables, convicted of the murder of toddler James Bulger. As far as the people of Preston knew, Shipman's was not such a horrific case. And his poor wife should be left in peace, the old ladies muttered.

But although this case lacked the violence, gore and hysterical reaction of the Bulger murder, it was still chilling.

First there were legal arguments, holding up the trial for yet another week. Shipman arrived in the dock thinner and paler than ever, sporting a grey suit and a prison service haircut. He looked daunted and, in that first seventeen-minute hearing, a pale shadow of his former self. In the public gallery sat Primrose and their youngest sons David, then 19, and 16-year-old Sam, still recovering from using his skills as a prop forward to protect his mother from the cameramen. All four children were to chaperone their mother over the coming weeks. Sarah came less frequently, her bright blonde hair now cut into a short style and dyed brunette, perhaps a disguise of sorts that would allow her to return to her preferred style when this was all over. Christopher, younger and without a beard but still the very image of his father, similarly attended less often. But young Sam, only just out of school, was there day after day by his mother's side.

Shipman's defence counsel Nicola Davies QC, who was to do a tremendous job for her arrogant client, had three applications. It took her two days to explain them. None were granted.

One was that the trial be stopped. Dr Shipman, Miss Davies said, could not have a fair trial following the 'unremitting, extensive, inaccurate, misleading' publicity about the case. It took her half a day to show how a range of newspapers had reported the investigation into her client, the rising toll of patients – up to 150 of them – the financial searches on them and, of course, the shocking litany of exhumations. On 23 February 1999, it culminated in the *Daily Express* headline 'Is GP Britain's biggest serial killer?' But prosecutor Mr Henriques insisted the publicity had not been sensational – 136 deaths were investigated, close to the 150 claimed by the papers – and had even been helpful. The *Manchester Evening News* exclusive report which revealed the GP was under investigation on 19 August 1998, some two weeks before toxicologist Julie Evans proved his last victim Mrs Grundy had died of morphine poisoning, had alerted the families of other victims. The *Manchester Evening News* had followed this with an interview with Coroner John Pollard, who promised a speedy investigation to reduce the anxiety of the families involved. 'They needed to know,' Mr Henriques insisted. 'They [the papers] were entitled to report it. Most of the publicity was accurate and responsible.'

The second wish was to sever the charges to make three trials. One trial for the two charges regarding Kathleen Grundy as it was the only case where the prosecution could allege a motive – in this case money. Another trial for the charges regarding patients who had been buried, as there was evidence of how the women had died – morphine poisoning. And a third trial for the charges relating to patients who were cremated, as there was no physical evidence of how they had died. Miss Davies argued that a case taking several months and involving 15 victims, 600 witnesses and a staggering 8,000 exhibits, all against a complicated medical background, would be too much for any jury to bear. But again Mr Henriques put a strong argument to try all fifteen together: that they were all highly probative of one another and put 'a proper picture' to the jury.

The third wish was a revelation – not to use evidence referred to as volume eight, which showed how Shipman had stockpiled morphine. Volume eight was a list of 28 patients, most of whom had died, from whom Shipman had taken the painkilling drug. Sometimes he had taken away their remaining ampoules after they died and, instead of destroying them, had kept them for himself. Other times he had prescribed morphine to patients even after their death, or even to healthy patients who had no need for it, in order to keep the ampoules for himself. Volume eight included names such as Len Fallows, the retired policeman who had regarded himself as Shipman's friend, taking Sam and David to the rugby and working hard to run the appeal fund. But apart from his asthma he was perfectly well and in no need of the opiate – he was simply being used by Shipman to build up his stock of the deadly drug. Another familiar name was Sarah Ashworth, a patient whose body was exhumed by the police, although it gave no evidence with which to charge Dr Shipman. This new evidence sent a frisson of excitement through the press box. Miss Davies argued that by referring to dozens more deaths, it would make her client look guilty of even more murders than those with which he was charged. And, she said, the pattern of stockpiling was that of a drug addict rather than a killer. But Mr Henriques said volume eight was essential to show that Shipman had access to the drug, despite the fact that he had taken himself off the Controlled Drugs Register following his pethidine addiction in 1977.

Volume eight was revealed to the jury by yet more ordinary Hyde folk called to the witness box. Healthy patients realised with horror that they had been prescribed lethal doses of diamorphine while heart-broken widows were forced to relive the pain of their loved ones dying from excruciating terminal illnesses. The 28 patients used in this way were listed to the court. It sounded like a roll call of Coronation Street characters – Olive Higginbottom, Nellie Mullen, Fanny Nicholls, Harold Eddleston – the names revealing their age and vulnerability. Dr Shipman could have agreed to the evidence and saved the witnesses from facing court, but he did not. He was to prove his own worst enemy again many times over the coming weeks.

Mr Justice Forbes carefully considered the defence's three requests before denying each of them, taking half a day to explain his decisions thoroughly. Then he adjourned the proceedings until the following Monday, 11 October 1999.

It took some time to make up the jury that morning. Many of those called up balked at the idea of spending three months on a trial that would take them away from their daily routines. But they found Mr Justice Forbes a hard man to convince. Those who had booked holidays were told they would have to cancel them, except for the man who had booked flights to Malta as a 40th wedding anniversary present for his wife. Those who knew anyone in Hyde or Todmorden, had been a health worker, or close to one were released. It left a jury of five women and seven men.

Shipman rose to his feet in the dock as the names of the jurors were read out, followed by the 16 charges in the indictment, name by name. It was time for Mr Henriques' opening address.

Greater Manchester Police were delighted to have Mr Henriques as their prosecutor. A leading barrister on the Northern circuit, he was a brilliant court talent. Born in wartime Lytham-St-Anne's, he had gone to Oxford and was called to the Bar in 1967. In 1986 he was made a QC. Ten years later he became Leader of the Northern Circuit. Rumour had it he was to become a Judge following the Shipman trial. Mr Henriques had the experience necessary for such an important case. His most famous case was the Jamie Bulger murder trial in which he guided the jury through the most horrific and unimaginable scenes of torture, made worse by the fact the victim was a tiny two year old and the perpetrators ten-year-old boys. His most recent case was prosecuting the 'wheelie bin killers' of pensioner

Lily Lilley, whose body was dumped in the canal in a wheelie bin. Again it was a difficult case, with two fourteen-year-old schoolgirls in the dock. If anyone could explain such a lengthy, complex case as Shipman's to the jury, it was Richard Henriques.

His opening address began slowly and steadily, fact by fact, but within six sentences he had explained the essence of the case. 'None of those buried nor indeed cremated were prescribed morphine or diamorphine, all of them died unexpectedly, all of them had seen Dr Shipman on the day of their death,' his deep, sonorous voice intoned. Mr Henriques, aware of the massive media interest in the case and of the jury's fear of being overwhelmed by a case that would last twelve weeks, hit home with a line that would never be forgotten. 'He was exercising the ultimate power of controlling life and death,' he went on, 'and repeated it so often that he must have found the drama of taking life to his taste.' It filled the front pages: Shipman's taste for murder.

As soon as Angela Woodruff stepped into the witness box, it was clear that her experience as solicitor meant nothing in the face of her emotions as a bereft daughter. 'Just a minute please,' she asked weakly. The whole courtroom stared intently at the small, slim woman who had finally brought Britain's biggest killer to book, shaking as she took a drink of water. Dressed in an expensive, understated grey suit, looking so much like her murdered mother Kathleen Grundy, she began her evidence. It was to take her most of the day, always on the edge of breaking down. Standing just feet away from the man who had killed 'mum', she gripped the top of the box, sometimes rocking to and fro as she spoke.

First Mrs Woodruff took the jury on a heartbreaking tour of Loughrigg Cottage, a place she now found too painful to visit, as police photographs were exhibited. Through the gate, past the false front door, to the side door and inside, every doorway, every room, even the lounge where Mrs Grundy was found dead. Mrs Woodruff struggled to remain composed.

Mr Henriques then reminded her gently of how she had heard her mother had died, at 2 p.m. on 24 June 1998, when the police at Hyde rang to tell her the terrible news. Later that day she had spoken to Dr Shipman. 'It's very hazy because I was very, very upset,' she recalled. 'Dr Shipman said he had seen her the previous day at his surgery. He said he had seen her on the morning of her death. He said he had seen her at home.' But, she added, she had been too devastated to remember if he said why he had been there.

Mrs Woodruff grew stronger as Mr Henriques turned to the tattily forged will, so out of character for her meticulous mother. She was proud of mum, and telling the world about this, and at the same time reliving happier times, seemed a little easier. This trait was seen in most of the witnesses: telling their loved one's story, showing how they loved and cared for them, was vital – almost as important as bringing Dr Shipman to justice. Their stories, sometimes sad, sometimes comic, were the most moving moments of the trial.

For her part, Mrs Woodruff explained with a gentle smile, 'she used to complain about my writing, mine's appalling.'

There were more smiles as Mr Henriques took her through her mother's full and fascinating life. 'She was just amazing,' she recalled. 'We would walk five miles and come in and she would say, "Where's the ironing?" without sitting down. We used to joke she was fitter than we were.' Even a burglary which left Mrs Grundy fanatical about security was remembered fondly: 'My husband would go out to the car to get something and then couldn't get in because she had locked the door behind him.' The court, already hushed by the poignancy of her memories, fell utterly silent as she revealed how her mother's postcard from Bakewell arrived the day before she died.

Mr Henriques turned to Mrs Woodruff's investigation and the ensuing police activity. As a solicitor, Mrs Woodruff knew what an exhumation and a post mortem would entail, but still she agreed to it. Her mum could be hurt no more than she already had been and the no-nonsense pensioner had not believed in life after death anyway. 'I don't think she cared one way or other [whether she was cremated], she believed when you were dead you were dead,' Mrs Woodruff explained. 'It was me who wanted her buried.'

Throughout the morning, Mrs Woodruff had remained strong. But her courage was tested to breaking point as she was cross-examined by defence counsel Nicola Davies QC.

Miss Davies spoke carefully and respectfully as she put her questions. 'You are not a family in need, are you?' she asked, having dissected Mrs Woodruff's finances for all to see. Mrs Woodruff, rocking back and forth in the box, had to agree. Yes, she and her husband David had inherited more than £1m from his father Cyril. Yes, they both had good incomes. And yes, she had put their home in his name in a bid to avoid losing it should her law firm be sued. This was normal practice for any solicitor, as Miss Davies knew, but to some it might suggest greed as well as grief.

Miss Davies pressed on, asking how difficult it was for Mrs Woodruff to quiz the witnesses to the forged will on that quiet Sunday morning. Mrs Woodruff, growing more agitated, explained: 'They were very helpful, very co-operative. Mrs Hutchinson invited us in but I was very distraught so in that way it was difficult.'

Miss Davies reminded her: 'It was suggested by the husband of Claire Hutchinson that you leave, wasn't it?'

Mrs Woodruff could only reply: 'I don't remember. By then I was upset. We certainly didn't want to impose ourselves on them.' She insisted she was not overbearing: 'Certainly not. I was shaking.'

When Miss Davies asked about the contents of her mother's handbag, Mrs Woodruff broke down. She had managed to sort through the bag but was too upset to help David search Loughrigg Cottage. Now even the thought of her mother's empty home drove her to tears. 'I haven't looked for medicine at my mother's house,' she wept. 'I just went through her handbag as I went through mum's things . . . I don't know if I was there, I don't like being in my mum's house.'

Mrs Woodruff was exhausted but somehow she found the strength to dismiss Miss Davies's suggestion there may have been a 'cooling off' between her and her mother. Miss Davies, referring to several of Mrs Grundy's now well-known diaries, had seized on the sparse entry for Easter 1998. Mrs Grundy had visited her daughter at Leamington Spa yet, unlike other years, had not recorded it in any detail. Mrs Woodruff grabbed at the 1998 diary and began pulling through the pages, her face flickering with emotion at the sight of her mother's handwriting, thoughts and plans. Finally she found the page she wanted and pointed it out triumphantly: 'I can see John Shaw's taxi, that's the taxi to take her to the train station, and then I picked her up from the station.'

Mrs Woodruff had last spoken to her mother five days before she died. She was as busy as ever: 'She was absolutely fine. She was thinking about getting a new back door, looking at back doors, changing her car. If my son was not going to Japan she would have given hers to him, she said.' Clearly this was not a woman about to disinherit her family. Choked, her voice so tiny it was almost childlike, Mrs Woodruff insisted: 'She loved my sons to pieces and they loved her to pieces too.' It was now, after hours in the witness box, that she finally looked at her mother's killer. She could only manage a momentary glance but it was enough to show her utter hatred of the man – her face was full of pain, and her eyes full of anger.

Over the following days a host of different characters gave testimony to Mrs Grundy's popularity in Gee Cross and Hyde. They were in the main examined by junior prosecuting counsel Peter Wright QC. A jovial man with a smiling freckled face, looking much younger than his 41 years, he put the witnesses at their ease. Clearly enjoying the high-profile case, he gently quizzed them about their last memories of Mrs Grundy and teased out a ribbon of fond tales.

Charity shop volunteer Irene Tovin took the box wide-eyed with concern but still smiling. The pensioner had made an effort to look smart, all made up, her fancy earrings and bright pink jumper bringing a shock of colour to the court, but she was without artifice. No doubt that had meant a lot to Mrs Grundy, her colleague at Age Concern for eight years. Asked what the former Mayoress had thought of daughter Angela, she replied simply: 'Oh, she loved her.'

Three meals on wheels workers followed. Again these were ordinary working women, daunted by the experience of giving evidence at court, but determined to tell their tale. They had seen Mrs Grundy the day before she died when she called in with her shopping list of 'veg' for the lunch club, as she did every Tuesday morning. As usual she had stood next to them as they rang in the order to make sure they got the right greens. Hazel Shaw, clutching her oversized black handbag to her chest, recalled with pride how she and Mrs Grundy had a bond – her son went to Warwick University, where David Woodruff was a physicist. 'She was very proud of her family,' she told the packed court. 'She often talked about her grandsons – one had just got a job in Japan and she was really happy that day. She thought the world of Angela.' She and her colleagues, Katherine Shaw and Linda Skelton, raised a laugh as they explained how they remembered Mrs Grundy's visit that day so well – Linda was celebrating her silver wedding, even though she had divorced the groom years back. 'I should have had a glass of champagne,' Linda had said to Mrs Grundy, who mistakenly congratulated her. She had replied poignantly: 'I've been widowed longer than I was married.'

Frail 91-year-old May Clark took the oath next. Her tiny frame should have been lost in the deep, dark wood witness box but the former Mayoress was undaunted by her surroundings and the formalities. She perched straight-backed and dignified, a picture of class and tradition in her pale blue twin-set and pearls, answering the questions slowly but with certainty. She and Mrs Grundy had been friends for years, their daughters both attending the prestigious Manchester High School for Girls and their husbands both in public office. The two women had sat on the same committees, helped the same charities, run the same lunch club and spent every Tuesday evening together, chatting about the week's events. Mrs Clark had been the last person to see Mrs Grundy alive – apart, that is, from Dr Shipman. She had been brought up to speak firmly when necessary, but her voice cracked a little as she recalled her friend leaving her home that night. Mrs Grundy had been looking forward to a visit from the GP: 'She thought it was very good of him to go along to her house and save her going to the surgery.' Miss Davies seized on the fact that Mrs Grundy had wanted to donate some of the Mayoress's Fund to Dr Shipman's appeal for equipment. But Mrs Clark put her straight: 'Well, she thought he was a great doctor. She thought it would be good for the practice and good for the people of Hyde. She admired his work. All the people of Hyde thought highly, all his patients thought highly of Dr Shipman, not just Mrs Grundy.'

Mrs Clark's undramatic delivery made the memory of waiting at the lunch club the following morning, unaware that her friend had been callously murdered, all the more painful to hear. 'She was usually punctual, even though she was well known in the village and she had a habit of talking to people that she knew,' she explained simply, creating a lasting image for the jury.

Lunch club caretaker John Green was not such a good witness. He found giving evidence an ordeal and grew flustered as he recalled finding Mrs Grundy's body with Ronald Pickford. This in turn made him embarrassed and annoyed, especially under cross-examination. He explained: 'She was a friend, a very great friend. That particular day I was well out of it.' Mr Pickford, older and much calmer, gave a more straightforward account.

PC John Fitzgerald remembered the men's distress when he was called out to Loughrigg Cottage. PC Fitzgerald turned up to court looking pin-neat, his beard trimmed and his uniform buttons gleaming, his smart appearance failing to hide the fact that he had missed his chance to catch Britain's biggest serial killer.

'I had a quick look round and once I thought there were no suspicious circumstances, dealt with it as a sudden death as we normally do,' he answered Miss Davies stiffly.

But Brian Burgess, the solicitor at Hamilton Ward, had been suspicious. When he received the forged will, on 24 June 1998, he thought it strange and left it on the corner of his desk. 'When I got a phone call at lunchtime saying Mrs Grundy had died I became suspicious,' he told the court. Again, despite working as a solicitor, he was not at ease in the witness box. Big and solidly built, filling his navy suit like an overstuffed sofa, his large, pale face showed his discomfort at what lay behind his vague suspicions and his part in Britain's biggest murder trial.

Claire Hutchinson was even more upset at her part, as a purported witness to the forged will. A respectable young mum of two, she had been distraught when confronted by Mrs Woodruff. Now, in the witness box, she was mortified. 'I felt quite upset really that this lady had been to see me at my house because of what we had signed,' she explained shakily. 'I felt quite a range of emotions. I went to see Dr Shipman and said we had this lady in the house and there seemed to be some question about what we had signed. He apologised and said he was very sorry, he would never ask anybody to witness a will again in the surgery.' Two weeks later, she recalled, Dr Shipman made a joke which she considered was in bad taste. 'Dr Shipman was behind the counter with the receptionists. He said, "Have you heard the latest? She's left it all to Age Concern." At that point he made some comment. I just didn't want to discuss it really, it just seemed odd,' she recalled.

Determined to defend her respectability, Mrs Hutchinson overcame her shyness to enthusiastically help Mr Henriques show how the whole will, including her signature, was a forgery. 'I don't think it's my signature, the C is small but I always join my C and L up, the U in Hutchinson is a V and I always write my U as a U and not a V,' she insisted.

Paul Spencer, the other witness to the forged will, arrived in the witness box in sharp contrast to Mrs Hutchinson. The tattooed skinhead, who took the stand sporting a black eye and heavy gold neck chain, was much more relaxed. But he too seemed embarrassed by the end of his evidence, when Miss Davies revealed how he had sold his story to a tabloid. 'Expenses, yes,' he admitted gruffly, going on to paint a seedy picture. 'He came to the house and we went for a walk.' Miss Davies asked him sternly how much he had been paid. 'Is it relevant?' he grumbled, wishing the moment would pass. He revealed the paltry sum: 'Two hundred and fifty pounds.'

At the end of the first week the tone of the trial changed as the case for the prosecution turned to expert witnesses more at ease with the proceedings. The trial ran more smoothly now, but although there was less emotion on display, their evidence was nonetheless fascinating.

Home Office pathologist Dr John Rutherford made the first of many appearances, having carried out post mortems on nine of the victims and three other women in the months leading up to the trial. Tall and slim, his luxuriant white hair contrasting with a deep tan but matching the pristine hanky in the breast pocket of his elegant navy suit, Dr Rutherford made an impressive witness. His deep, gentle voice made the catalogue of post mortems almost bearable. Mrs Woodruff, sitting in the public gallery, was assured he had given her mother and the other women every possible dignity as he carried out his work. Dr Rutherford carefully explained how he had removed Mrs Grundy from her body bag and shroud and measured her – she was five foot two. She also had embalming wounds, so the process had to be explained to a rather disturbed court – how a large needle was plunged into the body and a sheath inserted through it to deliver the embalming fluid. Dr Rutherford said that Mrs Grundy had been a very healthy woman with far fewer fatty deposits than could be expected in a woman her age. She would not have died of old age or any natural cause. She had died of morphine toxicity.

Fingerprint expert Ian Borthwick was another impressive witness, having worked on Manchester's infamous Woolworths fire, which had killed 10 people in 1979, and the Waco cult disaster, in which 87 died in 1993. He had helped identify the badly burned victims by taking their fingerprints. Mr Borthwick explained how he had taken ink prints from Mrs Grundy's lifeless fingers then photographed them. He said that there were other methods, but he had seen no reason to use them, especially destructive ones such as removing the upper layer of skin or even the hands themselves. Junior counsel Mr Wright referred to these horrific methods again, and in particular how they had devastated the families of the Marchioness partygoers, as he later demolished the evidence of defence fingerprint expert Graham Daniels. Mr Borthwick went on, explaining how a print needed sixteen ridge characteristics to identify its owner.

His colleague Andrew Watson followed with an explanation of what these procedures showed on the forged will. Once those of Brian Burgess and his secretary had been eliminated, there was only one full print remaining – the left little finger of Dr Shipman.

The red-purple blotch on the bottom left corner revealed all too clearly how he had gingerly handled the fake will. And, added Mr Watson, there were none from Mrs Grundy.

Document examiner Michael Allen, a thin unsmiling young man, labelled the signatures 'crude forgeries'.

He was followed by Detective Sergeant John Ashley, an officer from the computer examination unit who had unearthed some of the most damning evidence against Shipman. He had traced the GP's tampering of medical records to the very hour, minute and second, always on the day the patient died. It was his evidence that had brought Shipman to his knees in his third police interview. DS Ashley, making his first and only appearance, pointed to a large projector screen showing Shipman's bogus entries. 'Term: Malaise symptom. Comment: Nothing definite, just feels tired, nothing specific, . . . old? anything at all? Depressed although always happy. Lives on own. Socially active,' read one for 23 June 1998, the day before Mrs Grundy died. In fact, DS Ashley said, it had been created the day after her death at 08:21:39. The jury was left with a chilling image of Dr Shipman, busy inventing a new medical history for his latest victim before inviting in his first patient of the day.

In week two, the case was turned back to the ordinary Hydonians – this time the receptionists, nurses and surgery manager who had worked with Dr Shipman. Practice manager Alison Massey's face took on a defensive blush as she stood in the box, while practice nurse Gillian Morgan hid behind a magazine as she dashed past the cameras outside the courthouse. Some held hands as they ran the flashgun gauntlet. Horrified at what had been revealed about the fate of the people in their care, they now had to tell the world how they had worked with their murderer.

District nurse Marion Gilchrist took the oath on the verge of collapse and immediately dissolved into tears. Dr Shipman, who had sat impassively in the dock for days, suddenly wiped his eyes. He looked devastated as Mrs Gilchrist told the court how he had broken down in front of her, knowing his arrest was imminent. 'He said, "I read thrillers and on the evidence they have I would have me guilty," she recalled, her soft Scottish voice breaking as she stumbled over the words. The court fell silent, the jury stunned, as she went on: 'I took it as black humour when he said, "The only thing I did wrong was not having her cremated." He said, "If I had had her cremated I wouldn't be having all this trouble." '

It was followed by the statement of patient Lesley Pullford, read to the court by Mr Henriques. Shipman had again broken down in the days before his arrest. 'I remember thinking I should have sat in his chair and that our roles had reversed,' he intoned on her behalf. 'He said, if I could bring her back and sit her in that chair I would say look at all the trouble it's caused. I was going to say I didn't want the money but because of all this trouble I will have it.' Her bizarre account continued: 'He said, we have had a meeting, the staff and I, and decided what to do with the money if we get it. He said, we will all have a week off each and on the anniversary of her death, give so much to old people's homes, and if anyone had a baby that day, give the money to the charity of their choice.'

The Grundy case was wrapped up with the evidence of another expert witness, Derby GP Dr John Grenville, who had studied the medical notes of each victim. A small, sallow man with a quiet, serious air about him, he was the perfect foil for Shipman, who had been behaving in an increasingly bizarre way over the course of the trial. As it progressed, those involved in the prosecution case relaxed and began to enjoy a little banter between themselves and with the members of the press, but not Dr Greville. He sat quietly on the back bench, behind Mr Henriques, following the case intently. As a GP, he must have wondered how his colleague could have committed these cold, callous crimes, his close research giving little away of man himself.

Dr Grenville carefully deconstructed Dr Shipman's notes for each victim. Mrs Grundy was a fit, healthy woman and, even if she had been feeling tired and generally unwell as was claimed in her medical notes, still it would not explain her sudden, unexpected death. Dr Grenville told the court how he would have attended the scene of her death. It was very different to Shipman's cold, cursory efforts: 'I would ensure there were no suspicious circumstances, approach the body slowly, looking for signs of violence or a struggle. If there were none I would examine the body carefully to ensure death had occurred. Diagnosis of death is not always straightforward. If I found no pulse at the neck, I would look for more central point.' He went on, describing a procedure which would take some time, with even the possibility of resuscitation.

Mrs Grundy's case had taken more than a week. The following fourteen would be much quicker, taking just a couple of days each, but together they would last another four weeks. Each murdered woman had her own story, each with its own revelations. And even though they shared the same silent end, there were still shocking new details to be heard of those.

Bianka Pomfret's sad and sorry life was revealed to the jury at length. It was heartbreaking to hear, and seemed an unnecessary indignity for the 49-year-old

German. Her long history of manic depression, the breakdown of her marriage to Adrian Pomfret, the split between her and her son William at his wedding – all were spelt out to the court. By the time she died, on 10 December 1997, Mrs Pomfret was living alone with her dog and dreading Christmas. She knew it would be spent with other psychiatric patients and professional carers, rather than her family. In fact her body was discovered by her social worker Susan Adshead. And her post mortem was a further indignity, revealing not only that she had died of morphine poisoning, but also that she had breast implants.

Her ex-husband Adrian gave his evidence with a serious air and was well-spoken to begin with. A slight man with a neatly trimmed beard and small glasses, smartly dressed in fashionable clothes, he clearly took care of his image. Theirs had been an amicable break-up and he still visited her, he explained. A letter from Bianka read to the court later revealed she had despaired when he remarried. As he continued with his evidence, reaching the time of his ex-wife's death, the Hyde burr to Mr Pomfret's accent grew slightly stronger. She had complained of chest pains but, he insisted, they were the symptoms of a cold, not signs of a heart attack.

Bianka's son William, a big, gentle lad dressed in a smart navy suit, coped even better. It seemed he too had come to terms with the difficult relationship he had shared with his mother. He admitted easily that they had fallen out at his wedding but, he explained in a relaxed, easygoing manner, they had begun to patch things up. Still, he had not asked his mother to work at his corner shop, in the next street to hers, as she had hoped. And he and his wife Gaynor only invited her round for coffee when the children were in bed.

It was left to Bianka's psychiatrist Dr Alan Tate to give a more fitting account. Dr Tate, a tall, bearded academic with a high forehead and half-moon glasses, spoke candidly and thoughtfully about Bianka's mental illness and how her sudden death had worried him. He thought he had missed the signs of suicide, even though she had often sworn to him: 'I don't want to die.' Dr Tate, taking the court on a terrifying journey through severe mental illness, demonstrated her true courage and fighting spirit. His first note, from July 1986, stated Bianka had admitted herself to hospital. Adrian had told her, 'pull yourself together'. But she was not suicidal. Dr Tate explained: 'It's an expression people use to represent a state of distress but it doesn't always represent a determined intent to die or kill themselves. It's language people habitually use to express extreme distress.' Years of different medications, admissions to hospital, successes and failures followed, only just stopping short of electroconvulsive therapy. A letter from Dr Tate to Dr Shipman in November 1987 told of 'a rather gloomy cycle' where she would come out of an episode to feel the next one coming. By 1995, she was psychotic – her mental illness was producing physical feelings that she was 'under a layer', unable to reach out. A letter from Bianka in September 1997, after she had heard Adrian was to remarry and her first dog had died, read: 'Every morning during the past week or so I have felt I intended to kill myself. The only thing stopping me was my dog . . . This has become hard to resist . . .' Dr Tate saw her immediately: 'She said, "it takes all the joy away. I think negative, can't think positive. It makes me suicidal."' She reported that on crossing the motorway in Hyde to church she thought of jumping off the bridge. She further elaborated that with, "I don't really want to die."' It was obvious Dr

Tate had thought the world of his lonely, struggling patient.

Dr Tate was to do more than pay tribute to Bianka. He was to damn Dr Shipman with his meticulous notemaking of their telephone conversation following her death. Shipman, assuring him that it was not suicide but a heart attack, spoke of her being found with a 'thready pulse' by paramedics who tried to resuscitate her. He said he had previously taken an ECG reading but the result was 'insignificant'. In fact he had done no such thing and there was no last, weak pulse, no efforts to revive her, Bianka having been murdered by Shipman hours before.

Dr Grenville said without the five new computer entries on Bianka's medical records, creating a history of angina, there was no evidence of her suffering either that or heart disease, as was claimed on her death certificate. 'I would have telephoned the Coroner's office and said I was unable to give cause of death in a patient who was not seen at the time of her death,' he went on. 'The fact that no one had seen Mrs Pomfret in the moments before her death, and that she had a strong history of psychiatric problems as well as a strong history of angina, would lead me to conclude that it could have been suicide or a heart attack.'

Winnie Mellor's case was in complete contrast to Bianka's. Two days of evidence from her five children, parish priest Father Denis Maher and a selection of her many friends painted a rich and colourful picture of a happy, busy life.

Winnie's only son, RAF officer James Mellor, took the stand first. Smartly turned out in his navy, brass-buttoned blazer, he would have made his mother proud as he gave his evidence calmly and steadily. His military career meant he saw her less than his sisters did, but they spoke on the phone a lot, the last time being the night before she died: 'She was extremely excited. She told me she had just put her name down with local church to go to the Holy Land. She was a devout Catholic and it had been her lifelong ambition to go.' Two weeks earlier they had walked for two hours, to the top of Werneth Low, Hyde's infamous steep hill, and back. 'Not bad for 73,' he appealed to the jury. His sister Susan Duggan addressed the court confidently as she too told a similar story. 'She was my boys' favourite because she could still play football,' she recalled fondly, with only a trace of emotion as she thought of her bereaved sons. Winnie's youngest, Sheila Mellor, told the court that her mother had been quiet when they'd last met, but she put it down to her mother being a little depressed because of Sheila's plans to emigrate to Australia. Winnie's granddaughter Nina Adamski appeared in court sunburnt, fresh from working in Gran Canaria. She recalled Dr Shipman telephoning her mother Kathleen with the news. Kathleen recalled how a terrible game ensued: 'He basically made me guess my mother had died. I said, you mean my mother has died and he said, "I see you understand."'

Winnie's friends were called. Quietly spoken Josephine Barnes, who had known her twenty years and regularly attended St Paul's Church with her, put her best voice on as she described proud Winnie's busy lifestyle. 'She was always full of life, really she was,' she told the jury. 'She was always happy, you know.' Slipping into the present tense, she added with great pride: 'When she goes up Gee Cross she doesn't catch a bus, she walks.' Mary Ball, another friend of twenty years, spoke to her on the phone the morning she died: 'She was just her usual self.' And Margaret Nixon recalled how Winnie had bought some ham for her tea at her cold meat stall on Hyde Market. Mrs Nixon sighed as she explained: 'She always came on a Monday. She was great, jovial, happy.'

Winnie's next door neighbour Gloria Ellis was a simple girl, a young mum whose life revolved around her husband and children. She was an innocent, her round face smiling in awe of the wigs and gowns in court. But her evidence blew a massive hole in Shipman's defence. She had seen the GP go to Winnie's just a few hours before she was found dead. Later he called at her house asking for a spare key to next door as he could not rouse Winnie, who was slumped in a chair. 'You were here before, weren't you?' Gloria had asked. Shipman, shocked to discover that he had been spotted, ignored her. When she went on to ask him if Winnie had had a stroke, he snapped: 'You stupid girl.' His contempt was misplaced. Thanks to her dull, suburban routine, Gloria's evidence was clear and damning. She had been ironing, half watching daytime TV, half looking through her netted front window, when Shipman first called on Winnie. She knew the time exactly – three o'clock – because she was about to pick her son up from school. And she knew he had gone to Winnie's because she recognised the distinctive squeak of her neighbour's front gate. When Shipman called the second time, she had just cleared away the family's tea. Again she knew the exact time – six thirty – because this time she was washing the pots while the local news was on. Her confidence growing as she spoke, Gloria's recollections were unwavering in the face of cross- examination. And, she added impudently: 'I was surprised he was a doctor; I thought he was an insurance man.'

Still she admitted that she had been intimidated by Shipman, who had taken Winnie's fingers and flicked up her arm, saying, 'this lady's gone'. Gloria had left the scene as quickly as she could after that, saying she would telephone Winnie's family: 'I just stood in my house and I thought, I can't phone anybody. I went back then and I told him. I said, I can't find the numbers, but I hadn't looked.' In the dock Shipman looked down, his mouth open as if gasping, as she added: 'He was heartless.'

Winnie's good friend Father Maher said the same in a powerful performance that withstood a heavy cross-examination. Father Maher, a silver-haired Irishman with a strong, resonant accent, was used to speaking from the pulpit and made an excellent witness. He was nervous and emotional as he talked of losing Winnie, virtually spitting out her killer's name, but this made his evidence all the more striking. He had been called to Winnie's house to give her the last rites and to comfort her devastated daughters and granddaughter. He recalled how Shipman turned up and, brushing past him, coldly addressed the deeply shocked family about their mother's death. 'I got the impression that the person giving the news had little sympathy, was very uncaring, very insensitive, extremely insensitive,' the priest recalled, his face tight with anger. 'He followed this up immediately without pausing and questioned the family – have you got an undertaker? At this moment I felt very, very angry but I didn't feel it was a moment to show anger. At this moment I intervened – if you don't mind, doctor, I will help the family with that. But Dr Shipman didn't take any notice of what I said.' Father Maher's love for his parishioner and his need to guard the devastated 'girls' he knew so well was such that he took advantage of cool, confident junior defence counsel Ian Winter's tough questioning, using it to repeat and embellish his anger. 'I remember walking home and thinking, God, he didn't show much care or sympathy for that family,' he told the court. 'That was what I was thinking, I'm aware of feeling that.' Asked if he had lost his objectivity, Father Maher, angry but measured, retorted: 'I certainly have not lost my objectivity. I had great respect for Mrs Mellor, she was a woman of high standing, and I object very much you saying I have lost my objectivity, sir.'

Shipman's case was further eroded with another strong and emotional testimony from Derek Steele, boyfriend of the fourth victim, Joan Melia. Mr Steele was extremely nervous as he gave his evidence. He was a fiery man and his fury boiled close to the surface, having lost the woman he loved so dearly. But he was absolutely resolute and in the end won justice for his beloved Joan with a beautiful testimony that was both funny and sad. He recalled taking her to the surgery the day she died: 'She said, he said I've got pleurisy and pneumonia. I said, what the bloody . . . excuse my French . . . why aren't you going to hospital?' After that he had taken her home and left her to rest, promising to video a Deanna Durbin film for her. When he returned, she was dead. 'She was sat in the single chair I always sat in,' he said, fighting back tears. 'She never sat in that chair. I touched her and said, "Joan," and she was cold.'

Mr Steele maintained his composure but he took offence when Miss Davies cross-examined him about the time it had taken him to telephone Dr Shipman. As he became more muddled, his irritation showed. 'Without seeming to be facetious I didn't have a stopwatch on me at the time,' he said, embarrassed and fearful of losing the fight. 'It was a pretty damn good estimate.' Still he was triumphant when the Judge backed him up, as Miss Davies quizzed him about

Shipman's examination of Joan's body. Mr Steele had seen the GP carry out only a cursory check but added, 'he might have snatched a quick crafty touch at the neck'. Miss Davies seized her chance, causing him to become confused and defensive, vainly trying to explain himself. Eventually the Judge intervened: 'What he said, Miss Davies, was a crafty touch on her neck.' Mr Steele, relieved, caused a laugh: 'Exactly my Lord, I got it right.'

He was followed by his friend Raymond McKinley. He had seen Joan just a few hours before her death and when asked if she looked pale, he replied: 'Can't tell with all that make-up.'

Week three of the trial began with the extent of Shipman's true callousness finally being revealed. Ivy Lomas was the only one of the fifteen victims to die in the surgery. And when the police called in a bid to trace her family, Shipman cruelly made fun of her. Detective Sergeant Philip Reid, knowing how his words would shock the court, shifted uncomfortably in the witness box as he recalled: 'He was laughing. He said he considered her such a nuisance that he was having part of the seating area permanently reserved for Ivy with a plaque to the effect – seat permanently reserved for Ivy Lomas.'

Shipman had told DS Reid, who was then a constable, how he had left Ivy, who was grey and sweating, resting in his treatment room while he saw to other patients and found her dead fifteen minutes later. To the officer's amazement, he had not attempted resuscitation: 'He said she could have taken her last breath as he left the room.' Dr Grenville was also surprised that Shipman did not do more for Ivy: 'This was a medical emergency. I would have given my entire attention to this particular patient.' But that was no matter, for Ivy had not died of any natural cause but, like all the others, of morphine poisoning.

The court turned its attention to the sixth victim, Marie Quinn. Her son John, a thin, red-faced blond with small, round wire-framed glasses and a gentle, academic air about him, spoke quietly as he recalled being woken with the terrible news that his mother had died on 24 November 1997. He had moved to Japan in 1990 and, thanks to the time difference, got the dreadful telephone call in the middle of the night. 'I was coming home on 23 December that year and we were both looking forward to that, spending Christmas together,' he said shakily. John was confused as he recalled his conversation with Shipman some time later, having been woken from a deep unknowing sleep and left devastated. But he told the bizarre tale as best he could – how the GP had gone to his mother's because she rang him, suffering the symptoms of a stroke, and found her 'breathing her last'. As strange as the tale was, John had never imagined murder to be his mother's terrible fate. John was unable to look at Shipman, the man who had assured him that her death had been a blessing. 'He said mother could have led the life of an invalid, waiting a year or so for a second fatal stroke,' he recalled.

Marie's neighbour Celia Adshead had no such qualms. As she left the witness box, she gave Shipman a good, hard glare. Mrs Adshead looked grim as she took the stand, her red hair contrasting with her pale face as she stared straight ahead. John had asked her to go to his mother's house, let the undertaker Deborah Massey in and take care of the cat. She arrived at the same time as Dr Shipman and his wife Primrose – who was carrying a cat basket. 'The cat was having none of it,' Mrs Adshead recalled. 'I said, leave the cat, I will sort it out.'

Shipman grew more excited as the prosecution set out the case of Irene Turner. The police map of Mrs

Turner's street, showing where he had parked the day she died, was incorrect. The mistake was pointed out by her neighbour Sheila Ward, who had been set up by Shipman to find the body. Mrs Ward recalled how he had asked her to go to Mrs Turner's in five minutes to help her pack for hospital. She found her dead in bed: 'She looked beautiful.'

Dr Shipman made a great deal of the fact the prosecution's map was wrong, rolling his eyes and grinning wildly every time it was referred to. He revelled in the prosecution's embarrassment, even though it was a minor mistake which was easily rectified. Shipman saw the trial as a challenge – him against the judiciary. He constantly scribbled notes and at times like this, he truly believed he would beat his adversaries. Often he would lean forward, sharply tapping solicitor Ann Ball on the shoulder and shoving a sheaf of paper under the rail for her to pass to Miss Davies. His arrogance was fast approaching lunacy.

More domestic routines were illustrated. Shipman had thought he was being watched when he spotted Mrs Ward looking out of her window. But the grey-haired neighbour was only looking out for the milkman. She explained: 'Thursday is a ritual, two things always happen – my sister comes over and the milkman comes for his money. He always comes at 25 to 3, that's why I was standing at the window.' She was nervous in the box but her older, frailer sister Irene Groves fared better. She had seen Shipman, in a panic because he thought he had been watched by the two harmless old ladies, drive the wrong way to his surgery. Junior defence counsel Ian Winter seized on his chance when she got her street names wrong but Mrs Groves put him right: 'You have to go the other way to Mottram Road unless you go down the steps, and you can't do that in a car, can you?' As she left the box, she giggled: 'Sorry to cause a confusion.' DCI Williams, sitting with the other officers behind the witness box, in benches surrounded by more folders of evidence, smiled with admiration for the strength of yet another of Hyde's elderly.

Again Shipman had little sympathy for his victim's family – his main concern was to avoid a post mortem which would reveal the fatal dose of morphine he had given Mrs Turner. Her son-in-law Alfred Isherwood struggled to remember his conversation with the doctor, rocking in the witness box as he paused to collect his thoughts. Dr Shipman told him she had died of heart disease, with the blood rushing to her heart from collapsing veins. He assured them: 'She would have just fallen asleep and died.' And again, like Winnie Mellor, he said she had refused hospital treatment. This seemed odd, Mr Isherwood told the court: 'She took Dr Shipman's word. She thought he was a great doctor, she really liked Dr Shipman. She took every pill that he prescribed to her. Any medication, she did it, because she trusted her doctor.'

The case turned to Jean Lilley, a woman who, while not in the best of health, was not expected to die so soon either. The jury was visibly moved as her husband, big, burly lorry driver Albert Lilley, broke down in tears within minutes of taking the stand. Mr Justice Forbes, also moved by the harrowing scene, offered him a glass of water. 'I'm all right boss,' Mr Lilley replied in his Northern growl. 'No, I normally have tea.' He went on to describe how he lost his loving wife who, health problems aside, never let him lift a finger in the house and always had his tea on the table. 'I never do things like that, it's not my job, she wouldn't let me,' he said. Mr Lilley wept as he too described the guessing game Shipman played as he told him she was dead: 'He said, "I have been with your wife for quite a while now, trying to persuade her to go to hospital but she won't go." He said, "I was going to come home after surgery and have a word with you and your wife and I was too late." I said, "What do you mean too late?" He said, "You are not listening to me carefully." It just clicked. I said, "Has she died?" I couldn't say anymore. I put the phone down and came home.' Again this was not in Mrs Lilley's nature: 'She would have took advice, she had every faith in doctors, she would have taken his advice. She had only just come out for things, she had gone in on his say so.' Now he was lost without her: 'We could go anywhere, walk, and I got a wheelchair so I could push her round. We used to go Saturdays out to Blackpool, I'd push her around, we were happy.'

Her daughter Odette Wilson was six months pregnant when her mother died, yet remained calm, in contrast to her father. She recalled Dr Shipman kneeling by her side to break the news to her when she arrived at her mother's flat on the day of her death.

Mrs Lilley's friend and neighbour Elizabeth Hunter was almost as emotional as Mr Lilley had been. She and Jean had been very close, spending hours together every day, sharing the same housewives' routine – morning coffee in front of daytime TV and shopping. They had plenty in common and a favourite phrase, 'It's only me, missus.' Now Jean was gone. Mrs Hunter, her face stiff with nerves, her mouth set in a tense line, hobbled to the witness box with a walking stick. She recalled how she had gone to see if Jean was all right, having noticed that the doctor's car had been parked outside for some time. 'It's only me, missus,' she called. There was no reply. Jean was cold and lifeless, her lips blue. Mrs Hunter dashed outside to call the doctor back but he drove off, deaf to her cries. Mrs Hunter's desperate attempts to resuscitate her friend were to no avail, as were the attempts by the paramedics to do the same. When Dr Shipman returned, he told her: 'There's no point crying, she's already dead.' 'He didn't seem surprised,' she told the jury, shaking with nerves and anger. 'The way I felt at the time it was matter of fact, it didn't matter, it was irrelevant.' She was left with a last memory of their happy gossiping, just an hour before: 'I left her laughing.'

Muriel Grimshaw's daughter Anne Brown made seven statements to the police, one the day before she gave evidence to the court. Mrs Brown was determined to get all her facts right. Not only had Shipman murdered her mother, but he had stockpiled her dead husband's diamorphine as well. She was a nervous woman, refusing even to open the door when a reporter called months after Shipman was charged with the murders. She gave her evidence timidly but steadily, as if in a trance. But she remembered it exactly, to every little detail – the television echoing through the flat, the orange juice by the bedside where her mother lay dead. And Shipman saying: 'It was a nice way to go.'

The case turned to the six victims whose bodies were cremated. All the partners of the Brooke Surgery except Pamela Hillier were called to give evidence. All of them looked tired and seemed muted as they told how they had examined the body and, seeing no obvious signs of violence, signed the cremation certificate as required by law. The system had failed badly in these cases. And it was ironic that the only doctor who did a better job – snapping on rubber gloves, pulling the bodies out of their bags and rolling them about on the slab for a good, long look – was Dr Shipman.

The next witness, Marion Hadfield, seemed almost cheery as she took the stand. Mrs Hadfield had nearly caught the killer red-handed when he murdered her best friend Maria West on 6 March 1995. Unknown to him, she was stood in the kitchen next door, waiting for him to finish 'treating' her. He had looked shocked to see her but recovered his arrogant composure to flick up Mrs West's eyelid and say, 'This lady's gone.' Mrs Hadfield had just been having tea with Mrs West, who had been well enough to brew it and carry it. She was devastated. But, it seemed, Mrs Hadfield had bounced back from her close brush with death. Once helped up the steps into the witness box, the frail, old lady had a gentle smile on her lips. The whole court found some relief to see how well she had coped.

It seemed the old folk of Hyde were made of stern stuff. William Catlow, the dance partner of victim Lizzie Adams, gave a similarly heartening performance. Tiny and dapper in his clean, beige suit, his bright white hair cut into a sharp, straight fringe, he looked every inch a star of the dance floor. He and Lizzie must have made a striking couple. They had been partners for seventeen years and were so devoted to dancing, Mr Catlow proudly recalled, that Lizzie had turned up to one dance with her fractured leg in plaster. Another time they had danced at a fundraiser for Shipman's surgery. Mr Catlow told the court of the last time he held Lizzie. He had called to see her the day she died – and found Shipman looking at her eye-catching display cabinet of porcelain figurines and cut-glass crystal, as Lizzie slumped dying in the next room. A proud man, Mr Catlow maintained his composure as he described the heartbreaking scene: 'I just burst past him . . . I held her hand, she felt warm. I said, "I can feel her pulse." He said, "No, that's yours. I will cancel the ambulance."' The court was told there were no calls to the ambulance service from that address that day.

Shipman had known there was no point in calling one, let alone cancelling it: he had murdered Lizzie.

Lizzie's daughter Doreen Thorley, much younger than Mr Catlow and Mrs Hadfield but more nervous, struggled to maintain her composure in the witness box. Tall and slim, her dark eyes gleaming with tears, she shook as she gave her evidence and wept openly as she left the court. It was little wonder. Mrs Thorley recalled how she discovered her mother was dead, having been called to the house by Dr Shipman. She had collapsed and Shipman had held her up. Unable to look at him in the dock, she shuddered: 'He touched me.' The GP's sympathy was shortlived. As she knelt before her mother's body, dressed in the pink cardigan she had knitted for her, he said, 'You should visit old people more often, you know.' Mrs Thorley had felt a wave of guilt, even though she had taken her mother on an all-day shopping trip the day before.

Her sister Sonia Jones was a smart and strong witness, bigger built than Mrs Thorley and tanned, her hair permed and her make-up perfect. Yet she too had been persuaded by her mother's killer that a post mortem was not required. 'I was never happy with the death,' Mrs Jones told the court. When the story broke in the *Manchester Evening News*, she had checked with the ambulance service to see if Shipman had really dialled 999. But she was silenced before she got the chance to tell the jury the outcome, the evidence being inadmissable.

In week four, the bizarre story of Kathleen Laura Wagstaff's death was revealed. Gardener Andrew Hallas, dressed in a sweatshirt bearing his work's logo, his hands scrubbed but still stained with soil, was an ordinary, plain-speaking man. He told the jury of how he had seen Mrs Wagstaff the day she died, when she brought him a cup of tea and later going to the bank for her family's Christmas cheques. She seemed fine, he said quietly, still shocked at his part in such a case. Mrs Wagstaff's next-door neighbour, Margaret Walker, said the same. Mrs Walker, with the same grey helmet of hair as Primrose framing her plump face, wearing an old-fashioned embroidered blouse, looked kind and innocent and totally out of place in the courtroom. She had seen Mrs Wagstaff let Dr Shipman in, declaring, 'Fancy seeing you here.' An hour later she was dead.

There followed a terrible mix-up, as we have seen in the third chapter, as Dr Shipman told Mrs Wagstaff's daughter-in-law Angela that her mother had died. Receptionist Carol Chapman, a small, slight, unassuming blonde and a friend of the Wagstaff family, recalled how she told Dr Shipman of his mistake. 'He said, "Oh shit,"' she said quietly. Mrs Chapman was later to reveal how concerned she had been by Dr Shipman's behaviour. When her employer told her Maureen Ward had died, she recalled: 'I felt angry. I said, "She was alright yesterday."' And when he changed his story about how he came across Miss Ward's body, she told the rest of the staff, 'That's not what he told me.' Standing in the witness box, she willingly gave evidence against him, having found that the unthinkable – that a doctor could murder the old ladies in his care – was true.

The next witness was the only son of Norah Nuttall, John, better known by his middle name Anthony. He was a big man, in his 40s, but boyish, with dark brown eyes and a turned-up nose beneath his balding head and a sad look as he answered Mr Henriques like a well-behaved schoolboy. He recalled how he had gone to feed some ponies in a nearby field on the day his mother died. He was only away for twenty minutes but by then it was too late. Anthony found Dr Shipman leaving the house he shared with his mother, who had been to get a cough bottle from the surgery only that morning. 'It was a shock really,' he recalled slowly. 'I asked him what was wrong. He said, "Your mother's not so well. I have rung an ambulance for her." I ran in and she was sat in the front room. She looked like she was asleep in the chair. I took her by the hands and shook her, saying, "Mum, Mum". She was slumped in the chair. He came and stood at the side of her, I was knelt down in front of her on my knees, I had both her hands in my hands. I said, "Don't tell me." He said, "It looks like she has taken a turn for the worse." I said, "Can you do anything for her?" He touched her neck and said, "I'm sorry, she has gone." Then he opened her eyelid.' Anthony sounded like a lost boy as he told his tale. When junior defence counsel Ian Winter asked if his mother had problems with her health and weight, he replied: 'Not a very lot.'

Mrs Oldham had her own tale to tell. It was a shock to see that Norah's sister, tiny and slim with dark, permed hair, looked so different from Norah. And it was an even bigger shock to hear how she visited the surgery the day after Norah died for Dr Shipman to take her through her sister's medical records – in reception. 'He turned to the two females behind the reception and said, "I knew it would happen, I told you it would happen,"' she recalled. Dr Shipman said Norah had called the surgery because she felt ill and they paged him while he was visiting nearby Grange Road. But itemised billing showed that she'd made no such call. He was later to change his story, making his situation even worse.

Dr Grenville said there were no signs that Norah had died of left ventricular failure, as claimed on her death certificate: 'I have never seen a patient dying from this without frothing at the nose. It's a distressing mode of dying; the patient often struggles.'

The trial turned to the case of Pamela Hillier, a fit and healthy woman who had been moving furniture only days before her death. The jury was told how Shipman intimidated Mrs Hillier's family, both at the discovery of her body and on the following day, when they tried to demand a post mortem.

Mrs Hillier's daughter Jacqueline Gee clutched a handkerchief as she gave her evidence, rubbing her nose and placing her hand to her chest as she nervously recalled her last hours with her mother. They were close, talking and meeting up almost every day to walk their dogs or have a coffee and a chat. Mrs Hillier would have lunch with Jacqueline, her husband Martin and their two young daughters every Sunday. That week they were facing the first anniversary of the death of Mrs Hillier's husband and Jacqueline's father Cyril. 'We were all feeling a little bit sad,' Jacqueline recalled. No doubt that is why, when told that her mother had died too, she went to pieces. Jacqueline was so distressed that the paramedics who had been called to attend her mother stayed. Ambulanceman Stephen Morris said: 'We thought she might be our next patient.' But Shipman showed no such sensitivity. He had been abrupt as he answered her questions, shocking Mrs Hillier's neighbour Peter Ellwood and Jacqueline's husband Martin, who had arrived later. 'She was asking very sensible questions, and to my mind Dr Shipman was extremely unhelpful and uncaring for a daughter who had just lost her mother and a patient he had looked after for ten to twelve years,' Martin told the court, speaking curtly in a bid to control his anger. 'I will never forget Dr Shipman's words, "Let's put it down to a stroke." Now later on I realise it was a very imprecise way for a doctor to speak.'

Mr Ellwood was also angered by Shipman's treatment of Jacqueline. And he had heard the GP snap at a paramedic who suggested they call the police, 'I don't think there is any need to do that.'

Shipman's battle to quash any further enquiries had continued the following day, the court heard, when Jacqueline and her brother Keith Hillier visited him at his surgery. The devastated family were desperate to know what had killed their fit, healthy mother. But Shipman made the most of their distress, confusing and bullying them. No post mortem was ever carried out. Keith remembered how he had been confused by the GP: 'He said mum did have high blood pressure – not high enough to give him concern, but enough to kill her. We were going round in circles. I'm not a medical man.' Keith had suggested a post mortem: 'I was not happy.' But Shipman had other ideas. 'He said what an unpleasant thing to happen, what an unpleasant thing to happen to put my mum through,' he recalled. 'Reluctantly I did accept it. We did debate it and discuss the thing we would be putting mum through and it was something we really didn't relish the thought of. At the end of the day I was in shock and I was conscious of the pain my sister was going through.'

His sister was left feeling worse than ever. She looked terribly thin, her brown eyes small and tired, as she told the court: 'I can remember coming out and feeling guilty. He seemed to say mum had been poorly and we should have expected it really, that she might have died at any time and we weren't aware of this at all.'

The court was then told of Dr Shipman's frenzy of activity as he amended Mrs Hillier's medical records on the afternoon of her death, two hours before her body was found. He had described new symptoms that could have been the warnings of a stroke, such as 'headaches, feels unwell' for 6 January 1998. He also recorded raised blood pressure readings for four days and even a month before, complex figures that would not have been possible to recall days later. It was 160/100 on 6 January 1998. Of course Shipman had expected the records to be read for the days he purported the readings had been taken, not expecting the day he really created the files to be discovered. He was to give a ridiculous explanation of Mrs Hillier's detailed, backdated records later as part of his defence.

Dr Grenville agreed – Mrs Hillier had been very fit and her blood pressure extremely well controlled, discounting the newly created records. He could not imagine anyone remembering such readings 28 days after taking them.

The case turned to its final victim, Maureen Ward. She had successfully fought off cancer, a train of consultants and specialists told the court. Yet Shipman had certified secondary cancer in the brain and breast cancer as the cause of her death, on 18 February 1998.

Again there was a line of friends to tell Miss Ward's story, of how well she had been even on the day of her death. Her best friend Christine Whitworth told the court how Maureen had rung her the night before her death with some exciting news. Miss Ward's sense of fun was revealed as Mrs Whitworth explained that Maureen would not tell her until their Friday lunch date. It was a date they would not keep, thanks to Dr Shipman. Most moving was the evidence of Mary France, Maureen's elderly neighbour at the Ogden Court sheltered housing complex and her companion for the Carribean cruise she was never to take. Another frail old lady, all dressed up in a red jacket, pink jumper and scarf, innocent of the protocol of the Court. But she was unfazed by the formalities, asking the Clerk of the Court, 'Can I sit down?' and, 'Will you speak up, love?' as she gave the oath. Mrs France gave her evidence clearly and concisely but paused at the end of each answer as if wondering if she should go on. When solemn Mr Henriques asked her how Maureen had been on the morning of her death, she replied as if to an old friend on Hyde Market: 'Oooooh, smashing!' Then she described waiting for her friend to return for their afternoon 'brew', leaving the jury with yet another heartbreaking image. 'I put the kettle on,' she said, 'but she never came.'

Shipman was further damned by the evidence of Ogden Court's warden, Maureen's good friend Christine Simpson. Smartly dressed but shaking, Mrs Simpson told the court how Shipman had asked her to go with him to Maureen's first floor flat, as he had found her dead. 'I was very, very surprised, very shocked,' she recalled. 'I said I couldn't believe it. He said, "Well she had a brain tumour, you know."' Dr Grenville said a woman killed by a brain tumour would not have been carrying a big, black bin liner of washing to the laundrette and shopping for holiday outfits in Hyde, as Maureen had been.

It was still only the fifth of the prosecution's six weeks of evidence when the expert witnesses were called were called to consolidate the prosecution's case. With this came another thick volume of evidence. Mr Justice Forbes turned to the carousel of folders by his left elbow as the prosecution and defence teams, the jury and Shipman himself turned to their piles of paperwork. Mrs Grundy's daughter Angela Woodruff, who had returned to the public gallery for this latest evidence, also turned to her notebook.

First came morphine specialist Professor Henry McQuay. He was short and sturdy with a gentle manner, far from an aloof academic, and an ideal person to explain the effects of the painkilling opiate. His impressive qualifications and his post at Oxford University – an honorary consultant at the pain relief unit – were listed to the jury before he took them for a brief lesson. Professor McQuay explained how morphine was the standard strong painkiller into which diamorphine converted within a minute of ingestion. He added that diamorphine, used for terminal cancer sufferers, was twice as strong as morphine, used for accident victims. People could 'get good things from it,' he explained, as long as they were in great pain. But if you were not in need of it or you took more than you required, it would slow your breathing and possibly kill you. He described the molecules making their way along the 'A roads and B roads' of the human circulatory system to special receptors of the brain. If there was no pain to combat, the brain would slow the breathing instead. Professor McQuay said the most morphine he had ever given to a patient was seven milligrammes over a period of thirty minutes to a man who had broken his leg in an accident. 'I gave that with a lot of trepidation,' he added gravely.

Professor McQuay and his inquisitor, junior prosecuting counsel Mr Wright, made a good team. Together they made dry-as-dust medical evidence quite entertaining. 'What would be the effect of morphine on the breathing of a healthy individual?' Mr Wright asked, to drive home the fact that this drug could not be prescribed by accident. 'Can I use you as a guinea pig?' Prof McQuay enquired, to the amusement of everyone in court, except Dr Shipman. Mr Wright, enjoying the moment, said: 'Of course.' The comedy quickly passed as the professor described a chilling scene: 'We would expect to see slowing of your breathing within two minutes. By five minutes your breathing would be very slow indeed, two to three breaths per minute would be you normal rate ... You would appear to be asleep. Your lips and fingers might well be blue and your toes might have a blue tinge to them. If your brain can't get any oxygen because your breathing has stopped, you would die.' The court was silent.

Prof McQuay was followed by Julie Evans, the toxicologist who had tested samples of body tissue from the nine exhumed victims. Mrs Evans, heavily pregnant and wearing a padded velvet Alice band dotted with pearls, looked more like a housewife than a scientist. But as she answered her questions in an honest and professional manner, any such notion was roundly dismissed. She explained how she had taken samples from deep inside the thigh muscle, where decomposition was last to have an effect, and liquidised it into a 'soup' to be tested for various drugs, including morphine. She had also, where possible, taken samples from the liver. All nine women had fatal levels of morphine in their bodies, according to her analyses. Mrs Grundy, who had been buried for 38 days, the shortest amount of time, had 1 mg of morphine per gram of thigh muscle and between 4.5 and 4.8 mg per gram of liver tissue. She would have had to drink one litre of kaolin and morphine to get such a level, Mrs Evans added. The other victims followed. Bianka Pomfret had 0.6 mg of morphine per gram of thigh muscle and 0.8 mg of morphine per gram of liver tissue. Winnie Mellor had 0.7 to 0.9 mg in her thigh and 0.8 mg in her liver. Joan Melia had 0.7 to 0.9 mg in her thigh too and 4.5 to 5.2 mg in her liver. The remaining five victims could only give thigh muscle samples. Ivy

Lomas had 0.9 mg and Marie Quinn 0.3 to 0.4 mg. Irene Turner, who had been buried the longest at two years and four months, or 852 days, had the highest amount of morphine, 1.4 to 1.6 mg. Jean Lilley had 0.4 to 0.5 mg and Muriel Grimshaw 0.3 to 0.4 mg.

Defence counsel Miss Davies again did her best to discredit such damning evidence, determined to help her client. 'As a scientist you have been breaking pretty new ground in this analysis?' she asked Mrs Evans. 'Yes,' she replied. Miss Davies continued in the same vein – since Mrs Evans's work could only be compared to anecdotal studies, her findings did not prove how the drug was ingested. 'You cannot say as a scientist it reflects the level of the drug at the time of death,' she said. 'That is correct,' Mrs Evans replied reluctantly. 'Although you found the level, you can't say if it was one dose or more than one dose,' she went on. 'I can't say,' Mrs Evans admitted. It was no matter. For all Miss Davies's work, it was a dry, complex cross-examination, which did not seem to worry the jury unduly. They could think of no other reason for the morphine to be there than Dr Shipman, the medical man who knew how to administer the drug and had been with every woman at or near the time of her death.

Dr Karch Steven followed. A small, red-haired American with round, wire-framed glasses and a bright yellow tie contrasting with his blue shirt and navy blazer, Dr Steven was as striking as his unusual name. So was his long list of qualifications and posts at Stamford University, the Kaiser Foundation and the World Health Organisation. His evidence was also stunning. Dr Steven explained how tests on the women's hair showed they were 'morphine naïve' – that is, not regular users of the drug. Such analysis techniques were new and very important, he said. They had only been published in the *Lancet* a year earlier. It stunned the courtroom.

Week five was cut short, thanks to a bomb scare on the morning of Friday, 12 November. The court was adjourned with no evidence heard.

Week six began with embarrassment for the prosecution, as it was revealed morphine found in Shipman's house had lain unnoticed in the police exhibits store for a year. DC Dave O'Brien, a big, balding, middle-aged officer, had been the exhibits manager. He explained how the ampoules of the drug were not tested because they were in a box labelled for another drug, in which the police were not interested. It was the only physical evidence that Shipman had stockpiled his lethal doses.

The case picked up again as it turned to the police interviews with Dr Shipman. DS John Walker, a serious, thin-faced officer, played out his role while Mr Wright read Shipman's answers from the transcript of their interview. The GP's arrogance was re-enacted for the jury, by now looking with undisguised mistrust at the man in the dock. Shipman's use of medical terminology, his references to generic and trade names for drugs which gave no clue as to their use, and his irritating attempts to wrongfoot his inquisitor – 'that's two questions, which one do you want me to answer first?' – were defensive tactics first used in these interviews. They were seen again, when he was cross-examined by Mr Henriques – but this time they were to be altogether less successful.

Finally the witnesses to volume eight, the evidence which showed how Shipman had stockpiled the deadly drug, were called. Theirs was a sad and sorry part to play. Each recounted a terrible tale of terminal illness followed by a long and painful death. Christine

Harrison's husband Keith was only 38 when he died of cancer in June 1996. Mrs Harrison shook as she recreated the scene of his early death, in bed, with her by his side. District nurse Barbara Sutherland and community nurse Diane Fleet followed with their memories of that time, almost as upset as Christine, affected more than usual by the death of such a young man. Now they were devastated that there was an even more sinister result of his death – the use of his painkiller to murder other patients. Mrs Harrison quietly explained how Dr Shipman had come to the house an hour after Keith had died. He had nothing in his hand, there were no drugs with him, she insisted. Yet, records showed, Shipman had prescribed two lots of 500 mg of diamorphine to him that day. The two nurses agreed and said that they had destroyed the drugs left from a previous prescription, but none for one that day. Suggestions by junior defence counsel Ian Winter that they were too upset to remember that day properly only served to increase the jurors' sympathy for the witnesses.

More widows followed – Irene Henshall, who had lost her husband John, and Olwyn Neal, who had lost her husband Peter. And more nurses including, once again, Marion Gilchrist. She had broken down the last time she took the stand but she this time she was stronger. She was still upset, however, her voice shaking as she recalled how Dr Shipman had confused her as he filled in a drugs record card for a patient. There was some diamorphine missing and when she queried it with him, he said he had borrowed some from a friend because the patient had run out of it at the weekend. 'Dr Shipman kept going over the totals,' she said. 'I was trying to make out what they were but I still couldn't understand it.'

Volume eight continued with more patients of Dr Shipman, this time those who had been prescribed diamorphine by him for no good reason. Lillian Ibbotson, his patient for twenty years, was prescribed 30 mg of diamorphine in April 1993. But she had no recollection of it and no need. The only pain she had ever had was a minor problem with her elbows and a duodenal ulcer, neither of which required the strong painkiller.

The case for the prosecution was closed after six weeks, 26 days, dozens of statements, hundreds of exhibits and 120 'live' witnesses.

The contrast with Shipman's defence could not have been starker. There was no opening address, and nor could there be, as Miss Davies would have had to refer only to fact. There were few facts which would do Shipman any favours. The defence barrister simply stood up smartly and briskly announced: 'I call Dr Harold Frederick Shipman.'

7 The Case for the Defence

Doctor Shipman walked from the dock to the witness box with every eye in the courtroom on him. He looked small but unbowed between the two burly guards; his back straight and his movements precise as he swung sharply out of the dock. He took twelve steps, one for every juror, to walk from his seat facing Mr Justice Forbes to the stand facing the jury. It was Thursday 25 November, day 26 of the trial.

The courtroom was silent as Dr Shipman took the oath and began his defence. The atmosphere was bristling with tension, but the press, public and jury were denied any drama. Miss Davies was a skilled barrister and knew that emotionally charged scenes would do her client no good.

Carefully, she began to tell the simple tale of an ordinary family doctor. The tension that had taken hold of the courtroom gradually subsided as she began with the most innocent of images – how he was born in Nottingham on 14 January 1946 – then briefly described his career. Naturally, there was no mention of Todmorden. She also explained how he had married Primrose, his loyal wife who was sitting in the public gallery, and produced four children. Miss Davies painted a most unthreatening picture.

Dr Shipman played his part well too, the picture of the small town GP who was shocked to be standing before a jury, charged with the murder of his patients. In a pale-brown suit, white shirt and traditional red-and-green striped tie, blinking behind his spectacles, he looked like a faded, homely chemistry teacher. From his appearance, he should have been wiping the froth from half a pint of real ale off his beard in the snug of his local pub, rather than facing a murder trial. He answered Miss Davies's gentle questioning quietly but firmly. With his hands on the top of the witness box and little nods of his head, he gave off a mixture of worry at his predicament and pride in his achievements. At first he spoke with a gravelly voice and apologised to the jury, at the same time looking for their sympathy: 'I'm sorry. I am slurring my words with the tablets I'm on.' But as the tablets, which he had been prescribed for stress, wore off through the afternoon, he grew stronger. He spoke with little accent, a slight Midlands trace giving him the flat voice of authority he used to his patients.

As the defence case progressed, Dr Shipman developed a Northern burr to his voice and added a few colloquialisms to his speech. He described Marie Quinn as having 'dizzy dos', hardly a professional term. This was in stark contrast to his usual register – most of the time he spoke arrogantly in terms of his patients, using unnecessarily highbrow language. It seemed that Dr Shipman was trying to boost his small-town GP image with the warm accent of a local and his use of grass-roots phrases, in an effort to create a more innocent aura. But his act, an untidy patchwork of intelligence and arrogance set against simplicity and innocence, failed to convince the jury.

Miss Davies turned to the crucial point – Dr Shipman's time in Hyde. The mundane details of an ordinary doctor's life would stand the defence in good stead: into the surgery at 8.30 a.m., working through his appointments before seeing patients in the open surgery, sometimes not even stopping for a cup of coffee. After lunch he would make his home visits and perhaps make a few 'cold calls' before returning to his practice to do a little 'housekeeping', such as organising training courses for his staff and discussing matters with practice manager Alison Massey. After that he would see more patients, both with appointments and at yet another open surgery. In the evenings he was on call, when his duties included seeing the relatives of dead patients.

Miss Davies continued to build a fine picture. When Dr Shipman gave up his high rank in St John Ambulance in August 1988, it was to devote more time to his work as a GP. When he opened his own single-handed practice in August 1992, it was to give his patients the best of the new fundholding type of practice. He was hardworking and innovative. His patient list grew from 2,300 to 3,100 in six years. As the jury were taken a photo-album tour of 21 Market Street, Dr Shipman proudly explained how he had spent months renovating the old Provincial insurance building to make rooms for the practice manager, the practice nurse, the midwives – and the ECG machine.

Immediately the jury would have been reminded of Ivy Lomas's death: how she had been led to the treatment room, supposedly to use the ECG machine, never to return. However the defence team attempted to portray Dr Shipman as a devoted family doctor who had been wrongly accused, they were bound to fail. The facts would damn him at every turn.

And not only the facts – by taking the stand Dr Shipman would 'hang' himself. He put in a fair performance as the good doctor, but he could not go five minutes on the stand without revealing his true arrogance. Miss Davies's attempts to portray her client as an innovator, determined to give his patients the best service when he left the Donneybrook Group Practice to go single-handed, were thwarted by Shipman's own arrogant explanation.

'It was at the time of fundholding, and the other doctors were not as committed as I was to make fundholding work,' he told the court.

Dr Shipman seemed not to notice the jurors' cold expressions, and such condescending asides were to continue. A smoker with heart disease, such as Bianka Pomfret, he said, 'is silly and is looking to die'. Both Mrs Pomfret and Ivy Lomas 'did not give a good history' of health, he added, using unnecessarily florid language. These were not the words of a devoted doctor, but rather an arrogant power addict; a man vainly trying to discredit the testimonies of 120 bereaved relatives and friends, the people of Hyde who had lined up to seek justice for his victims. His plea of innocence seemed doomed from the outset.

That first afternoon the case turned to Kathleen Grundy. Almost immediately Dr Shipman's lies and excuses began to grate on the court onlookers.

Dr Shipman was standing by his assertion that tireless charity worker Mrs Grundy was a drug abuser. 'Abuse of drugs in the elderly is becoming recognised,' he stated knowingly. 'I couldn't offer her any medication and let the matter go.' He was discussing a note that referred to 12 October 1996 when there was no appointment for her in the surgery book. Miss Davies asked him to explain. 'As GP I occasionally see people who just want a word,' he said. Mrs Grundy's daughter, Angela Woodruff, watching from the public gallery, furiously scribbled notes on a big pad. Dr

Shipman went on. There was another note for 15 July 1997, again suggesting that he suspected Mrs Grundy had a drug problem, and again there was no appointment in the book. 'It looks like I had just taken her into my room,' Dr Shipman said dismissively. He added: 'I distinctly remember saying, "Are you taking anything that could make the IBS [irritable bowel syndrome] worse, or interfere with peppermint oil?" And she said, "No."' He had written the note on the paper records and not on the computer because, he said, 'If she had seen this questioning attitude she might never have admitted anything.' By now Dr Shipman was unstoppable. He said the note for 26 November 1997, when he was 50 miles away in York, had been made the following Sunday at his home and backdated to the wrong day. 'I took the notes home to consider the matter and how to progress with it,' he insisted. 'This entry was made with a lot of thought and recollection ... I was just suspicious that she was abusing a drug. It had to be an opiate, so codeine, pethidine, perhaps morphine.'

Miss Davies turned to the will. Dr Shipman recalled 9 June 1998, the day he had asked two patients to witness Mrs Grundy's signature. He had assumed that the folded paper she brought to him was a will with £200, or thereabouts, bequeathed to his surgery appeal, which was why he had not signed it. But he *had* touched the document, he added, firstly when he pushed it back at her, and then when he had picked it up and given it to her after the departure of the witnesses.

With that, Dr Shipman began his assertion that Mrs Grundy was fading. That day he had also taken a blood sample. 'She just didn't look well,' he insisted, his face creasing with concern. 'Normally when she came in she was bright and talkative. She didn't come in like that.

She was very much quieter and didn't talk about my family or her family, which was very peculiar. I thought she looked old – not ill, old. Going downhill.'

When he saw her again at her home on the morning of 24 June, she looked even worse. He took five blood samples using one needle and five syringes, hoping to find out what was wrong. Dr Shipman sighed as he recalled: 'She looked older than I had ever seen her. Her face was more crinkled than it normally was, and she appeared slow in her movements. Just going up the two steps to the room, I thought she would have strode over the steps, miss one step out, but she didn't.'

The blood samples he took that day disappeared. Dr Shipman had claimed that they were lost on the way to hospital, where they were to be tested, but the prosecution had shown that this had never happened to any other samples in his area. Now he suddenly remembered: he had left them under a pile of paperwork and, later that day, realising they were too old to be tested, had thrown them away. Dr Shipman recalled going to Mrs Grundy's cottage after her body had been found and speaking with her daughter, Mrs Woodruff. He believed that he was right to put old age as the cause of death, having seen her recent decline – even though she had died of morphine poisoning.

Finally Miss Davies put it to him: 'You are charged that, between 8 June 1998 and 24 June 1998, you made a document purporting to be the will of Kathleen Grundy, to induce Brian Burgess, at Hamilton Ward, to accept it as genuine. Did you do that?'

Dr Shipman, now in his stride, replied firmly: 'Absolutely not.'

Miss Davies asked, 'Did you on the morning of 24 June 1998 administer morphine or diamorphine to Kathleen Grundy?'

Dr Shipman, was firm again: 'I did not.'

Miss Davies went on. 'Did you, on the morning of 24 June 1998, murder Kathleen Grundy?'

'No, I didn't,' Dr Shipman insisted.

At the end of his first day giving evidence, Dr Shipman looked tired, almost too weak to leave the witness box. As usual he left the dock without looking at Primrose, who was sitting loyally in the public gallery. She was to turn up every single day and, at first, almost seemed to enjoy the day out. Whatever turn the proceedings took, she was smiling softly, as if she thought the case was going well for her husband. But when the summing-up began, Primrose grew more downcast.

As Dr Shipman walked down the steps from the dock to the cells after his first day giving evidence, his legs buckled under him and he almost collapsed. It was only a slight faint, but enough to convince Miss Davies that he would need more breaks. That was true, especially when it came to certain cases such as those of Ivy Lomas and Laura Kathleen Wagstaff. Dr Shipman would spend a total of twelve days in the witness box. At times he seemed to enjoy his moment in the spotlight, even his eight-day stretch under tough cross-examination by Mr Henriques. He believed, however misguidedly, that he was making a great success of sparring with one of the country's top barristers. But at other times, Dr Shipman struggled with the burden, breaking down after Miss Davies quizzed him about the death of Mrs Wagstaff. He had falsely claimed on Mrs Wagstaff's cremation form that her neighbour was present when she died. His excuse was blurted out and damned him. 'I don't think I can give you a sensible answer. This was one of the few times I was possibly more upset than the relatives.'

With that, Dr Shipman sank to his seat, his head down, so that only his bald spot was visible over the top of the witness box. His scalp reddened as he shook, crying into his hands, whispering, 'sorry' as the jury were led out. In the public gallery Primrose leaned forward, her hand on the rail, looking miserably and helplessly over at her husband. Angela Woodruff stared too, her face tight with anger. The court was silent. After a few minutes of silence Dr Shipman was led out of the witness box and down to the cells to recover.

But, on the second day of his evidence, when the case turned to Mrs Pomfret, Dr Shipman was still fresh for the battle. He was again the patronising family doctor who knew best. This had been easy with a mentally ill, vulnerable patient such as Mrs Pomfret. Dr Shipman, aware that the computer audit trail had revealed his tampering with her records, claimed that she had only told him of her angina attacks on the day she died. That was why he had backdated her records, to indicate the dates of the attacks. He was to claim this 'grand disclosure', as Mr Henriques later put it, for three more patients – Winnie Mellor, Pamela Hillier, and Maureen Ward.

It was an implausible new assertion, but Dr Shipman was confident. 'I asked what happened when she walked her dog,' he recalled. 'She said, "He runs, I walk." She recognised that there was limitation on her physical activity. The pain lasted from two to three minutes. She said, "If I stand still and have a cigarette, it goes away."' Enjoying his own performance as the caring GP, he continued: 'I was told she smoked forty plus a day. Although she spoke English very well, she was a very poor historian in English . . . I said, "Have you ever had pain before today?" and Mrs Pomfret, being Mrs Pomfret, said, "Yes, many times," but I think there were only three episodes. She was a fairly regular visitor – she wasn't one to hide problems – but she had her chest pains ... With a little struggle we managed to have a past history of chest pain established.' Dr Shipman said he diagnosed angina, planned to do an ECG and offered her medication, all to no avail. 'She pointed to the multiplicity of bottles on the table and said, "I'm taking a lot of tablets and I'm not taking any more,"' he recalled, again using the florid language he favoured, both as a local doctor and now as court combatant.

Dr Shipman was well into his stride by now, as they turned to his computer entries. Smiling, he asked Miss Davies, 'Would you like me to translate?' Then he turned to the court and told the jury how he was hurt by Mrs Pomfret's silence about her chest pains: 'I was very upset that she had seen me on the 8th and hadn't let me know, because we could have started something, sorted it out, two days prior. It was the only reason to visit her at home, which was difficult to understand when she was actually sat in front of me at the surgery.'

Dr Shipman clearly felt at the height of his persuasive powers. He explained that he had put the entries into Mrs Pomfret's computerised medical history on certain dates to show the progression of her illness. Moreover, if he wanted to collate all the female patients aged 40 to 50 who had angina, the computer could do this for him correctly only if the dates of her attacks were correct.

He continued, proudly, with a little more background on his practice, the one he had created and built up himself so successfully. 'Fifty-year-old men are very difficult to get into the surgery,' he said, almost beaming at the memory. 'We sent them a birthday card saying, do you want another forty years of life? So, very proactive.'

Again Dr Shipman discussed being called to Mrs Pomfret's home after her body had been found, a cup of coffee by her side, a cigarette burned out in the ashtray. 'She had obviously made no effort to get to the telephone or anything,' he surmised. 'Whatever happened was clearly rapid.' And, again, he firmly denied administering morphine to her or killing her.

The case moved on to Winifred Mellor. Dr Shipman, denying that he had visited Mrs Mellor on the day of her death as was claimed by her neighbour Gloria Ellis, again showed his true, cold colours. He said that Mrs Mellor had visited him, unofficially. 'I said, "It will have to be quick." She would have made an appointment but I was stood there at the reception desk and she took charge,' he grumbled. 'She cornered me.'

Again he told of a grand disclosure by her – that she had been suffering from angina. 'I think she was frightened that she was going down the same pathway as her husband,' he said, recalling how Mrs Mellor had nursed Sid Mellor in his last months.

Dr Shipman also denied calling Mrs Ellis a stupid girl. 'I would hope I didn't say that,' he said, putting on a professional demeanour. 'I may have made a comment like, "you are being silly."' He denied telling her family he had visited her at 3 p.m., and he dismissed his callous treatment of Mrs Mellor's grieving daughters as best he could: 'I spoke to them as I would speak to anyone who had a dear one die. I thought I was considerate and thought I gave them a long time to ask questions. They were extremely upset and I was glad I had made the decision to go back, and not have them come into the surgery.'

Another break was followed by the case of Joan Melia. Dr Shipman now seemed strangely lively as he examined the photographs of Mrs Melia's flat, pointing out where her body had been. Scratching his head as he flipped through the heavy folder of evidence, he talked as though he were an expert witness, very much accustomed to the witness box: 'If you look at pic 22, she was sat in the chair next to a cup of tea or coffee on the right-hand side. In fact I have just looked at pic 23 – that was where she was, sat in that brown chair.' Again the doctor gave the court the benefit of his wisdom as he explained the cause of her death, pneumonia. 'A small percentage of elderly people with lobar pneumonia die very quickly but a large percentage survive ... I diagnosed lobar pneumonia which is localised pneumonia. I said the majority survive it – less than 5 per cent die. I had no way of picking that up [i.e. that she was at risk], so the fact that I had sent her home was rational. I had said if she was worse to send for me.'

Still, it had been another heavy day for Dr Shipman. As the trial was adjourned early for the weekend, before moving on to the damning case of Ivy Lomas, he rubbed his eyes. The medication which caused him to slur his words but kept him calm under pressure was beginning to wear off. He had quickly gone from lively to shattered. As the press corps gathered their belongings from their annexe, they discussed when, rather than if, he would collapse. They decided that it would be better for him if he fainted before he was cross-examined or it would look like a sign of guilt.

Week eight started with Dr Shipman giving his evidence about the death of Ivy Lomas, the only one of the fifteen victims, for which Shipman was being tried, to die in the surgery. In fact, at least four patients had died there. This was an astonishing figure. Dr Shipman's former colleague from Todmorden, Dr John Dacre, said that only one patient had ever died in his surgery in twenty years, and that this was the case for most, if not all, GPs – far from four in six years, as at 21 Market Street.

Dr Shipman said that Mrs Lomas had collapsed as she climbed on to the examination bed and that he had tried to resuscitate her, all alone, for fifteen minutes. As usual he had thought he was right. As a first-aid lecturer, he explained, 'I'm committed to carrying it out better than the average person ... It seemed the most reasonable action to take.' But then there was a sudden admission of fallibility: 'In hindsight it may have been better to call for an ambulance immediately and allow them to take over.'

Still, he denied making fun of Mrs Lomas, answering Miss Davies's questions quite sniffily. 'Did you tell PC Reid you considered her a nuisance?' she asked.

Dr Shipman replied, 'Far from it.'

Miss Davies went on. 'Was there any conversation about mounting a plaque over her seat saying that it was permanently reserved for her?'

Dr Shipman explained, 'Yes. I have a small number of extremely regular attenders who aren't curable, and you have to accept that they are in surgery on a regular basis. With some of them I joked that perhaps we should put plaque above their seat, in this case for Ivy Lomas. In no way was it said except in a friendly jocular manner.'

Again Dr Shipman firmly denied murdering the 63-year-old widow. It would not be so easy to dismiss the case under a robust cross-examination by Mr Henriques, however, as he clearly demonstrated the GP's proximity to her within minutes of her death from morphine poisoning, an opiate which when injected intravenously takes five minutes to kill.

When the case turned to Marie Quinn, Dr Shipman made a shocking admission – he found her 'breathing her last' and left her to die. He seemed to think himself quite courageous to make such a decision. He told the jury bluntly, 'I'm sure GPs throughout the country have this situation. They have to decide whether to attempt resuscitation or let nature take its course. Whatever had happened to Mrs Quinn was on a major scale, not a minor scale – she was deeply unconscious. I made the decision not to attempt resuscitation and review the situation in two minutes. There were no signs of life and she had died.' He went on in the same vein: 'In my experience, patients who are deeply unconscious, as Mrs Quinn was, who survive, often have a loss of personality, a loss of use of the body, often end up in nursing homes. Mrs Quinn was an extremely independent, likeable patient and to go from that to be depending on someone you don't know was something I couldn't envisage her doing. Knowing Mrs Quinn, I decided not to attempt resuscitation for two minutes.'

That afternoon, as Dr Shipman gave his evidence on the death of Irene Turner, a mystery woman sitting in the public gallery said softly, but menacingly, 'You liar.' She disappeared soon after, her words unheard by the jury at the other side of the courtroom.

As in many of the cases, Dr Shipman told his tale wearily – the tale of a doctor whose patients were often difficult. When he visited Mrs Turner, her diabetes was 'totally out of control'. Since she refused to go to hospital, he said, he decided to test her urine at the surgery and show her the result to convince her to obey him. He had said to her, 'If I show you the sample, will you go?' Then, he went on, he drove the wrong way from her home because it was a dangerous junction to reverse on. The GP, totally unembarrassed by his poor explanations and excuses, was unaware that he might be failing to make a good impression on the jurors.

They were growing increasingly bored and irritated by Dr Shipman's evidence, which included lengthy medical histories of each of the fifteen women. It did not explain their deaths, on the very day the GP saw them, from morphine poisoning.

On the following day, Dr Shipman's fourth in the witness box, he looked red eyed and frail. But once back in the fray, he was as strong and firm as ever. The case turned to Jean Lilley, another patient with a long history of health problems. Miss Davies dwelt on this case for some time, the jury shifting in their chairs in a bid to concentrate. They were listening – they knew it was their duty to do so – but as ever they were struggling to see how the problems alone could explain Mrs Lilley's death.

Dr Shipman told the court how he visited Mrs Lilley. 'Well, this is funny. I've never seen you at home before – what's the matter?' he had asked. Dr Shipman was at pains to present a warm, affectionate relationship between a GP and his needy patient. But with almost his next sentence he destroyed it. 'She was a very interesting patient, and when she came to the surgery I would listen to her chest because I had never come across this condition before,' he remarked. 'When I visited this time there were more noises, squeaky noises, harsh noises. I would say she had severe atheroma.' It seemed a cold, calculated pretence when he added how impressed he was by her: 'Mrs Lilley always tried, all the time – she was a courageous patient.' He denied ignoring Mrs Lilley's friend Elizabeth Hunter as he left, said he stayed twenty minutes rather than forty, and recalled breaking the news to her pregnant daughter, his patient Odette Wilson. And again he denied killing Mrs Lilley.

Dr Shipman admitted that he should have had a post mortem for Muriel Grimshaw: 'In hindsight I would have had one.' But when asked by Miss Davies why, he replied: 'Because I would not be standing here now.' In fact he may well have been standing there earlier – Mrs Grimshaw's post mortem showed she had died of morphine poisoning.

The case turned to Marie West, the first of the cremated victims, who died when Dr Shipman visited her at home as her friend Marion Hadfield stood in the kitchen. Dr Shipman's evidence echoed that which he had given for Marie Quinn: 'In my thirty years of experience I have only seen two or three people collapse like she did. In both cases they had a post mortem and they had a stroke as the cause of death. It's likely, having gone from walking and talking to being floppy with no response, that there was a stroke in a major part of the brain, or a large stroke. In my experience, resuscitation is poorly rewarded and, if rewarded, the patient will be left with a lot of disability.' Miss Davies put it to him that he should have called an ambulance. He answered, even more coldly: 'I wondered what we would end up with. As I say, in my experience, you do not get someone living independently, enjoying life, as she did.'

Twice now Dr Shipman had recognised how his victims had been leading meaningful lives. Another time he had praised Mrs Lilley's courage. It made his performance in the witness box even more chilling.

The case took a colourful turn at the start of December. A serious matter of contempt of court arose, infuriating the judge, Mr Justice Forbes, but it added a lighter touch to the proceedings, just as Dr Shipman's lies and excuses were becoming repetitive. After a twenty-minute delay to the morning proceedings, Mr Justice Forbes took his seat, simmering with anger. He had a big, friendly face with kind brown eyes, which looked upon the court benevolently for most of the time. Normally he would stand straight backed, smiling as he gazed up at the white corniced ceiling when the clerk reconvened the court, but not today. But he did smile reassuringly as he turned to the jury and asked them not to be embarrassed by his request: 'Did any of you hear an obviously irresponsible comment on this trial on a local radio station?' The jurors, perplexed, shook their heads. Mr Justice Forbes immediately relaxed a little and, after praising the press's 'entirely responsible' coverage of the trial, allowed Dr Shipman to enter the witness box once more. He could say no more then, but the incident would be revealed in an unreportable court hearing the following day.

Mr Justice Forbes was again stony faced when he entered court at 10 a.m., half an hour early. Before him stood Michelle Surrell, the managing director of Red Rose Radio, a local station once owned by millionaire and convicted rapist, Owen Oyston. It was now one of many owned by the Emap media giant. It emerged that Mark Kay, a DJ on Rock FM, a subsidiary of Red Rose, had made an astonishing statement on his primetime show. 'Did you see the Harold Shipman trial? We have to be delicate because it's ongoing; I'm supposed to be delicate, but really I don't care,' the would-be shock jock began. 'We all know Shipman is as guilty as sin. Why don't we save the taxpayer a lot of money and end the trial now?' To make matters worse, travel presenter Judith Forbes had cried out 'guilty, guilty' in the background.

Mr Justice Forbes knew how close the court had come to a mistrial after so many weeks, if any of the jury had heard the presenters' outburst. He was furious. Ms Surrell was mortified. However she remained calm as she apologised unreservedly and assured the judge that she had immediately boosted training procedures. Mr Justice Forbes ordered the DJ to appear before him the following week along with 'the lady presenter – if I can call her that'.

The pair duly did so, trembling as they stood before the judge. Mr Justice Forbes could not contain his contempt for them as he told the court in relentless detail what they had done. It was a humiliating ordeal for them as the judge berated them as a headmaster would two silly schoolchildren. 'That broadcast was contempt of court and I am presently considering whether to refer the matter to the Attorney-General,' the Judge thundered. 'I have little doubt that, were I to do that, procedures would be taken, certainly against you, Mark Kay. Have you any idea what the outcome would be?'

Mr Kay, a short, slight, dark-haired young man, could not disguise his radio-bright voice, despite his nervousness, as he replied, 'There would be a fine.'

Mr Justice Forbes loudly corrected him. 'Don't limit it to a fine, Mark Kay. It would not surprise me if it were not imprisonment for a short time, just to bring home to you the seriousness of this matter. This would not be something you would enjoy.'

Mr Kay shakily replied, 'No.' Ms Forbes, no relation to the judge, paled too.

Still Mr Justice Forbes went on, asking the pair if they knew what could have happened if a juror had heard their programme. 'There would be a mistrial My Lord,' they replied meekly.

He sneered back, 'Fortunately for you, the jury has more sense than to listen to your sort of broadcast.' With a final twist of the knife, he added, 'I am going to remind you of your opening words, so that other members of the press and the public can be aware of your attitude. I unfortunately can't give it the same flavour, and I am not going to imitate your voice or air of bravado.' The pair's ordeal lasted some twenty minutes before the judge finally put them out of their misery. The jury had not heard their outburst and their boss had assured him training would be improved, so he would not refer the matter to the Attorney-General.

By then Dr Shipman had given all of his evidence. During the case of Lizzie Adams, he denied the claims of her dance partner William Catlow, who had said that he had called an ambulance. And he insisted that he was looking for a telephone when he was found gazing into Mrs Adams's display cabinet. As Dr Shipman explained how Mr Catlow had felt his own pulse, rather than Mrs Adams's, he left the jury with a chilling image: 'I think I put the hand on her neck to show him there was no carotid artery.' Like Cinderella's Prince Charming in reverse, he added, 'I took her shoe off and stroked the lower part of the foot. There was no response.'

After that, Miss Davies turned to the death of Mrs Wagstaff, who died as Dr Shipman visited her at home. His version of events contained some of the most implausible excuses of all. Mrs Wagstaff's neighbour, Margaret Walker, had heard her express surprise at the visit. Dr Shipman said that he visited because Mrs Wagstaff was expecting an ambulance, having telephoned him at the surgery complaining of chest pains. But there was no such call recorded from Mrs Wagstaff's home. He told the court that he was extremely concerned for Mrs Wagstaff, who was grey and sweating, having led him upstairs to her flat. Yet he took notes instead of dialling 999. By then, he said, she was dead, having silently collapsed in front of him. Instead of calling an ambulance, he tried to resuscitate her himself – as she sat in an upright chair.

Such lies and excuses came on top of the macabre mix-up as to who had died – Mrs Wagstaff or her daughter-in-law's mother Ann Royle, who had taken the GP a Christmas present that very morning.

It is little wonder that Dr Shipman broke down at the end of that case. But before then he was as clinical and cold-hearted as ever. 'When you have no pulse in your carotid arteries, you are dead,' he said. 'It's as simple as that.' Dr Shipman's tears when he broke down in the witness box were not for Mrs Wagstaff or her grieving family, but for himself.

After lunch, Miss Davies turned to Norah Nuttall, who also died as Dr Shipman visited her at home. This time, he said, it was a 'cold call' to see how she was getting on at her new house. But – the prosecution later revealed – Mrs Nuttall had lived at her redbrick terraced home for eight years.

Again Dr Shipman took on the mantle of caring family doctor as he took the jury through her medical notes. One blood pressure reading was 'sensationally good for her', he told them smugly, as if giving a lecture to an evening class of simple lay people. And, he ungallantly confided, he had to use the largest arm band because she was so fat. When he called to see Mrs Nuttall that day, she said she had been suffering from breathlessness. As with Mrs Pomfret, he was perplexed as to why she had not mentioned it at her morning appointment for a wheezy cough. ' "I'm afraid to say," she said, "I didn't want to bother you," ' he recalled sadly. 'I said, "You should have rung me." I said, "We had better have a look at you." ' But within minutes she was dead.

Dr Shipman again denied telling Mrs Nuttall's son, Anthony, that he had called an ambulance or pretending to cancel one on the telephone – 'I moved into the kitchen, the room behind the dining room, and stood there, collecting my thoughts, talking to myself about what had happened.'

More astonishing lies followed for the case of Pamela Hillier. Dr Shipman claimed that he had added precise blood-pressure readings to Mrs Hillier's medical notes, for appointments four days and even four weeks before, because she had told him about them that day. Practice nurse Gillian Morgan had taken the readings, and Mrs Hillier had remembered them or noted them down. It was yet another 'grand disclosure' by a woman who was within hours of death.

Dr Shipman then gave evidence on the last victim, Maureen Ward. Again, he told the jury of a grand disclosure by her about her failing health, this time the day before she died. At 1.30 p.m. on 17 February she popped into the surgery without an appointment and told him of 'funny dos'. He diagnosed a brain tumour. 'Miss Ward had worked as a nursery nurse and had reasonable medical knowledge,' he said. 'She said, "You think it has spread."' Yet three hours later Miss Ward returned for an arranged appointment – laughing and joking with receptionist Carol Chapman. A 'strange pattern of behaviour' following such terrible news, as prosecutor Mr Henriques put it. The following day, having found her body, Dr Shipman diagnosed brain and breast cancer as the causes of her death. And he had happened to put the details of her failing health into his computer just an hour before.

Finally Miss Davies turned to volume eight, which contained the evidence showing how Dr Shipman had used his patients to stockpile morphine. It was a brief session in which yet more lies and excuses followed. Dr Shipman denied keeping the controlled drug, although four ampoules of the opiate had been found in the back bedroom of his modest family semi. He explained that when he had taken away James Arundale's morphine following his death, he had decided to dispose of it at the surgery. Later on, his car had been involved in a crash and he had had to clean it out, putting his medicines, dressings and other items in the back bedroom. Somehow, he insisted, the ampoules of morphine ended up there. 'I was not aware they were there,' he asserted. 'I thought I had destroyed everything she had handed to me.'

Suddenly Miss Davies turned to her client. 'I have no further questions, Dr Shipman,' she said sharply. 'Thank you.' With that she quickly sat down. At exactly the same time Mr Henriques stood up. It was a smooth, almost synchronised movement that took Dr Shipman totally by surprise.

'The evidence is that on 1 August 1998 –' Mr Henriques boomed, promising a robust cross-examination. He got no further. A horrified Dr Shipman reddened and drew his finger across his throat, gesturing to Miss Davies to stop the proceedings.

'Excuse me,' he pleaded, his voice strangled with shock. 'I don't feel very well.' He was by now dark red and frowning, looking over to his barrister for an explanation. Miss Davies appeared impassive. Dr Shipman was led immediately to the cells, his legs shaking, his head down, looking more furtive and guilty than ever. The jury was sent out and Mr Justice Forbes ordered a break of not less than fifteen minutes.

'Miss Davies,' he smiled over to her, 'go and see how matters are.'

The press and public, waiting in the foyer, were buzzing following the dramatic break in proceedings. Miss Davies, who had seen to her client and returned to the foyer, had a conversation with junior prosecuting counsel, Peter Wright. She had done a great job with a difficult defence, concentrating on the mundane details of a family doctor's life and helping Dr Shipman explain away his strange behaviour as best she could. Miss Davies was to do even better with her summing-up, chipping away at the prosecution's seemingly watertight case as only a highly skilled barrister can.

Dr Shipman had struck gold with Miss Davies. She did not have Mr Henriques' high profile or his strong relationship with the Northern circuit. At an earlier hearing when she requested that the trial be held in London rather than Liverpool or Preston, which were too close to Manchester, Mr Justice Forbes had scolded, 'Yet again counsel comes up from London and cannot tell the difference between the major conurbations of Manchester and Liverpool.' With her three requests at the beginning of the trial also denied, it seemed that Miss Davies had begun on a back foot with a difficult case. But that was no matter to the determined barrister, who remained coolly professional and amazed the court with her prowess.

Grammar school-educated Miss Davies had studied law at Birmingham University in the early 1970s. She was called to the Bar in 1976 and took silk sixteen years later, having already worked on several major medical inquiries. In 1987 she worked on the Cleveland Inquiry into child abuse and in 1989 took part in an General Medical Council inquiry into the sale of human organs for transplantation. Since becoming a QC, Miss Davies has been leading counsel for even more impressive cases. In 1994 she was involved in the public inquiry into the death of mental health worker, Georgina Robinson, at the hands of a patient. In 1995 she was instructed by the Secretary of State for Wales to investigate allegations of abuse of children in care in North Wales and was leading counsel in the case against gynaecologist, Reginald Dixon, who was charged with procuring the miscarriage of a woman contrary to the Offences Against the Person Act.

From 1997 Miss Davies's caseload exploded both in volume and importance. She worked on the first-ever case, before the GMC Professional Conduct Committee, concerning an HIV positive doctor, as well as the Bristol heart surgeons' case at the GMC and the BSE Inquiry. In 1999, as well as working on the trial of Britain's biggest serial killer, she was representing Dr Ken Taylor, a GP charged with hastening a patient's death by instructing the withdrawal of a food supplement.

Such experience, added to Miss Davies's cut-glass, cool demeanour, made the barrister Dr Shipman's best possible defender. But still the evidence would damn him.

Miss Davies was backed by junior counsel, Ian Winter. Polite, well mannered and well spoken, the 32 year old had a wealth of experience for his age. He was educated at the Bishop Wand School, in Surrey, and studied at the Bristol Law School and the Inns of Court School of Law. He was called to the Bar in 1988, at the Inner Temple, had lectured at Thames University in 1987 and 1988 and spoke fluent Italian. His caseload consisted of white-collar crime, tax evasion, fraud and share-market offences. He had prosecuted eight defendants charged with defrauding the Abbey National of £2m and defended the chairman of Atlantic Computers for insider-dealing offences.

But Mr Winter was no fey academic working only on the driest of cases. His hobbies included international rally driving from London to Mexico in 1995 and

Panama to Alaska in 1997 and travelling to India and the Americas, as well as playing jazz piano and the saxophone, and collecting modern abstract art. And he had prosecuted the officers charged with fabricating the record of interview of Winston Silcott, accused of murdering PC Blakelock in the Broadwater Farm riots. He was tough, as well as polite, when tackling the prosecution's expert witnesses.

Dr Shipman's solicitors, Anne Ball and Ian Barker at Hempsons, were also experienced, especially with 'white coat' crime, as they described it. The volume of negligence cases involving alleged manslaughter, murder and sexual assault had increased for the firm, which was more than a hundred years old and whose Manchester team was headed by Ms Ball. Hempsons had acted in 203 criminal matters in four years, with 61 of them in 1999 representing a 65 per cent increase since 1996. Ms Ball had been with the firm since joining as an articled clerk in 1985. She had become a member of the Manchester team in 1991 and risen to the status of partner. Mr Barker, head of the London team, had successfully defended Dr David Moor, the Newcastle doctor charged with murdering a patient, in May 1999. They were supported by Katherine Sheldrake, a genetics graduate and biochemistry researcher, who was on a training contract with Hempsons.

But an impressive team would not save Dr Shipman from a roasting at the hands of Mr Henriques.

Mr Henriques was not without cause the North's leading barrister. He devoured Dr Shipman during cross-examination; he began tough and grew tougher as the days drew on, with no mercy for the tired defendant. Dr Shipman in turn grew more and more arrogant as his case weakened and his arguments grew ever more ludicrous and implausible. Mr Henriques was the angry head boy to Shipman's snide class weed as his bullying interrogation tore into the GP's protestations of innocence.

Mr Henriques' questions leaped from victim to victim; to the patients of volume eight; from the murders to the forging of the will; to the changes to medical records; and back to volume eight again. This gave Dr Shipman no chance to think his arguments through, or to consider how his jigsaw of lies would fit together. It was brilliant work by a barrister who had obviously studied and memorised the case in minute detail. In addition, Mr Henriques applied the full weight of his experience and powerful presence. Dr Shipman did not stand a chance.

Mr Henriques quickly turned to one the most damning pieces of evidence – the forged will. Only the GP would benefit from it, and only his fingerprints were on it. Mr Henriques accused Dr Shipman of forging the will, having invented an age survey so that he could get Mrs Grundy's signature and find out who her solicitor was. 'She told you her solicitor was her daughter, Angela Woodruff,' the QC stated.

'I can't remember her saying that,' Dr Shipman replied.

'Pretend you're looking at this as an outsider, like in your thriller books – that would scupper the plan, wouldn't it?' Mr Henriques pressed on with more than a touch of sarcasm.

'What plan?' Dr Shipman asked, with mock innocence.

'To forge a will in the doctor's favour,' Mr Henriques hit back, irritated by the GP's insolent pretence. Mr Henriques pushed on. He reminded Dr Shipman – and the jury – of his words the previous day – 'you cannot dig up ashes'. The will had been ticked in the box requesting cremation. 'You put the tick in the box, didn't you?' he asked.

'No,' Dr Shipman replied irritably.

Mr Henriques went on; Dr Shipman becoming in turn cold, petulant, snotty, arrogant, simpering, and again irritable. The GP now returned to a tactic he had enjoyed during the police interviews – pedantically arguing about the questions put to him rather than actually answering them. When Mr Henriques asked him why he had put the 'two words' silent coronary thrombosis on Mrs Grundy's notes following her death, Dr Shipman said, 'they are three words, not two'. It won him no friends on the jury.

Dr Shipman looked at his most foolish when Mr Henriques put an alternative explanation for Mrs Grundy's death, borrowing heavily from the GP's defence that she was a junkie. 'Had you prescribed diamorphine?' the QC asked.

'No,' Dr Shipman replied, quietly but firmly.

'So she might have got into her motor car and driven to some drug dealers and obtained diamorphine, and then gone home and administered it to herself?' Mr Henriques asked with dramatic sarcasm.

'I don't think it's my role to ascertain where she was getting the diamorphine from, if she was taking it,' Dr Shipman said sniffily, as he back-pedalled from the bizarre image of a rain-bonneted pensioner hanging out with the homeboys of Hyde.

Dr Shipman then revealed the terror he had felt as the police investigation got underway. Explaining his joke to district nurse, Marion Gilchrist, about having Mrs Grundy cremated, he sounded like a child being bullied at school rather than an adult responsible for his own awful predicament. 'I knew the police would go very hard and very enthusiastically to get me, and that explains my comment,' he whined. 'It was black humour so I could survive the next two weeks until I was arrested.'

As week nine began on Monday 6 December, Mr Henriques turned to the second victim, Bianka Pomfret. Again there were the same exchanges between a righteous Mr Henriques and a shifty Dr Shipman.

The QC began to leap from case to case as similarities arose between them, tying them all together – and revealing each one to Dr Shipman. When Mr Henriques asked him about his conversation with Dr Tate, in which he assured the psychiatrist that Mrs Pomfret had not committed suicide, he suddenly referred to the death of Laura Kathleen Wagstaff – some ten victims ahead. This threw Dr Shipman. Dr Tate had made notes on their conversation and included the phrase 'thready pulse', not one of his own. And Dr Shipman had used exactly that unusual phrase to Angela Wagstaff. Yet the GP had not been present when Mrs Pomfret died – so, asked Mr Henriques, why say she had a thready pulse? Dr Shipman, now firmly on a back foot, denied using the words.

Mr Henriques' determination was steeled still further when he turned to the case of Winifred Mellor. 'I am afraid she is not telling the whole truth,' Dr Shipman said dismissively of Sheila Mellor, the youngest of the four grieving daughters. She and her sisters had all recalled Dr Shipman, saying that their mother rang him, complaining of chest pains.

'So you can't rely on that family for the truth?' Mr Henriques stormed back.

'When I spoke to that family they were in a state of shock, extreme unhappiness,' Dr Shipman replied quickly.

'Your problem is that you cannot admit getting that call, because itemised billing shows there was no call,'

Mr Henriques hit back. 'You have been caught lying to that very decent family, haven't you?'

Mr Henriques fought a mighty battle for the patients' relatives, decent law-abiding people who had lost their loved ones to a callous killer. But sometimes, while impressive, this merely reinforced what the jury already knew. For often the plain, simple facts would damn Dr Shipman – such as in the case of Ivy Lomas, the victim who died in the surgery.

Dr Shipman looked cranky as he entered the witness box for the ninth day of the defence case, his fourth under cross-examination. Again he took to 'playing for time', as Mr Henriques put it, by quizzing his interrogator. Mr Henriques asked: 'Why take an ECG when she already had an irregular heartbeat?'

Dr Shipman asked in turn, 'Are you asking why I took the patient for an ECG?'

But Mr Henriques would not be put off: 'That was a plain question. You knew it. By asking if that's a question you are playing for time, aren't you? Why purport to take an ECG?'

Dr Shipman, forced to give his reply, said, 'I tried to get an ECG reading to give to the hospital, to get her into coronary care, not accident and emergency.'

But Mr Henriques was not finished – 'Why say the ECG was broken?'

Dr Shipman, sighing, explained that it would breach Mrs Lomas's patient confidentiality and upset the three patients in the waiting room. He added, 'It was so they did not think I had deliberately wasted time.'

With that, Mr Henriques suddenly turned to the case of Norah Nuttall, whose sister, Elizabeth Oldham, had been treated to a consultation on her death in that very waiting room. 'Do you remember that evidence?' he asked. 'You were holding forth about the death of

Norah Nuttall. There were two ladies in the waiting room and you said, with arms aloft, you knew this would happen; this had been going to happen for a long time.'

Dr Shipman could only mutter, 'I don't remember.'

Mr Henriques pressed on with the case of Mrs Lomas and the fact that he had lied to his receptionist, Carol Chapman, as well as to the three patients. 'Is it ever right for a doctor to tell untruths to an employee?' he asked.

There were more delaying tactics from the GP. 'I'm not quite sure what you are asking me there,' he said.

'I think you are,' Mr Henriques insisted. 'Is it ever right for a doctor to tell untruths to an employee?'

Dr Shipman was again forced to reply, 'On occasions, yes, and this was just such an occasion.'

Mr Henriques was on the home straight in the case of Mrs Lomas – it was the case most damning to Dr Shipman. 'Other people had substantial doses of diamorphine in their homes, but it doesn't work in Ivy Lomas's case, does it?' he demanded. 'Where did she get it from? She didn't seem to have opiate poisoning. Was she able to walk along a corridor?'

Dr Shipman answered, 'Yes, she was.'

Mr Henriques continued, 'Remember Professor McQuay's evidence, that five minute window?'

Dr Shipman replied, 'Yes, I remember him saying that.'

Now Mr Henriques was closing in – 'If this lady died at 4.10 p.m., she must have been administered or administered herself diamorphine between 4 and 4.10, mustn't she?'

Dr Shipman, misery written all over his pale face, said, 'You can put the evidence that way and yes, I would agree.'

Mr Henriques pointed out, 'You were with her at that time.'

Dr Shipman replied, 'I wouldn't disagree.'

Mr Henriques, making absolutely sure he had his quarry, turned to the entry in Mrs Lomas's computer records for 15:57 that day, 'seen in doc's surgery'. 'You were in her presence, then?' he pressed.

'I'm not disagreeing with that,' Dr Shipman replied again.

'How did she get the diamorphine in her body?' Mr Henriques asked.

'I have no knowledge,' came the weak reply.

Mr Henriques had won. 'Dr Shipman, there is simply no sensible answer, is there?' There was a long pause, Dr Shipman's defence in its last throes.

'Is that a question or statement?' the GP asked stupidly.

'Dr Shipman, there is simply no sensible answer, is there?' Mr Henriques repeated.

'I do not know of any explanation,' Dr Shipman countered.

'Save for your guilt,' Mr Henriques hit home.

Still Dr Shipman continued to dig his own grave. 'That is what you are saying, but I disagree with it strongly. I did not administer anything to this lady and therefore I have no idea how she got it into her body.'

Mr Henriques was happy to continue his winning line. 'Can you think of any other sensible explanation other than your guilt?'

Dr Shipman replied: 'I cannot think of anything at all.'

'Other than your guilt?' Mr Henriques pressed.

'I am not guilty,' Dr Shipman insisted.

When Mr Henriques turned to the case of Marie Quinn, he exposed Dr Shipman as a liar more clearly than ever before. The GP had claimed that Mrs Quinn had telephoned him complaining of weakness in her arm, yet no such call was made from her home. Furthermore, Dr Shipman recalled leaving the surgery immediately. As it was a wet and windy November night, there was nobody in open surgery. He had then got stuck in traffic on the way to Mrs Quinn's home. Mr Henriques then pounced – 'I'm going to ask you to look at this document, exposing what a sham your evidence is.' It was the open surgery book, showing that four patients had attended that night.

Dr Shipman appeared shocked but continued to argue. 'What it shows is that they appeared in open surgery and were dealt with.'

Mr Henriques would not accept that. 'It also demonstrates when they were dealt with. It also demonstrates that your story of being in a traffic jam for twenty to twenty-five minutes and arriving at Mrs Quinn's at 6.20 p.m. is an outrageous lie.'

And so the head-to-head battle continued, through the cases of Irene Turner, Jean Lilley and Muriel Grimshaw. The same irregularities were raised by Mr Henriques, and the same implausible explanations given in turn by Dr Shipman. The same anger and irritation of the interrogator was met by the same shiftiness and agitation of the defendant.

Then Mr Henriques turned to volume eight, the evidence showing how Dr Shipman had stockpiled diamorphine. His twisting, incisive questioning forced the GP to admit astonishing malpractice. Dr Shipman said that he had prescribed one patient, Frank Crompton, with 2,000 milligrams of the drug – even though he did not need it. This, he said, was in anticipation of Mr Crompton's prostate cancer developing painful secondary tumours. He had prescribed ten ampoules of 100 mg diamorphine to Mr Crompton twice, on 28 February and 18 March 1995, because the cancer sufferer had destroyed the first batch. 'He said he didn't want to be a drug addict. He broke them and put them in the rubbish,' Dr Shipman explained, coolly. 'He and I sat down and talked about it again. Mr Crompton agreed to keep them in the house.' It had been easy for Shipman to remain cool, knowing that Mr Crompton had died and would be unable to testify against him. But Mr Henriques was able to tell the court that Mr Crompton never needed such pain relief, nor a home help, nor a district nurse. Volume eight was to generate even more bizarre claims from Dr Shipman. He recalled a batch of diamorphine being posted through his surgery door and landing on the doormat. This he was able to use for a patient in need over one weekend but it led to confusing entries on the sick man's drug record card. Mr Henriques was incredulous as he swooped on the claim – a 'magic mat' where drugs appeared overnight.

Mr Henriques said Dr Shipman had been stockpiling the deadly drug using Mr Crompton's name, in order to kill Maria West. He reminded the jury of Mrs West's friend, Marion Hadfield, waiting in the kitchen, listening to doctor and patient chat to each other. Then, Mr Henriques recalled, 'there was a period of silence'. This, he said, was the few minutes it would take for someone to die of a diamorphine overdose – first they would fall asleep and their breathing would slow, as shown in evidence given by expert witness Professor McQuay. 'You were simply waiting for the diamorphine to take its course, weren't you?' he asked the beleaguered defendant.

Dr Shipman replied that he was not.

Dr Shipman admitted that he was surprised to find Mrs Hadfield in the kitchen – 'We almost collided' –

but he said he was not 'caught out' by her presence, as Mr Henriques put it. 'I have no doubt in my mind that the lady had a sudden lethal stroke,' Dr Shipman snootily insisted.

It gave rise to one of his combatant's best lines – 'That lady had a sudden lethal dose of diamorphine.'

Mr Henriques turned to Mrs West's cremation form, which was littered with untruths, as were those of Laura Kathleen Wagstaff and Maureen Ward. Dr Shipman denied that he had done this in order to make sure that they were cremated without further investigation. Again he appeared cold and unfeeling when asked why he had put Mrs West as his patient of eighteen months rather than three years. He replied, 'These things happen.'

Dr Shipman's personality crumbled still further with Mr Henriques' furious analysis of the death of 77-year-old widow, Lizzie Adams. The GP had been found looking in Mrs Adams's display cabinet of Royal Doulton figurines by her friend Bill Catlow, as she sat dead or dying in the back room. 'This was urgent, wasn't it?' Mr Henriques stormed. 'You had no business to stand about looking at figurines in a display cabinet, had you?'

When asked why Mrs Adams had her blouse tie and top buttons done up, even though he had purportedly fought to save her life, Dr Shipman said that she had had time to do that before she died. And he denied intimidating Mrs Adams's family in order to stop them asking for a post mortem.

Mr Henriques challenged him. 'This was another case in which the pressure was getting to you, as in Winnie Mellor's case, when it looked as if the family were going to question you, make things difficult. Do you remember how you pressurised Mrs Thorley?'

'I don't remember,' Dr Shipman replied.

Mr Henriques reminded him, 'You said you should come and see old people more often.'

'If that's what she heard,' Dr Shipman replied.

Mr Henriques added, 'Grief puts people in a state of weakness, doesn't it?'

Dr Shipman, as cold as ice, answered, 'Not always.'

Thursday 9 December, the 36th day of the trial, was also the second anniversary of Laura Kathleen Wagstaff's death. Before embarking on that case, Mr Henriques said to Dr Shipman, 'It is an unhappy coincidence that it was two years ago that she died. Are you disturbed that we should deal with this on the second anniversary of her death?'

The GP replied with a shrug and the sarcastic tone of a petulant teenager, 'No.' The Wagstaff family courageously braced themselves in the public gallery.

Again Mr Henriques played the righteous defender of the bereaved to perfection, as his questions thundered around the courtroom. Dr Shipman's dreadful mix-up of Mrs Wagstaff and her daughter-in-law's mother, Mrs Royle, proved rich material. 'Is it possible that you confused Mrs Royle with Mrs Wagstaff?' Mr Henriques asked bluntly.

'When?' Dr Shipman returned in amazement.

'That afternoon,' Mr Henriques replied.

'No,' the GP insisted.

'You had no reason to call on Mrs Wagstaff,' Mr Henriques went on.

'Mrs Wagstaff called the surgery, I answered the telephone and she complained of chest pains,' Dr Shipman insisted. Yet Mrs Wagstaff's telephone bill showed no such call.

Mr Henriques turned to Dr Shipman's assertion that he had recorded Mrs Wagstaff's blood-pressure reading

222

on a letter to a houseman at the hospital, which he threw away following the widow's death. 'You embarked on this letter as a flight of fancy in the witness box when you were cornered, and I'm going to cross-examine you until you admit there was no letter,' he threatened.

Mr Henriques returned to the mix-up and the pain it caused Mrs Wagstaff's daughter-in-law, Angela. With a vain hope of stopping the line of questioning, Dr Shipman admitted, 'I hold my hand up to a dreadful mistake.'

But Mr Henriques was unstoppable – 'Yes, but what is worse is you saying on oath that it was Angela Wagstaff's fault in part that she had not grasped that it was her mother-in-law, not her mother.'

Dr Shipman bleated, 'It was a mistake.'

'It was not a mistake, it was a deception,' Mr Henriques countered forcefully.

Throughout that day and all the others, the rest of the courtroom could only look on as Mr Henriques cut down Dr Shipman over and over again. At one point a juror seemed to snigger then cover it up with a cough. Just two yards away, senior defence counsel, Nicola Davies, QC, sat and stared straight ahead of her, listening. Her junior, Ian Winter, meanwhile, watched Mr Henriques' performance closely as Dr Shipman continued to explain his bizarre behaviour.

Mr Henriques again portrayed Dr Shipman as a bully when he turned to the case of Norah Nuttall and his treatment of her son, gentle giant Anthony Nuttall. Mr Nuttall had recalled that the GP said he had called an ambulance. Dr Shipman denied this. 'Is Anthony Nuttall to line up with the small army of witnesses who were mistaken as to what you said?' Mr Henriques asked. He went on, 'Is it possible you underestimated him? Did you take more trouble with some relatives than others? Larger families were more likely to cause trouble when it came to a post mortem.'

Mr Henriques finished with Dr Shipman on Friday 10 December, having discussed the cases of Pamela Hillier and Maureen Ward in great detail and then referring again to the infamous volume eight. He relentlessly linked the stockpiling of diamorphine with the deaths of Dr Shipman's victims. The GP's explanations moved from implausible to downright bizarre. Dr Shipman claimed he had 'got into the habit' of prescribing 30 mg of diamorphine for patients who needed only 5 mg or less while working at the Donneybrook Group practice, where other doctors did the same. But when Mr Henriques pressed him to name the doctors who did so, he refused. Then he added, 'You can have some names', and reeled off the list of GPs who had worked there so fast that it was barely audible.

Mr Henriques continued with the minutiae of volume eight then suddenly stopped, as if bored by the GP – 'My Lord, that's the end of my cross-examination.'

Dr Shipman looked surprised then collected himself. He began gathering the documents he had been asked to refer to and laughed softly when he almost dropped one of the heavy files. He either felt relieved or was again pretending to be an expert witness rather than a furtive defendant.

'You can leave the box now, Dr Shipman. Thank you,' Mr Justice Forbes said, politely but sternly.

The judge turned to the jury with a smile and wished them a 'very pleasant and relaxed' Christmas. Now the picture of benevolence, he made the twelve tired jurors laugh as he added, 'I should have something more profound to say to you since next time you meet it will be the next millennium, but I haven't, so I will confine myself to have a very merry Christmas.' Dr Shipman, only too aware of where he would be spending the season, looked morose.

He grew even more depressed once the jury was sent out and Mr Justice Forbes began to discuss his summing up with the two barristers. Dr Shipman sat silently and ignored behind Mr Henriques and Miss Davies, suddenly of no importance at all to the proceedings after twelve days in the limelight. His frown deepened as the three professionals discussed the case coolly and dispassionately, as if he were not there. And he reddened furiously when Mr Justice Forbes explained how he would tell the jury how to deal with the lies told during the trial. 'Defendants lie for various reasons,' he said. Dr Shipman gaped with shock.

Then he was led away, disappearing down the steps to the cells, again without looking once at Primrose. The next time he appeared in the dock, it would be a new millennium, a new start. But not for Dr Shipman.

8 Shipman's Legacy

There are two questions left burning in people's minds by this shocking case – why did Dr Shipman do it and how could he do it to so many for so long?

Had this case happened anywhere but Hyde it might have been understandable. We live in a high-speed world whose inhabitants don't have the time to gossip or the energy to love thy neighbour. We run blinkered through life, promising ourselves we will relax once we reach our goals. Once home, we batten down the hatches. We have created a hard, harsh world where crime often goes unchecked by the community, barricaded behind its locked doors and thoughtless self-absorption. Who among us would notice a creeping killer silently picking off the old women who were near the end of their journey anyway?

But Hyde is different – it is an old-fashioned little town where families live on each other's doorstep and everyone knows everyone else's business. From the stone-built cottages and swanky palaces of leafy Gee Cross to the boxy semis and tiny terraces of Godley, Newton and Hyde, it is a close community with a good heart. Yet even here, these women and countless other patients were not safe from Britain's biggest serial killer.

Worse still, the town's 'grapevine' was in fine working order. Dr Shipman was nicknamed Dr Death by the home helps for two years before his arrest. Taxi driver John Shaw, and his wife Kath, kept a list of customers they lost to the killer GP; bereaved families whispered their suspicions as they cried for their dead; undertaker Debbie Massey admitted to local GPs, Dr Linda Reynolds and Dr Susan Booth, that she had been checking bodies for violence as she embalmed them, such was her concern. Even the police investigated him, to no avail. The grapevine did not save Dr Shipman's victims. The message, now so loud and clear, was at that time unthinkable.

Of course Dr Shipman knew this. It was at the root of his cold-hearted slaying of the town's old and vulnerable. He was a doctor, a trusted carer, a figure of authority whom no one would even think of accusing. He loved his position of power in this small, respectable community. But it was not enough. Only when his arrogance spiralled so out of control that he sloppily forged Mrs Grundy's will was he finally caught out.

Dr Shipman was convicted of fifteen murders, but it is widely believed that he killed many more than that. Police took all of the 202 death certificates issued by Dr Shipman as a single-handed practitioner from 1992 to 1998. In addition, they spoke to families who had lost loved ones in Dr Shipman's care. In the end they investigated 136 deaths, going back to 1984, when he was still working at the Donneybrook Group Practice. Dr John Smith, his retired former colleague at the seven-strong practice, insists that he could not have murdered a patient and got away with it there. But Coroner John Pollard, not a man given to overdramatic statements, believes Dr Shipman could have killed as many as 1,000 people during his 30-year career.

The *Manchester Evening News* has been approached by the friends and families of dozens of other patients, certain they died at the hands of Dr Shipman. And it has spoken exclusively to two survivors of the GP – Jim King and Ann Royle, who was saved only because Dr Shipman confused her with Laura Kathleen Wagstaff.

Jim King believes Dr Shipman tried to murder him by prescribing hundreds of milligrammes of diamorphine after he was allegedly misdiagnosed with cancer of the urethra in 1996. But, Mr King says, his father, James senior, was not so lucky. Mr King believes that he was murdered by Dr Shipman on Christmas Eve 1997 after telling the GP earlier that year: 'I am on to you.'

Mr King has now made a complaint against Dr Shipman for the alleged misdiagnosis of his cancer, only a week after he married his American girlfriend Debbie, in May 1996. The couple had met through a singles ad when Jim was working as a pilot in Dallas. Four months later, Jim had to return to England but, as they said a tearful goodbye at the airport gate, he begged Debbie to marry him. He rang her when he changed planes at New York, swearing: 'I still mean it.' She joined him two months later.

Jim and Debbie moved in with James senior at his Ogden Court flat, the sheltered housing complex where Dr Shipman's victims Maureen and Molly Ward also lived. James was delighted to make his son and his new fiancé feel at home, bringing them breakfast in bed and helping them plan their wedding. 'He was a real gentleman,' Debbie recalled wistfully. 'He made me feel like a princess.' The couple made plans to settle in the town. Debbie glowed as she recalled their traditional English wedding in Flowery Field, an area of the town whose name seemed to reflect her new hopes of happiness. 'I had always dreamed of a beautiful fairytale wedding like that,' she said. 'Jim's dad walked me down the aisle. It was perfect.' But their bliss was shortlived.

Jim was transformed after the shocking diagnosis –
from a dashing newlywed and pilot into a desperate
unemployed junkie. He had been passing blood in his
urine and Dr Shipman arranged a future appointment for
him. But when he grew much worse, he was rushed to
hospital. There he was told the devastating news – he had
cancer of the urethra. Jim's father, James senior, was
heartbroken by the news.

After six chemotherapy sessions, between July and
September 1996, Jim was declared clear.

Jim claims that the consultant did not tell him all the
details of his case. Adrian Griffiths, director of surgical
services for the Tameside and Glossop Acute Services
NHS Trust, confirmed a complaint for medical
negligence was being investigated.

When Jim discussed the case with Dr Shipman at his
surgery, the GP told him he wasn't yet clear of the
cancer. That had spread to his bladder, and he had
eighteen months to live. Again Jim was alone when he
heard the terrible news. He walked the streets for hours
before facing his new wife. 'When I came home, I
couldn't tell Debbie,' he recalled, white with anger at
the memory. 'I kept looking at her, trying to say it, but
it wouldn't come out. Can you imagine it? How do you
tell her? I had walked the streets, wondering. You hear
all these stories and you think of all the things you will
not do.' But Debbie knew something was wrong and
eventually forced Jim to tell her.

By then, Jim had lost his job as a pilot; the
chemotherapy had made him violently sick. The
treatment does not distinguish between healthy and
cancerous cells and, as Jim's cells were all allegedly
healthy, it caused a great deal of damage. He was made
impotent within months of his marriage. 'We have lost
our intimacy,' he said. 'Of all the things we could have

lost, that's the worst.' They also lost their new home and their funds for a fresh start. But lionhearted Debbie loved him dearly. She had already shown her mettle when she refused to go on Shipman's panel after he asked her, 'Why are you marrying that old man?' She was offended by the question. Like Dr Linda Reynolds, who alerted the police to Dr Shipman's death rate in March 1998, she was new to Hyde and not in blind awe of the rude, brusque GP. 'He is young at heart,' she snapped back.

Despite Debbie's unwavering support, Jim was destroyed. He attempted suicide by gassing himself in the garage. His seventeen-year-old son Jamie kicked down the door and saved him. 'I didn't want her to see me die of cancer,' Jim explained.

Worse was to come. As Dr Shipman's morphine prescriptions slowly grew in strength and number, Jim became addicted to the drug. He suffered spasms, and Debbie took to hiding the opiate from her desperate husband. Dr Shipman had told him: 'Take as much as you like, you're dying anyway. This is a drug addict's dream.' Jim was shocked by the GP's flippant remarks but did not think any more of it. Then on 14 October 1996 he suffered respiratory depression. Debbie dialled 999 and told the paramedics: 'I don't know how much he has taken. He had been having pain the night before and had been up a lot.'

James senior was, by now, suspicious of Dr Shipman. He had warned his son that the doses of morphine were too high. 'He is killing you, lad,' he insisted. His warnings went unheeded. James senior also went to the surgery and 'had a go' at Dr Shipman.

In January 1997, Jim asked Dr Shipman to refer him to Christie Hospital for a second opinion. The GP did. The results of his examination were sent back to the

Market Street practice, but it was not until July that year that Dr Shipman finally told Jim the amazing news. Dr Shipman phoned Jim and asked him to go into the surgery 'for an update' at 8 a.m. the following Saturday. It was a bright, sunny summer's morning when Jim arrived. The GP let him in through the back door and, as he led him to his consultation room, Jim could see that the waiting room was empty. 'You should have called me,' the GP began, making sure he had covered his tracks. Then he suddenly announced: 'You've won the lottery. You haven't got cancer and you've never had it either.' Jim almost collapsed with relief. Such was his excitement and joy, he immediately left the surgery to tell Debbie the wonderful news.

Later, as the truth sank in, he grew angry. Angry at the GP: 'It was only later I thought, how dare he? He was trying to be the nice guy.' That same month, Jim filed a complaint against the GP and Tameside Acute Services NHS Trust, which runs the hospital where he was diagnosed. But his pain was far from over.

Six months later, Jim's spritely 83-year-old father was found dead at his flat – one hour after a visit by Dr Shipman. Jim's sister, Margaret, found him sitting in his favourite chair; it was Christmas Eve – just a fortnight after Laura Kathleen Wagstaff and Bianka Pomfret had died. Jim, Debbie and the whole family were heartbroken. 'I loved my dad so much, I adored him,' Jim said. 'When he heard I had cancer he said, "I wish I could have it for you lad, I have had my life". Now I feel like he did.'

Debbie had only known James senior for a matter of months but had grown close to the 'true gentleman' who always wore a shirt and tie and had welcomed her to Britain like a princess. 'He would give you his last £20 and the shirt off his back,' she said. 'He knew we were struggling and he only thought of his family. He was such a lovely man.'

Again, just like many of the other patients' families, the Kings asked for a post mortem. Again Dr Shipman said it would not be necessary, and signed the death certificate. He gave the cause of death as hypertension.

When the news broke, in August 1998, that Dr Shipman was being investigated over a string of patient deaths, Jim and Debbie realised the true extent of the pain caused to them by Dr Shipman. Jim is now certain that his father was murdered by Shipman because he knew too much. 'He was fit and well,' Jim insisted. 'He would walk from Hyde to Ashton along the canal. He didn't smoke or drink.'

The couple also recalled the sinister way the GP had broken the news that Jim had not had cancer. 'He didn't want Jim screaming through the lab, "This man has misdiagnosed me, I have lost my house, lost my job, lost my money",' Debbie explained.

'My dad said, "He is trying to kill you, lad", and I didn't believe it,' Jim added. 'It's really sad. We trusted these people.'

And they realised it was a miracle that Jim had survived Dr Shipman's attentions. Debbie explained: 'He kept it [the morphine] hidden for a year with us as the murders escalated. He was testing it on Jim, increasing the dose bit by bit. I would lie in bed thinking how much morphine he was on and, as I knew about it from my mum's death, wondering why he was not dead? Before that he didn't even have cancer. I believe we are being looked after.'

But now Jim's and Debbie's lives are wrecked. Jim, forever in fear of the disease, feels constantly angry at his situation: 'I can't tolerate anything, and all the time I see something else he has done. I daren't go to court.

I would kill him myself.' Debbie is now married to 'a changed man'. Gone is the lively, jolly Brit who wooed her with his smooth moves on the dance floors of Dallas. He is often too scared to leave his house, a tiny terrace on Sydall Street, in Hyde's town centre, let alone take Debbie dancing in crowded, smoky clubs. 'I was a captain in charge of 727s,' Jim recalled, angry with hopelessness.

Debbie too has changed. She is more aggressive and has lost all trust in people. Both of them are on Prozac. 'The only thing we have in common is what's happened to us,' she said. 'We have not known anything else since May 17, 1996. What life is there after this? Will we make it as a couple?'

The King family have also wondered if Dr Shipman killed some of their other elderly friends and relatives. Jim's aunt, Irene Berry, was found dead at her Hyde home in February 1998, again sitting in her favourite chair, and again having been visited by the GP an hour before. Family friend, Molly Dudley, had died four years before, in Dr Shipman's arms. He had called her sons, after giving her some kind of injection, and said, 'She won't last long', according to Jim. She was dead by the time they arrived. Such shocking tales are by no means unusual in Hyde these days.

The Kings, like so many others, had thought Dr Shipman was a good doctor who was looking after Jim with dedication and care. The couple were so grateful to him that they bought raffle tickets and attended a fundraiser for his surgery appeal fund at the Globe public house in Hyde.

Another family to show their appreciation that way was the Wagstaffs, who donated £245 to the fund when they asked mourners at the funeral of their mother, Laura Kathleen Wagstaff, to give money in lieu of flowers. The grieving family sent the cheque with a card inscribed: 'Just a few lines to thank you for all your care and attention to my mother as your patient, and it was comforting to know you were with her during her last moments. We greatly appreciate how you look after us as a family and we couldn't ask for a finer, more caring doctor.' But in fact Mrs Wagstaff had been murdered by Dr Shipman.

Worse still, he had murdered Mrs Wagstaff because he had confused her with her daughter-in-law's mother, Ann Royle, who had called into his surgery that morning with a bottle of gin for him for Christmas. It appears that Dr Shipman had intended to thank Mrs Royle for her gift by killing her in cold blood. A still-beautiful and smartly dressed lady with a sharp brain and sensible demeanour, she hides her distress well. In fact her blood pressure is 'sky high' and she has suffered many sleepless nights, coming to terms with the fact she came so close to an unnatural death. 'You do feel frightened,' she admitted at her neat terraced home. 'I have been awake at four in the morning, thinking about it.' She does not like to talk about it, even now, and even to the family. 'I don't want to be a burden,' she says proudly.

Mrs Royle ran the family chemist shop in Middleton for many years and continued to do so long after her husband died. She retired eight years ago and moved to Hyde to be close to her daughter, Angela, and two beloved granddaughters, Melanie and Louise. She takes pride in her no-nonsense approach to life, which led her to dismiss the news that Dr Shipman was being investigated over the death of Mrs Grundy. 'I thought she had left her estate to him after falling out with her family,' she recalled. 'You do silly things like that when you are old.'

Mrs Royle was finally forced to face the horrible truth when she was visited by murder-squad detectives. They had thoroughly investigated Mrs Wagstaff's death at the request of her sons John and Peter, Angela's husband. When they discovered that Mrs Royle had taken a gift to Dr Shipman on the day Mrs Wagstaff died, and that he had later confused the two women while breaking the news to Angela, they realised who his intended victim really was – Mrs Royle. She was devastated by the news and has struggled with her health ever since. Her blood pressure remains high and she was unable to face giving evidence in court – but she was proud to see Angela giving a courageous performance in the witness box.

One of the worst aspects of the case is, again, the fact that Mrs Wagstaff and Mrs Royle were not safe from Dr Shipman even while their families were so close. The two women would check Christmas lists with each other to make sure their granddaughters did not 'double up' on presents. They lived within minutes of each other and of both sets of children, as well as being close to the primary school where Angela was hailed by pupils as 'a brilliant teacher'. Mrs Royle was also friends with Norah Nuttall, another of Dr Shipman's victims. She recalled how, after Mrs Nuttall had died, she had spoken to Mrs Nuttall's son, Anthony: 'I told him, "Keep that front nice or she will haunt you".' But she added, with pride, 'I needn't worry. The lad's coping very well. I saw him recently and said to him, "I'll tell your mother how nice you've got that brass tonight".' These were close and loving families in a warm and affectionate community – yet these three women and so many others were living in constant danger.

'I feel so cross at him,' Mrs Royle said, her eyes finally glistening with the tears she had tried so hard to hold back. 'The way he has hurt Mrs Wagstaff, Peter and John, and especially my Angela. She is a good girl. He has hurt all of us, our family and the people of Hyde. He is a monster.'

There is no doubt that Mrs Royle and Mr King were extremely lucky to have escaped death at the hands of Dr Shipman. Week after week, sometimes day after day, Dr Shipman took his lethally loaded syringe and silently slaughtered yet another trusting patient. Bianka Pomfret died the day after Laura Kathleen Wagstaff. Mrs Wagstaff died two weeks after Marie Quinn. Maureen Ward died nine days after Pamela Hillier. Mrs Hillier died two weeks after Norah Nuttall. Jean Lilley and Ivy Lomas died in consecutive months, as did Winnie Mellor, Joan Melia and Kathleen Grundy. Mrs Melia and Mrs Grundy died just twelve days apart.

And then there are the patients believed by many to have died at his hands, who have not been the subject of any charge. Time and again, the details of their lives and their deaths bear a sinister resemblance to those of the fifteen women whose cases were tested in court.

Monica Sparkes, best known by her middle name Rene, died on 7 October 1992, just weeks after Dr Shipman went single-handed. Born Monica Rene Bilton, in Hyde, on 12 December 1918, she was the widow of estate agent John Sparkes. Her death certificate, signed by Dr Shipman, gave the cause as a stroke, narrowed arteries and congestive heart failure. It was co-signed by her son Terence, who lived in Romiley. Taxi driver John Shaw, who used to take her shopping for her grocery every Wednesday, took in her cat Dinky. John was surprised when Mrs Sparkes died – she had seemed fit and well, although she had been suffering from arthritis. Years later he put her at the top of his list of lost customers, convinced she was Dr

Shipman's first victim. 'She was a strong person,' he recalled. 'She always kept herself and her home right.' Her home was a flat, 15 Rock Gardens – the flat next door to that of Laura Kathleen Wagstaff.

Joan Milray Harding, a wealthy spinster, was one of five patients to die at Dr Shipman's surgery. Miss Harding, who died on 4 January 1994, lived on Joel Lane, just a few doors down from Kathleen Grundy. The retired social worker was a very smart woman, 'as fit as a flea', and ready to give anyone who crossed her a hard time. But she didn't bear a grudge once her peace was said, and she was never too proud to ask for a favour. Again she was a good customer and friend of taxi driver John Shaw. John got on well with her: 'She was an absolute character and a good friend, although I upset her on a couple of occasions. She had said she was stopping driving and she had a little Polo, then someone I knew was after a car and I told them about hers and they rang her. She went mad, she didn't want to sell the car. She had a go at me the next time I saw her.' But still they remained friends, Miss Harding confiding in John that she found driving a little difficult now that she was older. John spoke to Miss Harding on the day she died and almost drove her to her appointment with death. She had broken her shoulder in a fall a few days before and asked him to take her to Shipman's surgery, but his diary was full. Typically, she answered: 'Don't worry, John, I will make my own way there.' Within minutes of arriving, she was dead.

Netta Ashcroft died at her Meadowfield Court flat, in Flowery Field, on 7 March 1995 – the day after Marie West, the earliest of the fifteen victims Dr Shipman was charged with murdering. Mrs Ashcroft had telephoned her cousin Isabel Shelmerdine to say the doctor was visiting her but half an hour later, when Mrs

Shelmerdine rang her back, there was no answer. To her horror, Mrs Shelmerdine found Mrs Ashcroft dead. Yet again she had been quite well, apart from her arthritis. A retired railways clerk, Mrs Ashcroft had been born Netta Barratt in Manchester on 13 June 1923. She was the widow of dental technician Herbert Ashcroft and, again, a good customer and friend of John Shaw. 'Netta was a nice lady,' he recalled. 'I have a clock that was Netta's that her cousin said we should have when she died, so you can see I was more than just her taxi driver.' Mrs Shelmerdine signed Mrs Ashcroft's death certificate along with Dr Shipman, giving the cause as coronary thrombosis, heart disease – and schizophrenia. John angrily denied the cause: 'She was not schizophrenic. She was perfectly well apart from a bit of arthritis.'

Maltese-born Marie Antionette Fernley died at her Darwin Street home just six days later, on 13 March 1995, making three possible victims in one week. But when detectives flew out to have Mrs Fernley's body exhumed from her grave in Malta, her brother Alfred refused to give them permission. No charges could be laid against the GP without the evidence her body could have given up.

Mrs Fernley, born Marie Antoinette Falzon on 7 October 1941, had moved to Britain when she married an Englishman. The couple had two daughters before separating some years before Mrs Fernley's death. Dr Shipman attributed it to a stroke, hypertension and narrowing of the arteries. The girls, devastated by their mother's sudden death, were distraught when police revealed their suspicions but were then unable to confirm or deny them.

Postman's widow Ada Hilton, another neighbour of John and Kath Shaw, died at her home on 12 July 1995.

Mrs Hilton was born Ada Hampson in Hyde on 22 March 1907. She had worked as a textile worker at the town's print works and married Harry Hilton, who retired from the Post Office before his death. Mrs Hilton had just had lunch with her sister, who lived in the next-door block, when the doctor called. When her sister returned, having left so that Dr Shipman could tend to her, she found Ada dead. Her death certificate, signed by Dr Shipman and Mrs Hilton's nephew, Derek Godley, gave a heart attack, cardiac arrhythmia and heart disease as the causes of death.

Irish-born Muriel Ward died on 24 October 1995. Two years later, Dr Shipman returned and murdered her only daughter Maureen, in the very same flat the pair had shared so happily. Mrs Ward, better known as Molly, had been born Muriel Kimmitt in Londonderry on 20 March 1908. She married engineer Cyril Ward, with whom she had Maureen and a son. Mr Ward died after his retirement and Molly moved into Ogden Court. It was to become the scene of at least three deaths – those of Molly, Maureen and James King senior. Mrs Ward's death, at 77, was signed as heart failure by Dr Shipman. The devoted daughter was brewing tea in the kitchen when her mother died. Two years after co-signing her mother's death certificate, Maureen was dead too – killed by brain and breast cancer, according to the same cold-hearted GP. But, while police charged Dr Shipman with Maureen's murder, they were unable to do the same for her mother, as he had killed the only possible witness – Maureen.

Jane Shelmerdine died at her Napier Street terrace on 21 February 1996. Mrs Shelmerdine was born Jane Clarke in Stretford, Manchester, on 15 April 1915. She married mechanic William Shelmerdine and they had a son and a daughter. Mr Shelmerdine died after retiring, leaving Mrs Shelmerdine widowed and living in their old red-brick terrace. Her son Roy co-signed her death certificate on which Dr Shipman put the causes heart failure and breast cancer. The family home remained empty for months after Mrs Shelmerdine's death and became a target for local youths. Its broken, boarded windows were a sad and sorry testament to her untimely death.

Former landlady Val Cuthbert, who died in May 1996, was a good friend of Len Fallows, the manager of Dr Shipman's appeal fund. Now Len wonders if he could have inadvertently helped her to her death. Val, who ran The Cheshire Cheese pub with her husband Jim, had moved out of the area. When she returned, in 1996, she tried to get back on to Dr Shipman's patient list but it was too full. She asked her old friend Len to 'have a word'. He did, and Dr Shipman welcomed her to his practice. Weeks later she died at her Daisy Bank home, attended by Dr Shipman. Len was shocked to hear of her death. He had seen her only three weeks before, when they and another friend had lunch at The Highwayman pub, in Derbyshire. She had seemed well, if a little lonely after giving up her last pub, The Bull's Head, in High Lane, Stockport. She and Jim were popular hosts, well known for their wild sense of humour. Len recalled how he and Jim organised postcards to be sent to another landlord in Hyde from all over the world, from a mythical character Harry Horris. After many months, they 'bumped Harry off' – and informed their victim with yet another postcard. Then they sent the hearse carrying his 'ashes' – fertiliser in an urn – to the poor man's pub. Jim died while he and Val were still at The Bull's Head, and Val retired a few years later.

'We had had some great times,' Len said. 'When I had bumped into Val, I said, "How are you, love?" and she said, "Oh, it's so quiet now". So I invited her out with us. I paid for the meal and she said, "That was lovely, we must do it again – this time my treat". I will never forget those words.'

After she died, Len asked Dr Shipman what had happened. By way of reply he gave the same story as he had for Jean Lilley and Irene Turner, almost word for word. 'I got a call to go and see her,' the GP told Len. 'I suspected heart trouble and wanted her to go to hospital, but she didn't want to. I said I would go back later. I went back and the door was closed but not locked. I went in and found her dead in the chair.'

Len was shocked: 'I remember saying to my friend, "That's not the woman we knew".' When the news broke that Dr Shipman was being investigated by the police, Len could not believe it. But, as a retired police officer, he knew that they would not exhume Mrs Grundy's body without a great deal of evidence against Shipman. He began to wonder about Val's death and, after mulling it over for a while, telephoned Det Supt Postles. Len recalled: 'I told him what I knew and he said, "It's the MO". That is what we police officers call the method.'

The Smith brothers and their next-door neighbours, Thomas and Elsie Cheetham, were next – four people in two adjacent houses in eight months. Two other women died in that period too, Millie Garside and Irene Brooder, again living in the same street as one another. And still Dr Shipman was hailed as 'the best doctor in Hyde'. Retired gardener, Sid, died at the brothers' Garden Street home on 30 August 1996 as Ken made a cup of tea – just like Maureen Ward had been when her mother Molly died. Thomas followed on 4 December 1996. Ken, with unknowing foresight, said, 'Don't let that man near me – he is the angel of death.' It was to no avail – he died two weeks later. Soon after Dr Shipman had visited Ken, the window cleaner saw the pensioner sitting motionless in the chair and alerted next-door neighbour Elsie. She died on 25 April 1997, again soon after a visit from Dr Shipman.

Millicent Garside had died by then, at her St John's Drive home on 23 October 1996. Mrs Garside was born Millicent Coupé in Hyde on 2 September 1920. She married Frank Garside and the couple ran a shop. Frank died after they retired. Mrs Garside's death certificate was co-signed by her son Keith, who lived on nearby Fountain Street. Dr Shipman had given the causes as coronary thrombosis, heart failure, heart disease, diabetes and asthma.

Millicent Garside's neighbour, Irene Brooder, died on 20 January 1997, again at home. Mrs Brooder had been born Irene Ainsworth in Denton on 11 February in 1920, the same year as Mrs Garside. She married factory worker John Brooder, who died after retiring from the battery works. Just a few years before she died Mrs Brooder also lost her son, just in his middle age. But despite her troubles, she made the most of her life: she would visit her daughter-in-law, Joyce, who lived in Great Ashby, Cumbria, and her nephew Alan, who lived in Abergele, sometimes staying for several weeks. Mrs Brooder died after a visit from Dr Shipman. She had told a visiting neighbour he was on his way. When the neighbour called back later that day, she was dead.

Mrs Brooder was another good friend of John Shaw and his wife Kath. 'She was full of fun,' Kath recalled. 'Her death really affected me. She liked to garden, even though she had had her hip done. She would be in the garden with a stick, she couldn't resist doing something. She was a lovely person, I really liked her. Sometimes I would glance across to her garden and couldn't believe it.'

Lena Slater, another strong character well loved by the Shaws, died at her Newton Hall Court home on 2 May 1997. She was a spinster, born in Hyde on 7 April 1929, who had made her living as a seamstress. Miss Slater died within half an hour of a visit from Dr Shipman and her body was found by her sister. An expensive new sewing machine was also missing. Miss Slater's brother, Alfred, co-signed her death certificate, on which Dr Shipman gave the causes as carcinomatosis and breast cancer, a condition for which she had been treated earlier. John Shaw recalled, 'She was a smashing woman.'

Nancy Jackson died at her Gower Court home on 1 September 1997. Just like Kathleen Grundy, she lived in Gee Cross, and Dr Shipman gave the cause of her death as old age. Mrs Jackson was born Nancy Morris in Bramhall, Stockport, on 9 June 1916. She married rates assessor Philip Jackson, who died after retiring. Their daughter, Rosalind Farrell, co-signed her death certificate. Coincidentally Rosalind Farrell lived in Todmorden, where Dr Shipman had begun his career in general practice.

Flo Lewis died at her Mansfield Road home on 10 November 1997 – two weeks before Marie Quinn and four weeks before Laura Kathleen Wagstaff, yet again soon after a visit from Dr Shipman. Mrs Lewis was born Florence Windebank, in Hyde, on 10 April 1918. She married steelworker Albert Lewis, who died after retiring. Their son, Brian, who lived next-door-but-one to Lizzie Adams on Coronation Avenue, co-signed Mrs Lewis's death certificate. Dr Shipman had given the causes as a stroke, narrowed arteries and hypertension. She was another of John Shaw's regulars, taking a taxi to her weekly night out at The George public house every Saturday. 'All of them were smart ladies,' he said. 'Again she was very, very outgoing, very with it.'

Mary Walls died just days before her old friend Marie Quinn – who had been to Mrs Walls' funeral on the day she died: 24 November 1997. There are many such horrible coincidences to this case: there is not a person in Hyde who is untouched either directly or indirectly by the case, not a street in the town not visited by him in some terrible way. Sheila Ward, the neighbour who found victim Irene Turner dead in bed after being sent across by Dr Shipman, not only lived opposite her but had also lived opposite Mrs Walls some years before. And Sheila Ward lived next door to Lizzie Adams, then in her 30s with two young daughters and an impish son, when she was at home with her parents. 'It's strange to think I have lived so close to three of the women who died in his care,' Mrs Ward said. 'It makes me very sad.'

Cissie Davies, better known as Pat Davies, died at her Lodge Lane home on 3 February 1998. Mrs Davies was born Cissie Patterson in Maryport, Cumbria, on 14 May 1924. She married factory foreman Eric Davies, who died after retiring from his engineering works. Their daughter, Norma Lenthall, who lived in Sheffield, co-signed her death certificate. Dr Shipman had put the cause as bronchopneumonia and diabetes.

Coronation Street actress Joan Dean died three weeks later, on 27 February 1998. Again, she died after a visit from Dr Shipman at her Joel Lane home, just a few doors away from Kathleen Grundy. Just as in the case of Joan Melia, her watch and diamond ring were missing. Joan was born Joan Briggs at Heaton Park, in north Manchester, on 9 February 1923. She was a glamorous, fun-loving woman who won the heart of company director Eric Dean, who owned a big furniture shop in Stalybridge, and she bore him two sons. One of them, Brian, suffered a breakdown following his mother's death and the end of a ten-year relationship with girlfriend Elaine. Brian's relationship with his mother had been strained before her death because she did not like Elaine. Brian turned to Dr Shipman for help. The GP had put coronary thrombosis, heart disease and hypertension as the causes of her death. Brian knew of the investigation into the GP but refused to believe that he would murder his patients.

Dr Shipman prescribed work as the antidote to stress. 'He said, "I've been expecting you",' Brian recalled. 'He said, "Do you want to do what I do? I work. You know about Mrs Grundy, don't you? Well I knew her from sitting on various committees".' At about the same time Brian was visited by murder squad detectives, who told him they were investigating his mother's death. 'I still could not believe it,' he said. 'Then I thought about things he had said and I began to wonder.'

Brian has coped well with his loss and the subsequent investigation, thanks to the happy memories his mother left him. His childhood was one of music and laughter and parties for the people Joan met while working as an extra in *Coronation Street*. 'Mother was a very, very touchy-touchy, huggy-huggy person,' he explained. 'The house was always full of theatrical people. She knew Pat Phoenix well and we were at the Alexander Hospital when she died. Mother was a hoarder. She loved playing charades, dressing up, entertainments with instruments. We had a ukelele, horn and drums. She always had lots of friends. You would have to rub her nose in it quite a few times before she would fall out with you, but I've seen her in action and, my God, when she was, you kept well clear. Her use of language was vast but I never heard her swear in 70 years.' Joan's funeral at Holy Trinity Church was a wonderful testament to her fascinating, fun-filled life. Actor John Savident, who plays *Coronation Street*'s loudmouthed butcher, Fred Elliott, gave the oration. But because she was cremated, there is no evidence to prove she had died of morphine poisoning.

Ada Warburton died at her Grange Road North home on 20 March 1998. She was born in Hyde on 21 June 1920 and worked as a packer. She had retired before she died, from a stroke, according to Dr Shipman. Her death certificate was co-signed by her great nephew, Alan Hadfield, who lived in nearby Marple, Stockport. Miss Warburton was another regular customer of taxi driver John Shaw. 'She was full of fun, full of life, there was no sign of illness,' he recalled.

Nurse Margaret Waldron was the last to die before Dr Shipman's final three victims, Winnie Mellor, Joan Melia and Kathleen Grundy. Mrs Waldron died at her Woodend Lane home, in Gee Cross, on 6 March 1998 – the third anniversary of the first of the fifteen victims, Marie West. She had been born Margaret Platt in Manchester, on 20 April 1932. She married civil servant Ronald Waldron, who died after retiring. Their daughter, Sally Freeman, signed Mrs Waldron's death certificate, on which Dr Shipman gave the causes as coronary thrombosis, heart disease and hypercholesterol anaemia. Mrs Waldron was just 65 when she died, and was yet another regular customer of taxi driver John Shaw. 'She was not old or ill at all,' he said.

West Pennine Health Authority [WPHA], responsible for the Tameside area where Dr Shipman practiced, has shown remarkable restraint in its recommendations to Health Minister, Alan Milburn – even though it was kept in the dark about Dr Shipman's past, particularly his drugs convictions.

Mr Milburn has ordered a public inquiry into the case and taken a report from WPHA, which does not want to ban single-handed practices but rather to change them. It has recommended that lone GPs be linked to others or group surgeries for some aspects of their work. It has also suggested that the General Medical Council inform health authorities of a doctor's criminal record. WPHA did not know of Dr Shipman's drugs conviction when he first came to Hyde, nor when he went single-handed in 1992. The partners at the Donneybrook Group Practice knew of his pethidine problem, but agreed to give him a chance. No one thought to tell WPHA when he left to go single-handed. Even though the WPHA was his paymaster, using public money, the authority had no legal right to know of his past convictions, as it only contracted the work of GPs rather than actually employing them. That should all change following this horrific case.

Coroner John Pollard was more forthright. He believed that there should be an end to single-handed practices. He also wanted to see more deaths reported to the Coroner. 'People don't know the procedure and maybe one of few benefits of this case will be an education of the general public on what the Coroner does and how he can help resolve problems, causes of death.' However, Mr Pollard hoped there would be a carefully considered, pragmatic approach rather than a knee-jerk reaction condemning all GPs to unnecessary draconian measures. 'The law should evolve, not rapidly change; special hard cases create bad law,' he explained. 'Doctors are unaccountable, and have to be by the very nature of their job, but 99.9 per cent are good, honest people.'

Dr Linda Reynolds, who first alerted the police to Dr Shipman's killing spree, also believes that single-handed practices should be banned. According to Dr Reynolds, murder was the reason Dr Shipman decided to 'go it alone'. If any GP had anything to hide, they would want to work alone – although this is not, of course, to say that all single-handed doctors have something to hide. Dr Reynolds also believed that there should be changes to the cremation forms, so many of which were signed by her partners at the Brooke Group Practice. At present the forms contain a section asking if the relatives and carers have been consulted, allowing the doctor co-signing the document to answer yes or no. Dr Reynolds said it should have to be yes. Finally, she said, the General Medical Council should take more responsibility for the public: 'They should have greater power and use it properly.' However Dr Reynolds did not want patients to feel unable to trust their doctor just because of this one man's actions. 'I am concerned people will stop trusting their doctor and I hope they don't,' she said. 'Most are good, hardworking, caring people, although patients should question the way they are being treated and know what is happening to them. Shipman is a one-off.'

Dr Shipman did it simply because he could.

Harold Shipman's mother, Vera, died after a long struggle with lung cancer when he was just seventeen. No doubt she would have been given morphine by her family doctor, as she sat in her favourite chair, looking out of the window, a cup of tea by her side, just like so many of the women in this case. The similarities are striking. Young Fred never publicly expressed his grief. Instead he ran for hours in the rain in the dead of night. But there were differences too. Some of the victims may have been men – Sid and Ken Smith, Thomas

Cheetham. Some of the women died in the surgery – Ivy Lomas, Joan Milray Harding. And the circumstances of his mother's death alone are not enough to explain away Dr Shipman's vile actions. As one psychologist put it: 'We all have bad things happen in our lives, but we do not do this. It goes back further than that. Dr Shipman has a personality disorder.'

Det Supt Bernard Postles was more blunt: 'The opportunity was there – he was a trusted individual, he was invited into people's homes – but there was no motive. We could indicate from that – just because he got the chance to do it he did.'

The Coroner, too, took a blunt view of why Dr Shipman had decimated a community's old folk. 'I think he is a genuinely evil man,' Mr Pollard said. He believed Dr Shipman was in the thrall of 'the perverted pleasure' he derived from killing. He went on: 'I just keep coming back to the belief that he enjoyed power and control. If you link that to the fact that he was regarded by many as a good doctor with a surgery which had high expenditure on pain-relieving drugs for the terminally ill, he was controlling when they died as well as those he was killing.'

Det Supt Postles added: 'A clue to the motive is his attitude – "I'm superior, I want to control situations".'

His second in command, DCI Mike Williams, agreed: 'We have lived this 24 hours a day for more than twelve months. Our first question was why? It's the ultimate control, over life, over death.'

Dr Richard Badcock, the police psychologist who profiled Dr Shipman to diagnose whether he was fit for interview, believed that the GP suffered a form of hands-off necrophilia – that he got a sexual kick out of injecting his patients and watching them quietly slip away. Dr Badcock told the police that Dr Shipman had a fascination with death, which manifested itself in his love of technology. He, like many serial killers, was motivated by control, rather than anger or revenge. Of course, the power of life over death is the ultimate control. And who would have better access to that than a well-loved family doctor? Dr Badcock added that the sense of control was often allied to obsession – the killer's obsessive need to exercise that control, as he felt insubstantial in normal life but powerful in the act of murder. And, Dr Badcock added, this psychological condition may have had its root in his relationship with his mother.

Dr Shipman was an arrogant power addict who took the ultimate satisfaction from extinguishing the lives of those who had turned to him for care.

It chills the blood to think how his victims' last words must have gratified him even more.

'Thank you, doctor.'

Afterword

On the 31st of January 2000 at 4.35 p.m., Dr Harold Shipman was found guilty of murdering fifteen of his patients. The jury had been out for longer than many had imagined – they had clearly wanted to consider the merits of each case separately. But by the end there was no doubt in their minds: Dr Shipman was guilty of murdering his patients in cold blood, and Britain's biggest serial murderer had been brought to justice.